ROMAN CATHOLICS IN ENGLAND

ROMAN CATHOLICS IN ENGLAND

STUDIES IN SOCIAL STRUCTURE SINCE THE SECOND WORLD WAR

MICHAEL P. HORNSBY-SMITH

Senior Lecturer in Sociology
University of Surrey

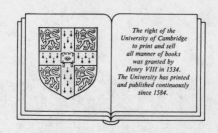

The right of the
University of Cambridge
to print and sell
all manner of books
was granted by
Henry VIII in 1534.
The University has printed
and published continuously
since 1584.

CAMBRIDGE UNIVERSITY PRESS

CAMBRIDGE

LONDON   NEW YORK   NEW ROCHELLE

MELBOURNE   SYDNEY

Published by the Press Syndicate of the University of Cambridge
The Pitt Building, Trumpington Street, Cambridge CB2 1RP
32 East 57th Street, New York, NY 10022, USA
10 Stamford Road, Oakleigh, Melbourne 3166, Australia

© Cambridge University Press 1987

First published 1987

Printed in Great Britain at the University Press, Cambridge

British Library cataloguing in publication data

Hornsby-Smith, Michael P.
Roman Catholics in England: studies in
social structure since the Second World War.
1. Catholics – England – History – 20th century
1. Title
305.6'2'042   BX1493.2

Library of Congress cataloguing in publication data

Hornsby-Smith, Michael P.
Roman Catholics in England.
Bibliography.
1. Catholics – England – History – 20th century.
2. Catholics – Wales – History – 20th century. 3. England –
Social life and customs – 1945–   . 4. Wales – Social
life and customs. 1 Title.
BX1493.2.H67 1987   305.6'2'042   87–20705

ISBN 0 521 30313 3

CE

CONTENTS

———— ❧ ————

FIGURES

———— ❧ ————

TABLES

—— ✣ ——

PREFACE

———— ✣ ————

how many of you were wise in the ordinary sense of the word,
how many were influential people, or came from noble families?
(1 Cor. 1:26)

I write these words from the Epistle read at Mass on the day I started
to write this book. They seem strangely relevant to the questions
which first exercised me ten years ago when I decided to explore the
impact of post-war social change on the Roman Catholic community
in England. How had Catholics benefited from the expansion of
secondary and higher education and the general post-war affluence?
And how had these social changes affected the nature of social relationships, especially between the parish clergy and the laity? At the
commencement of this research the Second Vatican Council had
ended a bare eight years earlier and the liturgical reforms it had
instigated and the fuller participation of the laity in the everyday life
of the Church it had encouraged were only just beginning to
percolate through to the parishes. Did the ordinary Catholic favour
the reforms? And did he or she welcome the increased involvement
expected? How was the nature of religious authority changing in
response to both social change and religious innovation? After a
decade's research and five successive research projects I believe we
are in a position to answer some of these questions and some others
which emerged in the course of our surveys.

The focus of our attention will be Roman Catholics living in
England and Wales in the 1970s and 1980s. For simplicity these will
be referred to as English Catholics though some of our data will refer
also to the Catholics in Wales who comprise about 3% of the

Catholics under the authority of the single hierarchy of England and Wales. For our purposes, too, we have included in this term all those Catholics who were born abroad, notably Catholics born in Ireland or the Catholic countries of eastern or southern Europe who are currently living in England and Wales.

In attempting to answer the questions outlined above I will draw on research from five different studies, each of which will be described in detail in the main text. For the moment I wish to pay tribute to all those who have contributed to this substantial research programme. The original inspiration for this research came from Asher Tropp who first encouraged me to investigate the impact of post-war social mobility on the Catholic community in England and persuaded me that a Roman Catholic could legitimately and from a sociological perspective investigate his own religious community. Valuable advice and encouragement was given in these early stages by the late Robert Bogan, Joan Brothers, Tony Coxon, Graham Dann and Margaret Norris.

I gratefully acknowledge two research grants from the Social Science Research Council which enable the first two studies to be undertaken. It was my good fortune to have as colleagues Penny Mansfield, Ray Lee and Peter Reilly who were the Research Officers on these studies. We were indebted to the four parish priests in our London and Preston parishes for their trusting and generous help. During our field work in Preston we were particularly grateful for the hospitality give by Liz Bond and Patsy Manda. During the study of *Roman Catholic Opinion* Ray Lee and I received much constructive advice and great encouragement from Joan Brothers, Tony Coxon, David Gerard, Chris Harris, Bishop Harvey, Gordon Heald and Noel Timms. Several invaluable analyses of these data were carried out by Kathy Turcan.

I am also pleased to acknowledge two small research grants from the University of Surrey which facilitated the National Pastoral Congress (N.P.C.) study and the early stages of the study of the Pope's visit. I am also indebted to them for two terms of sabbatical leave which facilitated the early stages of data collection in the S.S.R.C. studies and a further sabbatical year in 1985–86 which enabled me to complete the writing of this book.

Archbishop Worlock kindly arranged to make available the lists of delegates to the N.P.C. The Nuffield Foundation awarded two small grants, one at very short notice for the Pope's study. Much of the analysis of this study was undertaken by Ann Scurfield, Joan O'Byrne and Jennifer Brown. In the analysis of the N.P.C. data I was fortunate to have Betsy Cordingley as a collaborator. On numerous occasions I have been grateful for the computing skills of Jane Fielding and Lyn Rajan. Mike Procter has always been generous with his advice on data analysis. Peter Abell counselled me to continue my research on Roman Catholicism at a crucial stage and Christian Heath offered me valuable and encouraging criticisms and comments on various drafts.

I am grateful to all those who have allowed me to quote extensively from publications we originally produced jointly: Jennie Brown, Betsy Cordingley, Angela Dale, Ray Lee, Penny Mansfield, Joan O'Byrne, Mike Procter, Lyn Rajan, Peter Reilly and Kathy Turcan. I would like to acknowledge special debts of gratitude to all my colleagues in the Sociology Department at the University of Surrey and to the members of the Sociology of Religion Study Group of the British Sociological Association for their continuing support and critical comments on various working papers over a number of years.

I wish to thank the editors of *The Month*, *The Newman*, *Sociological Review*, *Sociology*, and *The Tablet* for permission to quote from articles originally published by them. My thanks are also due to Gordon Heald for permission to include extracts from *Roman Catholic Opinion* written on the basis of Gallup's 1978 survey and Omnibus and also to Angela West for permission to quote from her article 'A Faith for Feminists?'.

For over a decade a succession of dedicated, competent and good-humoured secretaries in the Sociology Department have typed various drafts of what has emerged in this book. I am particularly grateful to Alwyn Whitehead for so carefully and patiently producing the final copy.

Finally, I am pleased to record my love and gratitude to my wife, Lennie, for her tolerance and support for the work I have chosen to do. In the hope that our children will be committed to the process of transformation of the loveable but flawed Roman Catholic Church I am pleased to dedicate this book with love to: Andrew, Gillian, Stephen and Richard and also to Tom Messinger whom I was honoured to sponsor at his confirmation on the day this book was completed.

CHAPTER I

INTRODUCTION

———— ⚜ ————

1.1 HISTORICAL SIGNPOSTS

This book is about the Roman Catholic community in England in the decade from 1973 to 1983. It is concerned to explore the state of this community four decades after the Butler Education Act of 1944 and the subsequent expansion of both secondary and further educational opportunities had paved the way for socially and geographically mobile Catholics to escape from the working-class parishes in the inner cities. At the same time it will report the responses of Catholics to the liturgical and social changes resulting from the reforms of the Second Vatican Council which had been held in Rome from 1962 to 1965.

Five years after the end of the Second World War, in 1950, the Catholics of England and Wales had celebrated the centenary of the Apostolic Letter *Universalis Ecclesiae* by which Pope Pius IX restored a full Catholic hierarchy of bishops to England and Wales. The last survivor of the medieval Catholic hierarchy to refuse to take the Oath of Supremacy of Queen Elizabeth I had died in 1585 and until 1850 the small body of Catholics had a variety of religious leaders but no diocesan bishops. The restoration of the hierarchy in 1850 had infuriated the prime minister and public opinion although Cardinal Wiseman substantially defused the situation with his famous *Appeal to the English People* (Albion, 1950).

The celebrations of 1950, which included a massive open-air Mass at Wembley stadium, were triumphant and self-congratulatory. By contrast the Mass celebrated by Pope John Paul II in the same stadium in the course of the historic first visit to Britain, in 1982, by a reigning Pope on the vigil of the feast of Pentecost, was pastoral, reflective and challenging in tone. Between these two events the Second Vatican Council, called by Pope John XXIII, had been held in Rome. In the four sessions of the Council the Catholic bishops of the world had endeavoured to reform the Church in order that it might more readily respond to the rapidly changing social and political conditions of the post-war world. The religious teachings of this Council (Abbott, 1966) constituted a radical break, with a 'pre-Vatican' model of the Church. In concrete terms their effect was shortly to be experienced in a series of liturgical changes which aimed to encourage lay participation in the Mass, the central act of worship of the Church, and in the increasing involvement of lay people in advisory structures and decision-making processes at all levels.

The culmination of this process of lay participation was the first open congress involving all the bishops and representative priests, religious men and woman, and lay people from all the dioceses and the main Catholic organisations. The National Pastoral Congress (N.P.C.) which was held in Liverpool in 1980 was a milestone in the life of the Church in this country. Some commentators regarded it as the 'end of adolescence' in the growth to confidence and maturity of English Catholics in the 130 years since the restoration of the hierarchy.

This book aims to bring the disciplines of social research and sociological analysis to bear on this English Catholic community at this important transitional period in its history. It will attempt the interpretation of its processes of adaptation to the social changes in British society in the post-war world and to the religious reforms emanating from the Second Vatican Council. The period of our empirical investigations closes with the visit of the Pope and with evidence, for example, in the much-publicised case of Mgr Bruce Kent, formerly the General Secretary of the Campaign for Nuclear Disarmament, that the Catholic community remains seriously divided on the proper relationship between religion and politics.

It was perhaps inevitable that the visit of Pope John Paul II to Britain in the summer of 1982 should have generated so much interest. It was bound to arouse controversy among those protestants who regarded any hint of papal pretensions with suspicion; other protestants had come to regard the Pope as a world Christian as well as a Catholic leader.

English Catholics, too, had anticipated his visit with a mixture of pride and apprehension. They were, perhaps, rather surprised that the Pope was accorded such a warm welcome by their fellow countrymen whom they continued to suspect nurtured a latent hostility towards Catholicism, seeing it as basically 'unEnglish'. Progressive Catholics feared that a conservative Pope would arouse this latent hostility towards a Catholic community which had successfully maintained a low political profile in the previous decade or so. They also suspected that he would reverse some of the trends which had emerged so clearly at the 1980 National Pastoral Congress. The enthusiasm for an 'open' Church engendered by the Congress had led to optimistic expectations which the bishops did not meet in their official response to the N.P.C., *The Easter People* (Anon., 1981). In their disillusionment at the frequently hostile response by priests and laity at the local parish or deanery level, many delegates feared that the Pope's visit would restore a more traditional and authoritarian model of the Church and would alienate many by an aggressive reassertion of official teaching, especially on contraception.

In the event these fears did not materialise and in his homilies (John Paul II, 1982) the Pope referred to many of the themes which had emerged from the N.P.C. On the other hand, critics pointed to the fact that at no stage during his visit did the Pope formally meet any of the key leaders of the Congress nor was any opportunity provided for him to listen to representations from lay leaders. For all the enthusiasm and media attention during the visit, too, there has been little evidence of any significant or long-term impact of the Pope's visit.

1.2 CONTEMPORARY SIGNIFICANCE

Granted the general improvement in the circumstances of the English Catholic community, what reasons are there for paying them any special attention? First of all there is the increase in their size (from around 5% in 1850 (Spencer, 1966a) to around 11% in 1978 (Hornsby-Smith and Lee, 1979) and the potential this might have for political or religious mobilisation. The Catholic population has grown considerably in recent decades. From under 40,000 Catholics at the beginning of the seventeenth century and still only 80,000 in 1770, it had grown to around 900,000 at the time of the restoration of the hierarchy of England and Wales in 1850 (Bossy, 1975: 193, 298;

Currie, Gilbert and Horsley, 1977: 153-5; Spencer, 1966a). In the last
130 years, however, it has increased sixfold to around 5.4 million. A
century ago Catholics were still a beleaguered minority fighting for
survival in a hostile society. By 1982 the warmth of the reception
accorded Pope John Paul II demonstrated clearly that they had
largely been accepted as an integral part of British society.

In Cardinal Hume they have a leader who is widely admired and
respected. In recent years, too, Catholics have held such posts as
Secretary of the Cabinet, leadership of both Houses of Parliament,
editor of *The Times*, and General Secretary of the Trades Union
Congress. The Earl Marshal is a Catholic. The assimilation of
English Catholicism can also be judged from the fact that as many as
1 child in 11 attends a Catholic school where the teachers' salaries
and 85% of the grant for capital building are paid for by the State
(Hornsby-Smith, 1978a), a fact that is now largely accepted as
uncontroversial.

Catholics' religious significance, too, can be judged from the fact
that in the late 1970s there were more Roman Catholic adult
'members' than members in all the Protestant Churches in England.
More than one-third of adult attenders at church services were
Catholics and there were more Catholic Mass attenders than
attenders in the established Church of England (Anon. 1980a: 23).

Secondly, they are of considerable social and political importance
because they are a community with overwhelmingly immigrant
(especially Irish) origins and they represent an important example
of assimilation to British society over many generations. At the turn
of the century a largely impoverished Irish Catholic working class
was concentrated mainly in the inner-city parishes especially in
Liverpool and the north-west and in London, Now they are more
generally dispersed throughout England and Wales. There has been
considerable movement into the industrial midlands and the south-
east and, more generally, with rising affluence, a move out of the
inner cities and into the suburban estates.

Thirdly, a study of the Roman Catholic community is important
not only because of its size and social significance, but also because it
provides a valuable opportunity to monitor in some depth the wider
issues of religious change and to explore further processes of secularisation in the post-war world. It also enables us to monitor transformations of religious meanings among ordinary members when the
boundaries protecting them from the influences of the wider society

become eroded, not only by social change generally, but also as a result of theological developments or shifts of dominant religious ideologies within the religious collectivity.

In recent years a high proportion of the concern and attention of sociologists of religion has been focussed on the study of sects and new religious movements (Barker, 1982, 1984; Beckford, 1975, 1985; Wallis, 1976, 1982; Wilson, 1970, 1982). While this academic concentration, if not obsession, might be justified in terms of some supposed prototypical characteristics of such developments, it is important to stress that the vast majority of religious adherents remain members of the more established churches and denominations, which are also subject to the same global forces of social change. Their members, too, have to face the same problems of religious meaning and the significance of everyday life in a changing world, and these established churches and denominations are transformed in the process. It is argued here that there is a need for serious sociological investigations of the transformations of the Roman Catholic, Anglican, Methodist and other major denominations in the post-war world and it is hoped that this study of these processes of adaptation and adjustment to the new social and religious circumstances by the English Catholics might have relevance, not only comparatively for the Roman Catholic Church in other countries, but also for the other major denominations in England who clearly face the same problems and have the same tensions and conflicts between traditional and progressive groups.

1.3 MAJOR THEMES

The problems of continuity and change, consensus and conflict, traditionalism and progressivism for the Roman Catholic Church in England were, then, the starting points for this study in the early 1970s. Who were the English Catholics? How did they differ from their fellow countrymen? Were the barriers which once separated them from 'non-Catholics' breaking down? How homogeneous was the Roman Catholic community? How had it been affected by post-war social and geographical mobility? How distinct were those Catholics with Irish origins? What was happening to Catholic marriages and family life? Who were the dominant elites in the contemporary Church? How had the Catholic parish survived post-war changes? How had the nature of religious authority been

transformed? Were Catholics seriously concerned to encourage ecumenical developments? To what extent did the traditional defensiveness and 'ghetto' or 'fortress' mentality of English Catholics
persist? What political weight did Catholics wield?

Five distinct factors in the changes taking place in English
Catholicism were postulated:

1 The largely immigrant origin of earlier generations of Catholics,
   notably unskilled and semi-skilled manual workers from Ireland,
   but more recently refugees from Eastern Europe. In the early
   stages these immigrants found security and a sense of identity in a
   hostile environment largely through their membership of ghetto
   churches serviced by co-cultural priests.

2 Catholics have participated in equal measure with the rest of the
   population in the massive expansion of secondary, further and
   higher education provision since the Second World War. In
   consequence they are now more informed and articulate than
   ever before and increasingly critical of authority based on
   traditional rather than legal–rational forms of legitimation.

3 With the increasing certification of large numbers of Catholics,
   there has been a significant amount of upward social mobility. For
   the first time there is now a sizeable 'new Catholic middle class',
   assertively self-confident and less deferential towards traditional
   forms of authority. In this respect, Catholics have participated in
   the broad process of democratization in industry, universities,
   schools and homes in the wider society.

4 The recent developments in the media have produced revolution-
   ary changes, not only in the speed of mass communications but
   also in the exposing of authority figures to public scrutiny. This
   scrutiny concerns not only the cognitive content of communications but also non-verbal and affective aspects.

5 For Catholics, the teaching of the Second Vatican Council has had
   a profound influence in changing the dominant emphases and
   orientations which make up the normatively prescribed belief and
   value system.

(Hornsby-Smith and Mansfield, 1974: 62–3)

It was anticipated that the 'new Catholic middle class', upwardly
mobile from the working class as a result of the post-war expansion of
educational and occupational opportunities, would be central to the
outcomes in the tightly structured, rigid and hierarchically organised
Church of the 1950s. Tensions and conflicts between those Catholics

favouring the certainties of the traditional orthodoxies, on the one hand, and those, on the other hand, who felt that their religious beliefs and commitment needed to be expressed in new ways which they claimed were more appropriate to the changing circumstances of the moment, were only to be expected. For example, it was apparent that some of the most successful products of the expanded Catholic system of secondary education were the most articulate critics of the effectiveness and desirability of this system in a plural society (Spencer, 1971). The tensions could be seen, too, in the diminution of the traditional docility and deference to the dominant clerical leadership in England and a corresponding change in the nature of the cohesion of the Roman Catholic community. Conflicts were also manifest in the approach of Catholics to the ecumenical movement and in their reception of the recent changes in the liturgy and the reiteration of the traditional viewpoint on the birth-control issue. However, it was suggested that overt conflict might be avoided by the strategy of reducing the area where the authority and guidance of the Church was thought to be relevant. There were also latent conflicts surrounding the wider social, economic and political issues of justice and peace and the international ramifications of post-colonial capitalism. In all these conflicts the role of the 'new Catholic middle class', subject to the twin pressures towards secularisation in an advanced industrial society, on the one hand, and the attempts to achieve a reform and a renewal of purpose by the Church, on the other hand, was expected to be crucial.

These, then, were the hypotheses, hunches and assumptions with which this programme of research was initially undertaken. They explain why it was that our first studies were of lay members of the bishops' national advisory commissions. If the 'new Catholic middle class' was rising in prominence we anticipated that its members would be found in the new participatory structures. Secondly, we expected they would be found in significant numbers in the expanding London commuter and suburban parishes. A feasibility study in one such parish was later expanded and surveys were subsequently undertaken in four parishes: the original commuter parish and an inner-city parish in the London area and a suburban and an inner-city parish in the Preston area in north-west England. Given limited resources these four parishes were chosen to reflect as far as possible both regional and social-class differences.

As these two studies proceeded, and especially as a result of our

field-work experiences, some of our initial assumptions were shown
to require some modification. Vertical conflicts between priests and
lay people, for example, were nothing like as salient as we had at first
anticipated. More significant were the horizontal tensions between
traditionalists and progressives. Even more important was the
growing evidence of a cleavage between the articulate 'activists',
largely familiar with the shifts of religious ideology in the Church,
and the inarticulate, nominal Catholic, whether 'practising' or not in
terms of regular Mass attendance. This led to a shift in the focus of
the research (Hornsby-Smith, 1983a). From the testing of hypotheses
about social mobility and adaptation to religious change, our
in-depth interviews became increasingly tentative and exploratory as
we sought to interpret the significance of a Roman Catholic identity
as 'common' (Towler, 1974: 145–62) or 'customary' religion
(Hornsby-Smith, Lee and Reilly, 1985). These more qualitative
data, concerned primarily with the social reality of the religion of
English Catholics (Berger and Luckmann, 1971; Berger, 1973) will
be reported in a sequel to this present book.

The more quantitative data presented in this volume will indicate
the broad structure of beliefs and practices and enable us to specify
some of the parameters for the subsequent interpretation of the more
in-depth interview material. In particular we will be able to draw on
the data from the 1978 survey of a nationally representative sample of
Catholics in England and Wales (Hornsby-Smith and Lee, 1979) in
order to identify a number of distinct types of English Catholics
(Hornsby-Smith, Lee and Turcan, 1982).

One of the limitations of the 1978 survey was that it did not permit
the detailed examination of the nature of Catholic 'traditionalism'
and 'progressivism', nor was it possible to construct adequate
measures of a 'post-Vatican' theological orientation on the basis of
the questions asked. A survey of the delegates to the N.P.C.
(Hornsby-Smith and Cordingley, 1983) provided the opportunity to
pursue these matters further, at least with a national sample of
Catholic 'activists'. Finally, the visit of Pope John Paul II in 1982 led
to a piece of opportunistic research (Hornsby-Smith, Brown and
O'Byrne, 1983) and the further exploration of people's attitudes to
papal authority. The occasion also provided a favourable opportunity to check some of the conclusions of the various researches over
the previous eight or nine years.

It can be seen, therefore, that the research programme reported in this book has been a dynamic process. The questions which informed the initial studies of lay activists and the four parishes led to new research questions. The resources needed for a national survey were not available at the beginning of our work but once undertaken answered many questions about Catholic schooling, marriage patterns, the heterogeneity of belief and practice, and so on, but in turn raised other issues, notably about the nature of progressivism and in particular Catholic attitudes and behaviour in the politically sensitive areas of justice and peace. Following this, two opportunistic pieces of research in connection with the N.P.C. and the subsequent visit of the Pope, enabled more fundamental questions about the coherence and compliance of Catholics within the socio-religious community with its changing authority structures to be addressed more directly.

1.4 DATA SOURCES

A summary of data sources in the five studies has been given in table 1.1. It has already been stressed that the starting point for the present research was the 'new Catholic middle class' which was thought to have emerged in the affluent post-war years especially as a result of the general expansion of secondary and higher education provision. In a feasibility study funded by the British Social Science Research Council (S.S.R.C.), tape-recorded focussed interviews, on average two hours long, were obtained from 71 of the 83 lay members of five of the bishops' national advisory commissions in 1974–5. In these interviews four areas were investigated: the social and religious background of the respondent, his/her religious beliefs, views on recent changes in the Church, and observations on the work of the commissions. In a postal survey of the 68 lay members of the remaining commissions and listed advisory bodies, including the Catholic Education Council, 39 completed schedules were returned. Overall, therefore, data were obtained from 110 of the 151 lay members of the national Catholic advisory bodies, a net response rate of 75%, allowing for death and other serious reasons.

A study of a parish in the outer London commuter belt was subsequently extended in a second S.S.R.C. funded project 'Tradition and Change in the Roman Catholic Community in England' from 1975–7. In all four parishes were studied: an inner-London parish and a commuter parish about 20 miles from the centre of

Introduction

Table 1.1 *Summary of data sources*

Research stage	Years	Respondents	Research Instrument	Number	Length (av. hours)	Net response rate %
1. Commissions	1974–5	Lay members	Focussed interviews	71	2	88
			Postal questionnaires	39	na	57
2. Parishes	1974–7	Non-Catholic electors	Structured interviews	1164		
(a) Stage I					3/4	60
		Catholic electors	Structured interviews	266		
		Catholic activists	Structured interviews	84	3/4	94
(b) Stage II		Catholic electors	Focussed interviews	183	1/2–2	84
		Catholic activists	Focussed interviews	77	2	92
		Priests	Focussed interviews	15	1/2–2	100
3. National survey	1978	Adult Catholics	Structured Interviews	1023	1 1/4	
National Gallup omnibus	1978	Non-Catholics	Structured interviews	8915	na	
	1978	Catholics	Structured interviews	1150	na	
4. National Pastoral Congress	1981	Delegates (other than bishops)	Postal questionnaires	1276	na	65
5. Pope's visit	1982	Attenders at public events	Structured interviews	194	under 1/4	
	1982	Catholic attenders (after 4 months)	Postal questionnaires	120	na	72

London and an inner-city parish and a suburban parish in Preston, Lancashire. In each parish random samples of electors were selected using sampling fractions adjusted to achieve around 60 Roman Catholic electors. In addition, in each parish, around 20 parishioners identified by parish priests as being actively involved in the life of the parishes were interviewed. In each parish the priests were also interviewed, in several cases on more than one occasion.

Two types of interview were conducted with the parish samples. First of all, basic social and religious data were obtained from random samples of electors using a structured interview schedule (Hornsby-Smith, 1987). These Stage I interviews typically lasted three-quarters of an hour and were the main source of data on social mobility experiences. In addition, second, focussed interviews were obtained with the Roman Catholic electors identified in the first stage and also with activists. Similar interviews were obtained from the parish clergy. The Stage II interviews, which were generally tape-recorded, were more variable in length, ranging from half an hour to two hours. They focussed around four main areas: the respondent's social and religious background, religious beliefs, responses to recent changes in the Church, and observations on their own parish.

In the four parishes considered together, Stage I interviews were obtained with 1,164 non-Catholic electors, 266 Roman Catholic electors and 84 activists. In the rest of this book, except where indicated otherwise, parish data relating to random samples of electors have been given on the basis of a simulated sample of 1,430 electors, weighted to take account of the different response rates (averaging 60%, allowing for those who had moved away and not been replaced, the dead, ill or incapable categories) and different sampling fractions in the four parishes. It should be noted that the results relate to the aggregate elector samples in these four parishes only and no claim can be made that these are representative of the country as a whole. For example, the Roman Catholic densities in the four parishes were 18%, 8%, 33% and 27%, respectively, and in the weighted parish sample 17%, i.e. much higher than the national average of 11%. In addition to the Stage I interviews, Stage II interviews were obtained from 183 Roman Catholic electors (a net response rate of 84% of the available Stage I sample), 77 activists (87% of the original sample) and all 15 priests in the four parishes.

The third data source for this present study was the 1978 survey of *Roman Catholic Opinion* (Hornsby-Smith and Lee, 1979; this report reproduces the survey instrument and reports sampling procedures). The interviews conducted by Social Surveys (Gallup Poll) Ltd averaged around $1\frac{1}{4}$ hours in length with a national quota sample of 1,023 Catholics aged 15 and over, selected from 105 sampling points throughout England and Wales. Quota controls for age, sex and Mass-attendance frequency based on earlier aggregated Gallup omnibus data were used. In the analyses reported in the remainder of this book the results have been weighted according to the Mass-attendance and socio-economic status distributions revealed by 1978 omnibus survey data for a national sample of 10,172, including 1,150 Roman Catholics. The national sample of Roman Catholics in England and Wales was the best ever achieved in this country and it can reasonably be inferred that the weighted results from the 1978 survey substantially represent the views of Catholics a decade and a half after the Second Vatican Council.

In November–December 1981, 18 months after the N.P.C. had been held in Liverpool, all the delegates other than the 42 bishops were surveyed by postal questionnaire (Hornsby-Smith and Cordingley, 1983). A total of 1,276 usable replies was obtained, which represents a response rate of 65%. This survey, which is our fourth data source, had three aims: to elicit the reactions of the delegates to the Congress and its subsequent follow-up especially at the diocesan level, to describe the demographic, social and religious characteristics of the delegates in ways which enabled direct comparisons to be made with the findings in *Roman Catholic Opinion*, and to provide a basis for the construction of a new scale of 'progressivism' or aspects of a post-Vatican theological orientation. In addition, it was possible to make comparisons between 176 priests, 94 women religious and 959 lay delegates.

Finally, 211 tape-recorded interviews were obtained from people attending six of the public events of the Pope's visit to England and Wales in May–June 1982 at Wembley, Coventry, Liverpool, Manchester, York and Cardiff. Of these, 194 interviews, each averaging 10 minutes in length, were available for analysis; some interviews had been lost as a result of the malfunction of the tape or tape-recorder or because the conversation was obscured by extraneous noises, such as enthusiastic hymn singing over the public address system in the period before the arrival of the Pope. Each interviewer contacted people randomly, usually in or near their own corral or designated area, in order to ensure equal numbers of males and females in both the over and under 35 age categories. Interviewees spanned the age-range 13 to 75 and all social classes and included isolated individuals and stewards but also people in family or friendship groups. The interviews were chiefly concerned to explore people's motives in coming to the event, often at some considerable personal discomfort, and their attitudes to papal authority and obedience to the teachings of the Church. Apart from the interviews, participant-observation was carried out at all six events and Catholic interviewees were followed up by postal questionnaire in September 1982, four months after the visit. One hundred and twenty usable questionnaires (72%) were returned and included in the analysis. This questionnaire was chiefly concerned to identify demographic, social and religious data so that respondents could be compared with the findings in *Roman Catholic Opinion*, and also to test models of lay people's perceptions of the Pope's leadership style and attitudes to his teaching.

Taken together, the five studies reported in this book represented a substantial programme of sociological research on the changing nature of English Catholicism. The data sources, summarised in table 1.1, are unique and include not only a considerable body of quantitative material which enables the social and religious characteristics of English Catholics to be compared with those of their non-Catholic fellow countrymen, but also the biggest single collection of in-depth interview material with English Catholics, covering the whole range of institutional involvement from members of national advisory commissions to self-identifying Catholics at the parish level who had had no contact with the local church, sometimes for decades.

1.5 OUTLINE OF BOOK

In this chapter it has been argued that a study of the Roman Catholic community is merited by its size and social and religious significance 130 years or so after the restoration of the hierarchy of bishops. There are good grounds for anticipating that this community has been transformed as a result of post-war changes and by the gradual filtering through to the parish level of the reformulations and emphases emerging from the Second Vatican Council. Five distinct studies have been carried out over the past decade in the attempt to address the large number of themes identified.

In order to understand its emergence, it is necessary to try and place the contemporary English Catholic community in its social and historical context. It is suggested in chapter 2 that it comprises at least four distinct strands: recusant gentry, converts, Irish immigrants, and European refugees and immigrants. The contribution of each will be considered in turn and it will be asked whether the triumph of the Pope's visit in 1982 and its loose connection with the N.P.C. in 1980 can be interpreted as the growing to maturity of English Catholicism in a more tolerant society.

The popular model of Catholicism is one of monolithic homogeneity of belief and practice. It will be shown in chapter 3 that the reality is rather different. A typology of English Catholics has been constructed on the basis of survey data. These types will provide the basis for special analyses in subsequent chapters. Particular attention will be paid to the contrasting religious world-views of the 'activist' minority and the 'passive' majority. In this chapter, too, the evidence of major cleavages between generations will be presented and the implications for the cohesiveness of the Catholic community will be considered.

The original starting point for the present series of studies was the hypothesis of substantial Catholic social and geographical mobility in post-war Britain. The relevant evidence will be reviewed in chapter four and the 'mobility momentum' hypothesis will be tested. In addition, comparisons will be made between various groups: national advisers, N.P.C. delegates, parish activists, Catholic and other electors at the local level. The chapter concludes with an analysis of the relationship between social mobility experiences and religious and attitudinal variables.

Among official apologists in the Church, the ideology of the happy Catholic family has pride of place. Yet not only has there been widespread 'unspoken divergence' and opposition to the birth-control encyclical *Humanae Vitae*, but increasingly there is evidence that Catholic marriages are just as likely to break down as other marriages. In chapter 5, using data from the 1978 survey, a classification of Catholic marriages will be constructed on the basis of their religious endogamy or exogamy, their canonical status, and the timing of any switching of religious affiliation. The relationship between marriage type and processes of religious disaffiliation will be reported.

Separate analyses of first- and second-generation Irish Catholics will be reported in the following chapter. Surprisingly little has been written about the Irish in Britain since the 1960s in spite of their being the largest immigrant group. The evidence for the social mobility of Irish immigrants and its relationship to outgroup marriage will be reviewed and it will be suggested that there is evidence of substantial structural and cultural assimilation over two generations.

In the post-Vatican 'People of God' model of the Church there has been an emphasis on lay participation both in liturgical worship and in pastoral decision-making. In chapter 7 the focus will be on those activists, on the bishops' national advisory commissions, delegates to the N.P.C., and lay people at the parish level, who are most involved in the new structures. These new elites will be shown to be disproportionately highly educated, middle-class and middle-aged Catholics with a religious orientation which is predominantly 'progressive'. It will be suggested that these progressive elites are in latent conflict with the older, more established 'traditional' Catholics at all levels in the Church.

English Catholics have traditionally maintained a low political profile – the fruit of defensive responses learned in a hostile society over many generations in the post-Reformation period. In chapter 8 it is argued that they do not constitute a major political force in contemporary Britain. A review of their attitudes on a wide range of social, economic, political and moral issues suggests that in many ways English Catholics can be characterised as a 'domesticated denomination'. Even so there is a growing number of groups within the Church who have been challenging this stance and urging a 'preferential option for the poor'. This chapter also includes a brief review of the embryonic Catholic feminist movement and it is suggested that conflict with the male clerical leadership of the Church might be anticipated in the future.

In the following chapter four types of involvement in the community life of the Church will be distinguished and the implications of the density of Catholic friendships and the number of parish activities for religious practice and beliefs will be indicated. Secondly, three types of religious commitment will be distinguished. The chapter concludes with some observations about the Catholic parish and its quest for community. It will be argued that while the Catholic parish is adapting to some extent in response to social and religious change there is generally a divergence between the rhetoric of 'community' and the concrete reality. The problem of the parish as a 'greedy institution', consuming all the disposable resources and energies of activist Catholics is also noted.

The book concludes with some final reflections on the broad sweep of the research findings and the conflicting patterns of continuity and change, progressive activity and traditional passivity, conflict and accommodation. An underlying theme of the present work is the dissolution of the defensive walls around the English socio-religious community and its gradual cooptation by and assimilation to British society. In the process, religious authority has also been transformed and it is this theme which, in particular, will be explored in the sequel to this present volume.

It is, I think, important to try and explain my own research orientation so that the reader can better identify and allow for any biases in my selection of data or in my interpretation of them. My early research demonstrated positivist tendencies, a reflection no doubt of my previous training as a fuel technologist and chemical engineer. I continue to believe that in the last analysis good social research must appeal to the empirical evidence. I was particularly concerned to stress the patterned nature of religious beliefs and practices and to interpret them in terms of causes which constrained individuals. In this book there will be much quantitative analysis of survey data which demonstrate this type of approach. I would not wish to withdraw any of these data which, it seems to me, tell us a great deal about the patterns of religious belief and practice of English Catholics. They also enable us to test hypotheses about the effect of higher education or social mobility experiences or Irish immigration or parental religious behaviour on the current religious behaviour of English Catholics and they suggest new hypotheses or areas which require further exploration. In our work we frequently found it necessary to complement structured survey data with focussed interviewing in order to explore further the meanings which certain types of religious behaviour held for different types of Catholics. In practice it seems to me that multiple triangulation (Denzin, 1970) makes sense. So I have come to the view that in researching change in the English Catholic community good empirical research generally needs to combine survey methodology with focussed interviewing and participant-observation research strategies. As Max Weber observed

there is no absolutely 'objective' scientific analysis of culture ... of 'social phenomena' independent of special and 'one-sided' viewpoints according to which – expressly or tacitly, consciously or unconsciously – they are selected, analysed and organised for expository purposes ... The type of social science in which we are interested is an *empirical* science of concrete *reality*. Our aim is the understanding of the characteristic uniqueness of the reality in which we move. We wish to understand on the one hand the relationships and the cultural significance of individual events in their contemporary manifestations and on the other the causes of their being historically *so* and not otherwise. (Weber, 1949: 72)

If I am honest I will admit to a sense of awe when confronted with self-conscious theorising in sociology. Yet exemplary work in sociology rejects any sharp dichotomy between theory and method. My own position is fairly eclectic. I believe, with Durkheim, that to a very considerable extent human actors are constrained by external social forces. I also believe with conflict theorists that the outcome of much social interaction is determined by power differentials and the ability to mobilise resources or bias in the interests of the powerful as against the weak. I accept that Marx was right to direct our attention to economic interests, in particular, and to the ideologies employed by the powerful to legitimate decisions which operated in their favour. But I also believe that Weber was right to stress that the individual human being in interaction interprets and gives subjective meaning to that interaction and bargains and negotiates in an active manner in any concrete empirical situation. In other words, it seems to me that in the work of those empirical sociologists I most respect, there is a humility to recognise both the structural constraints within which social interaction takes place and that individual human beings actively interpret accordingly. In the area of religion as in industrial relations there is a dialectical relationship between structure and action.

Apart from methodological or theoretical predispositions it is also necessary to record that I am a life-long 'practising' Roman Catholic, actively involved in the life of the Church in this country at various levels and concerned as an individual to promote the 'renewal' of the Church along the lines encouraged by the theology of the 'open' Church and the participating 'People of God', which emerged in the teachings of the Second Vatican Council (Abbott, 1966). Thus I favour liturgical reform, lay participation at all levels of the Church, a much greater concern for the poor and for social justice and a recognition that religion cannot be divorced from politics in the real world. These are my personal beliefs, but I hope that as a social researcher I do not allow them to cloud my judgement about the evidence, for example about the latent effects of lay participation in the Church on nominal, working-class Catholics. But that must remain for the reader to judge. For the moment I regard the institutional Church in this country as loveable and flawed and much in need of reform and renewal so that it can more effectively serve as a witness to justice, truth, liberation and love.

CHAPTER 2

THE EMERGENCE
OF MODERN CATHOLICISM

2.1 INTRODUCTION

In order to interpret the empirical findings from our various surveys of English Catholics in the 1970s and early 1980s, it is necessary to locate them both historically and culturally. The importance of history for the sociologist has been observed by both C. Wright Mills and E.H. Carr:

We cannot hope to understand any single society, even as a static affair, without the use of historical materials. (Mills, 1970: 165–6)

We can fully understand the present only in the light of the past. (Carr, 1964: 55).

Two major purposes of a historical review of the roots of English Catholicism might be identified. The first purpose is to understand more completely its present composition and characteristics. Who are the English Catholics? Where do they come from? What are their beliefs and practices? What is distinctive about them? What historical experiences have shaped their present position in English society? The second and related purpose is to locate with some accuracy their position at some critical earlier times in order to explore more precisely what changes and trends there have been and what explanations can be offered to interpret them.

This exercise may help us to understand why it was that some Catholics viewed the Pope's historic visit in 1982 with some ambivalence. Broadly speaking five factors will be considered:

(a) the social and cultural heterogeneity of the English Catholic

community and the identification of at least four distinct strands in
its emergence over the past 130 years;
(b) the historical background of English Catholicism and its
nineteenth-century emphasis on loyalty to the Pope and deference
to decision-making by a centralist Roman bureaucracy, what is
called the 'ultramontane' tradition;
(c) the significance of the theological shifts of orientation legitimated by the Second Vatican Council held in Rome in the early
1960s and the many and far-reaching changes which have taken
place in the Roman Catholic Church generally in the ensuing
years;
(d) the manner in which the renewal of the Church in this country
in particular has been promoted, leading up to the National
Pastoral Congress in 1980 and the bishops' official response to it in
The Easter People (Anon., 1981: 307–98); and
(e) the emergence of a strong Pope, his reaffirmation of traditional
Catholic sexual morality and clergy–lay distinctions, the maintenance of a strong Roman centre *vis-à-vis* the local Churches, and
the impact of his visit to Britain in 1982.

Each of these will be discussed briefly in turn. The chapter will
conclude with a brief social portrait of the contemporary English
Catholic community and the identification of some of its distinctive
features in comparison with the general population.

2.2 HISTORICAL ROOTS

A recent authoritative account of the roots of twentieth-century
English Catholicism has argued that there have been three major
periods in the history of its evolution (Bossy, 1975). The first period
was brought to a close by the Protestant Reformation. The Act of
Supremacy of 1534 declared Henry VIII and his successors to be the
'Supreme Head on Earth' of the English Church. Refusal to accept
the Oath of Supremacy led to the executions of Bishop John Fisher
and Sir Thomas More. There followed the suppression of the
monasteries, the brief reigns of Edward VI, which saw attempts to
protestantise the Church, and of Mary, who attempted to restore the
traditional Catholic Faith. The accession of Elizabeth I witnessed the
final break with Rome by the passing of the Act of Supremacy and the
Act of Uniformity in 1559, early in her reign, and the establishment of
an English national Church claiming to be the Christian Church of

the land: 'the Church of England'. This ended the history of 'pre-Reformation' Christendom in England and heralded the emergence of 'the old Catholic community in England' about 1570 (Bossy, 1975; 4–5).

In Bossy's account, the second period was concerned with the English mission, which may be dated from the foundation of the English College at Douai on the continent in 1568. It was not until 1791 that penal restraints on the practice of Catholicism in England were abolished and not until 1829 were the civil disabilities of Catholics substantially removed. This second period ended in 1850 with the 'restoration of the hierarchy' of diocesan bishops and 'the climax of Irish immigration' in the years immediately after the famine. In Bossy's interpretation:

the history of the post-Reformation Catholic community in England is not to be envisaged as process of continuous decline reaching its nadir in the eighteenth century, but as a patient and continuous process of construction from small beginnings in which the eighteenth century represents a phase of modest progress and of careful preparation for the future. (Bossy, 1975: 297)

Arguably, Bossy's third period since 1850 continued until the changes emanating from the Second Vatican Council which ended in 1965. The Church in England, especially after the First Vatican Council in 1870, took on the monolithic characteristics of a rigid and unchanging bureaucracy. Various metaphors have been used to describe this model of the Church. At the 1980 Synod of Bishops in Rome, Cardinal Hume described a fortress model; Gabriel Daly (1981) refers to the enclosed village. Both metaphors emphasise the defense of strong outer walls against outsiders, prohibitions of breaches in the walls, the elimination of excursions beyond them, disciplined training and absolute obedience to superiors. In historical terms the definition of the dogma on papal infallibility resulted in the increasing use of papal power and an increasingly centralised and Roman bureaucracy. It has been suggested that the English Church, in response to 'virulent anti-papal prejudice in England' was particularly prone to ultramontanism (Coman, 1977: 12) which Daly defines as:

the wish for *total* conformity with papal ideas and ideals in *all* things and not merely in those which are essential to the unity of Christian and Catholic faith. Ultramontanes seek to derive their theological, political, and even cultural ideals from the Pope and Curia of their time. They may also promote 'creeping infallibility', but this is less important to their position than a disapproval of legitimate local autonomy, regional diversity, and freedom to explore issues in theology and church policy on which Rome is particularly sensitive. Ultramontanism treats the Bishop of Rome less as a bond of unity and charity in the Church than as an oracular figure to be reverenced in his person with quasi-sacramental fervour ... Ultramontanism is, in short, the predominant form taken by fundamentalism in a Catholic context, and it trivialises theology by reducing all issues to questions of authority and obedience. (Daly, 1981)

At this point a note of caution should be registered. The evidence of ultramontanism among English Catholics, especially in the more hostile environment in the nineteenth century, relates almost entirely to the Catholic elites and in particular to the bishops. The extent to which the 'ordinary' Catholic was familiar with this orientation (or that of its converse, gallicanism, the tendency to stress the prerogatives of the national Church), accepted it and acted in accordance with its assumptions, must remain an open question for further investigation by historians of the Catholicism of ordinary adherents in England in the late nineteenth century and the first half of the twentieth century.

In this connection it should be noted that there has been no significant social history of English Catholicism since the restoration of the hierarchy in 1850. Perhaps we are still too close to achieve a proper, detached perspective. Nevertheless there does seem to be some value in distinguishing three distinct phases in the emergence of the 'new English Catholic community' since the restoration of the hierarchy and the assimilation of successive waves of Irish immigrants. Broadly speaking, the period from 1850 to the Second Vatican Council in the early 1960s corresponds roughly to the model of the fortress Church. The 15 years from the end of the Council to the holding of the National Pastoral Congress represent a transitional period, perhaps an adolescent period, in the emergence of a new open, pluralist, participative, 'explorer' model of the Church. Arguably the Congress represented a *rite de passage* to a mature, adult, responsible, local Church, loyal to and in close relationship with the Pope and the Roman Curia but also proud of its proper independent contribution to the rich diversity of cultural traditions in the global Church. It remains to explore in more detail the extent to which this local Church in England and Wales will live up to this potential for strong, independent growth.

In the historical emergence of the contemporary English Catholic community, four distinct strands can be identified: recusant Catholics, converts, Irish immigrants and other immigrant groups.

(a) 'Recusant Catholics' are those Catholics who, very broadly, can be said to trace their Catholicism in some sort of unbroken line from pre-Reformation days. The term recusant referred to those Catholics who refused to attend the Anglican services and who were, in consequence, subject to penal taxation and fines. In the main, what Bossy calls 'the old Catholic community' emerged around the Catholic landowning gentry and their households, servants and tenants, especially in the remoter areas of the North and Lancashire. However, in the eight decades leading up to the restoration of the hierarchy, the English Catholic community grew enormously, became more geographically mobile and regionally dispersed, and experienced

an occupational and social transformation: congregations of labourers, handicraftsmen, tradesmen, the simply poor, their wives and children, topped by a stratum of business and professional families, replaced in the centre of the scene congregations of gentry, farmers, agricultural labourers and rural craftsmen. (Bossy, 1975: 298)

With religious and ethnic group intermarriage and leakage over many generations it is not possible to give any precise estimate of the significance of this source of contemporary Catholicism. However, if the assumption is made that the English Catholic population grew at the same rate as the total population, there would now be around 650,000 recusant Catholics in England and Wales (Currie, Gilbert and Horsley, 1977: 50).

(b) Converts to Roman Catholicism have made a substantial contribution to the growth of English Catholicism over the past two centuries. There is evidence that by the late eighteenth century a number of converts were being made as a result of the general missionary endeavours of Catholic priests after about 1700. It has been reported that

there were about 740,000 adult conversions to Catholicism in Britain between 1900 and 1960, perhaps a half or three-quarters of which represented a lasting increment to the Catholic population. (Currie, Gilbert and Horsley, 1977: 50)

Undoubtedly, the best known convert was John Henry (later Cardinal) Newman in 1845, but relatively few of his associates from the

Catholic movement in the Church of England, the Oxford movement, joined him, and so the trickle never became a stream nor Newman's 'Second Spring' an actuality. Many consider that Newman's great intellectual, theological and ecumenical contributions only bore their full fruit at the Second Vatican Council. In recent years receptions into the Church reached a peak of over 16,000 in 1959 but declined to one-third of his level in the 1970s. The 1978 survey of *Roman Catholic Opinion* (Hornsby-Smith and Lee, 1979) indicated that around 11% of Catholic adults, or around 460,000 English Catholics, are converts. The significance of convert marriages will be considered in some detail in chapter 5.

(c) Irish immigrants constitute the third, and numerically the largest strand in contemporary English Catholicism. In spite of Bossy's stress on the fact that a transformation and expansion of the *English* Catholic community was already well under way by 1770 (Bossy, 1975: 298–9), there is no doubt that the dramatic increase in the size of this community since the late eighteenth century can be attributed to what he calls 'the Irish deluge, beginning about 1790' (Bossy, 1975: 322). Even in the four towns in Catholic Lancashire that he considers for special analysis he reports that 'a ratio of three Irish-descended to one English-descended Catholic ... in 1851 seems likely' (Bossy, 1975: 308). Emigration in search of employment and opportunities and to avoid poverty and starvation has been a major feature of the history of Ireland at least since the last two decades of the eighteenth century (Kennedy, 1973). While many went to America or Australia in search of a better life, many, and since the mid-1930s, most, of these emigrants came to Britain. Census returns since 1841 have indicated sizeable numbers of Irish-born in Britain. Only in the changed economic circumstances of the late 1970s does it appear that there has been a net return flow of Irish from Britain.

The significance of immigration for English Catholicism can be judged in the first instance from an analysis of the country of birth tables of the 1971 Census. Making the simplifying assumption that the proportion of Catholics among immigrants is the same as their proportion among the indigenous population of the sending country, estimates have been made in table 2.1 of the number of Roman Catholic immigrants using data published in the *Statistical Yearbook of the Church* (Central Statistics Office of the Church). The full details of this analysis are not reproduced here but the contribution of immigration to English Catholicism is apparent. One-quarter (1.4

Table 2.1 *Estimates of Roman Catholic immigrants in England and Wales in 1971 by country of birth*

Countries of birth	Resident population ×10³	Estimated average %RCs	Computed Roman Catholics in England and Wales	
			×10³	%
Ireland	892	75.4	672	12.5
Old Commonwealth	129	32.5	42	0.8
New Commonwealth	1,121	12.5	141	2.6
Europe	603	70.1	423	7.9
Other	537	14.5	78	1.4
All outside Great Britain	3,283	41.3	1,356	25.2
Great Britain	45,338	8.9	4,026	74.8
All countries incl. visitors	48,750	11.4	5,382	100.0

Sources: O.P.C.S., Census 1971: Great Britain Country of Birth Tables, 1974. Statistical Yearbook of the Church, Rome, 1977.

million) of those who identify themselves as Roman Catholics are first-generation immigrants. Further analyses indicate that an additional 20% of Catholics (1.1 million) are second-generation immigrants (Hornsby-Smith, 1986).

Thus, in 1971 there were 3.3 million people living in England and Wales who had been born outside Great Britain. Of these some 892,000 had been born in Ireland. It is estimated that 75.4% of the combined population of the Irish Republic and Northern Ireland are Roman Catholics. Assuming that the proportion of Catholic immigrants is the same, it appears that some 672,000 Irish-born Catholics were living in England and Wales in 1971. Further analyses suggest that an additional 640,000 Catholics were second-generation Irish immigrants, that is British-born children of Irish parents. In sum, between one-fifth and one-quarter of English Catholics are either first- or second-generation Irish immigrants. The patterns of their assimilation to British society will be considered in chapter 6.

(d) Further analyses of the 1971 Census returns suggest that apart from the Irish immigrants there were around 684,000 Catholics in England and Wales who were born in countries outside the British Isles (table 2.1). Very little is known about them. Under 1% of the Catholics come from the substantially white 'Old Commonwealth' countries: Australia, Canada and New Zealand. It appears that

around 2.6% Catholics are from the 'New Commonwealth' countries. These include about 100,000 black Catholics from African,
West Indian and Asian countries and about 38,000 Catholics mainly
from Malta and Gibraltar. About 8% of the English Catholics (or
over 423,000) were born in European countries. The largest numbers
come from Italy (100,000), Poland (100,000), Germany (57,000),
Spain (48,000) and France (29,000). Finally, there are around 1.4%
Catholics who were born in other countries, including about 20,000
from the United States.

In sum, the estimates suggest that approximately one in eight
Catholics are in each of the following categories: recusants, first-
generation Irish, other immigrants, and second-generation Irish.
There are around 8 or 9% converts (allowing for children) and a
similar number of second-generation immigrants with origins outside
the British Isles. The balance of around one-third of English Catholics has a variety of other and mixed backgrounds but it is likely that
the bulk of them will have an Irish ancestry which originated three or
more generations ago.

2.3 THE MYTH OF A GOLDEN AGE

In order to understand more clearly recent changes in the Roman
Catholic Church it is important to demythologise the past so that
comparisons will not be made to some supposed golden age of Catholicism whether in the Middle Ages or the years immediately before the
Second Vatican Council. In the first place it is important to note the
weight of historical evidence which suggests that not only were the
urban working classes of industrial England lost to the various
churches but also that agricultural labourers and the 'common
people' of England never were significantly attached to organised religion at least from the sixteenth and seventeenth centuries. The evidence suggests that it is quite erroneous to suppose that low levels of
religious adherence and practice are relatively recent phenomena
caused by the nineteenth century processes of urbanisation and indus-
trialisation. Historians have described the ignorance and indifference
towards religion in the sixteenth and seventeenth centuries (Chadwick, 1975; Gilbert, 1976; Thomas, 1973). It is, then, not surprising
that at the end of the nineteenth century the Revd Winnington-
Ingram observed that 'it is not that the Church of God has lost the
great towns; it never had them ... ' (Quoted in Inglis, 1963: 3).

In seeking to describe the situation of Roman Catholicism in England and Wales before the Second Vatican Council it is also important not to paint too rosy a picture, for example, on such issues as the 'lapsation' rates (i.e. cessation of Mass attendance not necessarily involving disaffiliation or switching of religious adherence) or the cohesiveness and consensus of belief and practice of the Catholic body. In the first place it is historically inaccurate to suppose that practising Irish Catholics lost their faith only after arrival in Britain. It has been shown that the weak structural position of the Church in Ireland before the famine resulted in 'a low level of participation in the cycle of parish rituals and general ignorance of orthodox Catholic doctrine' (Lees, 1979: 166; see also Connolly, 1982).

Indeed the Irish Catholicism of recent years was imported into Ireland by Cardinal Cullen only a century ago. It is not surprising, therefore, that there was widespread concern over the 'leakage' of Catholics from the Church well before the end of the nineteenth century (Holmes, 1978: 161–7, 207–8, 211–15; Inglis, 1962: 122–42) by which time it was estimated that nearly a million Catholics had fallen away from the faith. Mass attendance among improverished Catholics struggling to exist in the urban slums of London and Cardiff was only about 20–30% (Hickey, 1967: 90–4; McLeod, 1974: 34–5). Generally the evidence suggests that in the nineteenth century the strains associated with migration and poverty may have lessened relations with the institutional Church for many Catholics, if indeed for some they ever existed (Bossy, 1975: 313–16).

A second reason for stressing that there was no golden past in English Catholicism is that one cannot uncritically assume that the Catholic Church during the nineteenth century and up to the 1950s was a cohesive, tightly knit body, sharing the same values and beliefs, substantially united under a clerical leadership, and manifesting an absence of divisive conflicts. Again, there are good reasons for modifying this view. In the first place it has already been indicated that the Catholic community was not homogeneous in its origins or allegiance. In particular the recusant Catholics and Irish immigrants differed not only in terms of their national identities and cultures but often also in respect of social class (Holmes, 1978: 30, 158–61, 178–83). It has also been suggested that in the nineteenth century the English bishops were responsible for a lack of Irish priests for the Irish immigrants in England (Gay, 1971: 91).

Liberal Catholics such as Cardinal Newman and 'modernists' who attempted 'to reconcile Catholicism with contemporary developments in the social, political and especially the intellectual world' (Holmes, 1978: 254) were also in conflict with ultramontanes such as Cardinals Manning and Vaughan and with 'integrism', or the defence of theological orthodoxy as 'an alleged "whole" which had to be defended against modification of any of its parts' (Daly, 1980: 187). This orthodoxy and 'its monopolistic imposition by authoritative decree' (Daly, 1980: 220) found its most notorious expression in the *Syllabus of Errors* of Pope Pius IX in 1864 and the encyclical letter *Pascendi* of Pope Pius X in 1907. The consequences were an English Catholicism which was 'chiefly engaged on practical rather than intellectual activities' (Holmes, 1978: 254). Arguably the contemporary conflict between 'traditionalists' and 'progressives', which will be considered further in chapter 7, has its roots in these nineteenth-century conflicts.

The cleavage between the mainly English upper middle classes and the mainly Irish urban working classes has perhaps never been bridged completely and class differences were apparent in the support for different sides in the Spanish Civil War in the 1930s (Hastings, 1977: 118–19). It is perhaps doubtful if even the great campaigns on behalf of Catholic schools following the 1944 Education Act united Catholics of all social classes, given the size and prestige of the Catholic independent schools for the upper middle classes. Hence it is not surprising that Fitzsimons, in a cross-national analysis of the Catholic Church in the mid-1960s, observed of English Catholics that

each constituent group ... had little knowledge of the others and neither theology nor their devotions promoted a lively corporate sense. (The English Catholic world was one) of unbourgeois extremes, of an upper class and an abundant mass. (Fitzsimons, 1969: 309–44)

Priest–lay relationships are often assumed to have been good and there is certainly strong evidence of Irish priests in particular sharing the miseries of their fellow countrymen in ghetto parishes in the major urban centres. This assumption should probably be qualified, however, in at least two respects. First, with the restoration of the hierarchy in 1850, prominent Catholic lay leaders were particularly concerned to retain the control which they had hitherto exerted over their priests and to resist the imposition of a foreign, Roman, clerical jurisdiction which would create further public antagonism against the Catholic community (Bossy, 1975; Hastings, 1977).

Secondly, there are good grounds for suspecting that some Catholic priests did not always act with sympathy and understanding in the confessional on the matters of birth control and marital difficulties. It seems likely that wherever there was a lack of pastoral sensitivity on such issues, large numbers of Catholics ceased to practise their religion and expressed resentments and antagonisms towards a Church which they considered had not cared enough about their real problems. For various reasons, therefore, it is necessary to be cautious in presenting a picture of a tightly disciplined, united and uniform Church in this country up to the 1950s.

Historical studies of religion in London and post-war empirical studies in Liverpool have both contributed to the construction of a social portrait of Roman Catholicism before the Second Vatican Council. A recurring theme is the authoritarianism of the parish priest in the Catholic community (McLeod, 1981: 128–31). In some cases this resulted in an atmosphere of 'spiritual totalitarianism' and on occasion led to a reaction against 'overbearing ministers' or 'benevolent tyrants' (McLeod, 1974: 74) and revolts against coercive Catholic schools. With the gradual expansion of educational opportunities in the post-war years the laity increasingly resented being treated as a 'spiritual proletariat' (O'Dea, 1958; quoted in Brothers, 1964: 81) and there were strong indications of a change in the relationships of educated Catholics to the parochial structures (Brothers, 1964).

A series of empirical studies in Liverpool in the 1950s provides us with a clear picture of the tightly knit, defensive, ghetto-like Irish inner-city parish. The rigidity of the ritual in this highly structured institution provided security but also dependence and an inconsistent social morality (which rejected birth control but tolerated abortion up to three months) (Kerr, 1958: 137, 170). Residential stability contributed to the functioning of the Catholic parish as a conservative force (Wyatt, 1976) and the parish school contributed to the religious socialisation of the child and ensured a minimum level of religious conformity and loyalty to the tribal institutions. Worship and prayer with non-Catholics were strongly discouraged and there were formidable sanctions against 'mixed marriages' which it was feared would endanger the faith of the Catholic partners. Even allowing for the distinctive elements of Liverpool Catholicism, it is not surprising that Catholics had a reputation as recently as the late 1960s for 'keeping themselves to themselves', for their 'defensive, cautious attitude', their 'attitude of introversion, of "anti-world"', their 'proud, sometimes arrogant attitude in its certitude of being right – and of everyone else being wrong' (Scott, 1967:13).

It has been argued that in the pre-Vatican years the leadership of the English Catholic community displayed all the characteristics of a distinctive, ultramontanist subculture, with a special emphasis on allegiance to the Pope and obedience in all religious matters (often widely defined) to the Roman See; characteristic norms and values of marital, sexual and familial morality; a unique identity and separateness fostered by peculiarly Roman Catholic practices such as the retention of Latin in the liturgy and Friday abstinence (Douglas, 1973) in supportive inner-city parishes (Hickey, 1967; Rex and Moore, 1967; Ward, 1961); a strong sense of boundary-maintenance and a fear of the erosion of values, resulting in a tendency to defensiveness and an emphasis on all-Roman-Catholic marriages and on a segregated Catholic schools system; and finally, particular views on social issues with a special emphasis on the family, property ownership and the principal of subsidiarity (Coman, 1977). While the cause of Irish Home Rule, 60 years after the Anglo-Irish treaty, is no longer the main integrating element in the Irish Catholic community in England, the political allegiances of Catholics continue to reflect a pronounced bias against Unionism (Jackson, 1963: 127; Hornsby-Smith and Lee, 1979: 37–9). On the other hand, with the decline of a recognisable Roman Catholic subculture in the affluent post-war years, there was a weakening in the presentation of a distinctive body of socio-economic teaching (Coman, 1977). In general, therefore, while there is much of value in the notion of a separate English Catholic subculture, it is probable, for the reasons already noted, that the historical social homogeneity of the Catholic community was exaggerated and the extent of heterodoxy in its doctrinal and moral beliefs and practices was underestimated.

A number of writers have stressed the 'other-worldly' nature of Catholicism. Bishop Beck, for example, quoted Evennett's well-known statement that 'the quintessential left by a Catholic education is a lasting consciousness of the fact and meaning of death' and at the centenary of the restoration of the hierarchy proclaimed a defiant and intransigent separateness from the world on the part of the Catholic claiming that 'the "other-wordliness" in a Catholic must always be his dominant if not immediately evident, characteristic' (Beck, 1950b: 604). There seems to be some evidence, however, that this other-worldliness had its price in a lack of concern for others (Lawlor, 1965) and the poverty of the contribution of Catholics to the great social, political and economic issues of the times (Coman, 1977; Hickey, 1967; Mays, 1965). It is necessary to take note of all these historical findings and impressions in order to avoid the danger of romanticising the past. While there is insufficient historical data to allow proper comparison of the Catholic Church in England and Wales in the early 1980s with the situation, say up to the end of the 1950s, it is important to stress that the information we do have is more than adequate to prevent our assuming that there ever was a past 'golden age'. While there may have been major changes in recent years, it does not follow necessarily that there has been a decline.

2.4 COMPETING MODELS OF THE CHURCH

What then was the character of the Roman Catholic Church in England and Wales as an institution in the years immediately after the Second World War and prior to the big social and economic changes which accompanied the era of post-war affluence in the late 1950s and Pope John's calling of the Second Vatican Council? From the preceding discussion it seems clear that the institutional model identified by Avery Dulles (1976) corresponds most closely to the sociological reality of the Church in the 1950s. The emphasis here is on the Church as a structured community led by office holders with clearly defined rights and powers. Dulles suggests that by itself this model tends to be doctrinaire and to result in rigidity and conformity. In a stable, unchanging world the Church manifested the character- istics of a 'mechanistic' organisation, such as a distinct hierarchical structure of control, authority and communication, tendencies for interaction between superiors and subordinates to be vertical, and for normal behaviour in the institution to be governed by instructions and decisions issued by superiors, and an insistence on loyalty to the institution and obedience to superiors as a condition for membership (Burns and Stalker, 1966). The hierarchical authority structures were seen as mediating grace and truth to the laity and there is a marked tendency for the institution to be concerned with its own survival and maintenance (Winter, 1973).

The pre-Vatican Church stressed the virtues of loyalty, the certainty of answers, strict discipline and unquestioning obedience (Greeley, 1972). In this model the priest was viewed as a 'man apart' and the 'sacred' ministry of the priest was asserted over the priesthood of all believers (Moore, 1975). In the pre-Vatican theology with its fidelity to tradition (Pro Mundi Vita, 1973), God was seen as remote, unchanging and perfect (Neal, 1970). There was a close relationship between an emphasis on a transcendent God, a hierarchically structured Church, an authoritarian clergy and social distance between the clergy and the laity (Sharratt, 1977). At the parish level there was an emphasis on the objectivity of the sacramental system and a discouragement of full lay involvement in liturgical worship. The sermon provided an opportunity to legitimate traditional practices and reinforce traditional status and power differentials. Control of information was monopolised by the priests who discouraged ecumenical ventures and independent lay initiatives. The 'sacredness' of the separate Catholic community was preserved by insistence on marital endogamy and religious socialisation in separate Catholic schools. Separation from contamination by the world was emphasised and, though there was the exercise of charity in order to save souls, social and political involvement as a requirement of the gospel was rejected (Leslie, 1980).

There seem to be good grounds, however, for believing that the Roman Catholic Church was unable to contain a growing 'underworld of dissent' with the ghetto strategy. The need to address the prevailing concerns of the contemporary world was becoming increasingly apparent. The strategy of suppression which had been ruthlessly followed for over half a century since the condemnation of modernism was beginning to break down. Coleman (1978) has suggested a seven-stage model of structural differentiation to explain the process and, in organisational terms, the Vatican Council's emphasis on collegiality and participation by all the 'People of God' can be interpreted as a shift to an 'organic' management structure in a changing world with far more emphasis on lateral consultation than vertical command (Burns and Stalker, 1966). The Church was to be transformed from a pyramid of organisation and power into a community of service and mission on the march (Moore, 1975: 34–5). There was increasing emphasis on the community, sacrament, herald and servant models of the Church (Dulles, 1976).

A number of attempts have been made to characterise the paradigmatic shift which has occurred. In the United States, Andrew Greeley (1975) has suggested that what is involved is a completely 'new agenda' for the Church with less emphasis on the defence of the Faith and more on the interpretation of religious symbols. There was a shift from assertions of immortality and the importance of the salvation of souls, Sunday Mass attendance and the indissolubility of marriage to a concern with how Christians live fully human and liberated lives in the community of the faithful.

These changes, remarkable in such a powerful organisation as the Roman Catholic Church, resulted from fundamental shifts of theological orientation legitimated by the Second Vatican Council. Daly (1980: 220–2) has bluntly characterised this as one from 'tyrannous transcendentalism' to 'radical immanentism'. Theology is said to have become more humanistic and in the post-Vatican period has stressed that

God acts in history, through people, in ever new ways. We must be ever ready to listen and respond to other persons, since he is always speaking to us through human encounter, the very diversity of which reflects the life of God expressed in the Trinity. The breaking through of cultural barriers; service rather than command as the stance of those in authority; singing and celebration together; acting to make just the social conditions of our times; protesting what is evil – these are the ways to come to know God and to realise the kingdom he promised. (Neal, 1970: 13)

Thus a new theological culture has emerged

around the themes of collegiality, dialogue, democratization, pluralism in theology, free theological inquiry, and free speech in the church. New theologies of creation, salvation, revelation, and grace have undercut rigid nature–supernature distinctions or too-facile divisions between the sacred and the profane. These new theologies have implications for the way in which the roles of priest and laity are defined in the church, and the way in which they allow the appeal to experience (instead of to trans-physical fiat) as the basis for the church's understanding of its own symbols and 'the signs of the times'. (Coleman, 1978: 17–18)

In consequence, there has been a shift from the traditional missionary strategy to a new cultural–pastoral strategy with an ideology of pluralist participation. Instead of the layman being viewed as simply an agent of the bishop, his role is now that of the Christian citizen, responsible as a co-participant by virtue of his baptism for transforming the political society (Coleman, 1978: 11–16). Whereas the pre-Vatican Church had been top-heavy with 'duty-language', the Second Vatican Council had

created a new rhetoric system which stressed the reciprocal duties of higher officers to respect the rights of lower agents: service, dialogue, pluriformity, collegiality, and consultation were called for. (Coleman, 1978: 198)

McSweeney interprets the shifts of theological orientation as manifestations of the latest stage in the long search for relevance by the Church in the modern world. In this view, the period since the Second Vatican Council has seen the victory of progressive theology which had originated in various attempts at reform and, in particular, the French worker-priest movement, the drive for Christian Unity, and the liturgical revival.

The newly emerging theology, therefore, marked a shift of emphasis from Christ's divinity to his humanity; from the Church as institution of salvation to the Church as community; from the objective to the subjective aspect of liturgy; from God's transcendence and otherness to his presence among men and in all creation; from the resurrection as a discrete event in the past and in the future to the kingdom already present in this world and in process of fulfilment; from a moral theology of sin to a moral theology of human development and interpersonal relationships. The effect of this attempt to redress the balance of tradition was to create a sense of the openness of dogma reflecting the openness of the human experience from which the meaning of dogma must be derived. (McSweeney, 1980: 112-13)

In order to facilitate the analysis of changes in the Church in recent years we have followed Weber in constructing 'ideal-types' of theological orientation before and after the Second Vatican Council (Weber, 1949: 90). These are grounded in empirical reality but by accentuating certain elements they enable us to identify key variables in the search for explanation and understanding. Thus it can be suggested that in contrast with the pre-Vatican Council situation where 'antimodernism became a species of ecclesiastical patriotism enforced by an oath' (Daly, 1980: 218) and neo-scholasticism was the stipulated theological orthodoxy, the post-conciliar period has been characterised by a plurality of theologies. Recent empirical studies have indeed demonstrated a wide range of theological orientations, for example among missionary priests in their understanding of God, revelation, tradition, and the role of the priest in the contemporary world (Pro Mundi Vita, 1973).

McSweeney has argued that a major feature in the post-Vatican theology is its doctrinal relativism. Thus, although there is a rhetoric of theological pluralism, in practice there has been a transition from theological uniformity to theological individualism since there is no longer any genuine, concrete unity of faith, belief or practice among Roman Catholics, who are now linked only by their common origin and by habit. This extreme version of the impact of the shift of theological orientation occasioned by the Vatican Council, while it usefully draws attention to the implications for social control within the Church of the 'desacralisation of authority', nevertheless appears to exaggerate the extent to which theological uniformity and a unity of faith and practice prevailed up to the 1950s. He has, however, usefully identified at least three conflicting theologies in what he sees as the fragmentation of Catholicism in recent years:

1 Political Catholicism which 'identifies the transformation of society as the necessary condition, if not the realization, of salvation' (McSweeney, 1980: 198) and which has been articulated powerfully by the liberation theologians of Latin America;

2 Charismatic Catholicism which is primarily concerned to transform the style of prayer but which 'is so individualistic as to reduce the possibility of a social activism to the level of charitable works of a politically ineffective kind' (McSweeney, 1980: 213); and

3 Traditional Catholicism which rejects the new theology and doctrinal tolerance 'in favour of the dogmatic certitude and authoritarian government of the old Catholicism' (McSweeney, 1980: 222).

What is of interest to the sociologist is the social location of these competing theologies within the Christian community, the political role which they perform, and the resources which their various proponents are able to mobilise in their defence and advocacy. In this connection it is salutary to note that the shift of theological orientation legitimated by the Vatican Council in the main represented a victory for certain European intellectual elites. From the perspective of the Latin American Church the new theology, however, looks decidedly bourgeois and the liberation theologians, in response to their analysis of structural injustices, stress that Christianity should not be simply a compensation for oppression and misery but should be concerned to liberate man and transform social relationships (Baum, 1980).

It would be impossible to give a full description of English Catholicism both immediately before the Second Vatican Council and in the post-conciliar period. However, the models which have been outlined do provide standards of comparison based on the identification of key features of the actual social realities. In the earlier period of stability a 'mechanistic' or bureaucratically administered Church ensured a high level of loyalty and conformity through its monopoly of control over the agencies of socialisation, ideological legitimation and the maintenance of group solidarity using an imposing array of religious sanctions. The post-Vatican period has been one of transition and of adaptation to the modern world. It has therefore been characterised by an 'organic' form of authority structure which has been legitimated by the ideology of participation in a joint undertaking by all the 'People of God' and by theological pluralism which distinguishes between the content of belief and its culturally bound modes of expression.

In the transition from the earlier 'mechanistic' model of the Church to the newer, post-Vatican 'organic' model, two events in particular had considerable importance for English Catholics. On 2–6 May, 1980 over 2,000 delegates attended the first N.P.C. in Liverpool. This was an elaborate attempt to 'renew' the Church in the light of the teachings of the Second Vatican Council and it had been preceded by wide discussion and consultation within the Catholic community over a period of some two years. Three months after the Congress the bishops published their official response to it in *The Easter People* (Anon., 1981: 307–98). When presenting this to the Pope, Cardinal Hume and Archbishop Worlock had invited him to make a pastoral visit to the Roman Catholic community of England and Wales in 1982. In spite of the uncertainties surrounding the visit beforehand because of the Falklands conflict, it was widely judged to have been a most successful ecumenical venture. It is tempting to regard these two events as marking the end of the period of adolescence of English Catholicism, its 'coming-of-age', the final shedding of the uncertainties and defensiveness of the fortress Church, and its emergence as a significant social and religious force in British society. It is one purpose of this book to evaluate the force of this view. In the two following sections of this chapter the N.P.C. and the visit of Pope John Paul II will each be discussed briefly in the context of the historical emergence of the English Catholic community and its adjustment to the social and religious changes of the past decade or so.

2.5 THE NATIONAL PASTORAL CONGRESS

The Congress was a key event in the attempts of the Church in these countries to come to terms with a rapidly changing world. It was attended, mainly by lay people but included 42 bishops, 255 clergy, 150 religious men and women and 36 ecumenical observers. In the two years preceding the Congress, the attempt had been made to involve as many Catholics as possible in the preparations and, to a considerable extent, the agenda was framed on the basis of responses of discussion groups at the parish level and by Catholic organisations (Anon., 1981). The bulk of the delegates were selected at the diocesan and deanery levels on the basis of one delegate for every 1,000 Sunday Mass attenders. Roughly equal numbers of men and women attended and there were over 300 delegates under 25 years of age, including about 100 still in their teens. The attempt was made to ensure representation of minority groups such as the Poles and members of the Latin Mass Society but there is evidence that the delegates were disproportionately articulate, educated, middle class and active members (Hornsby-Smith and Cordingley, 1983).

At each stage of the deliberations the bishops, clergy and members of the religious orders were all fully involved as participating members of the discussions. Before the Congress, doubts had been expressed that the whole exercise would simply be an elaborate, 'triumphalist' celebration but that serious debate and probable confrontation on such controversial issues as contraception or the morality of nuclear deterrence would be carefully stage-managed. The fears that the Congress proceedings might be manipulated in this way were sufficiently acute for some discussion-group leaders at a preliminary briefing on the first evening to challenge the desirability of playing a video-taped message from the Pope at the first session. They feared that this might be an attempt to pre-empt the agenda construction and discussion. In the event Pope John Paul II congratulated the delegates for the initiative they were taking in shared responsibility and the bishops shared fully in the discussions as participating members. There was no evidence that tolerance was not extended to minority views and the Congress was widely regarded by the delegates to have been a 'conversion' occasion and a remarkable and exhilarating experience of an open, participative, sharing and celebrating Church, unfamiliar to many delegates from parishes where liturgical worship was more traditional and ritualistic and where priest–lay relationships were more formal. Not surprisingly, therefore, the Congress concluded with considerable euphoria and the highest expectations for the future of the Church in the two countries.

The reports presented by the sector presidents on the final morning of the Congress were in many ways remarkable documents, characterised by an absence of obsequiousness to ecclesiastical authority but a firmness in expressing the views of the delegates on a wide range of religious, social and moral concerns with an unassertive tact. The bishops were urged, for example, by an overwhelming majority of sector A delegates to 'consider the possibility of making provision for eucharistic hospitality in certain cases' such as inter-Church marriages (Anon., 1981: 135). Sector B delegates hoped that 'the possibility of admitting women to the ordained ministries' would be explored (ibid.: 156). Sector C delegates voted overwhelmingly for 'a fundamental re-examination of the teaching on marriage, sexuality and contraception', the majority feeling that this 'should leave open the possibility of change and development' (ibid.: 170, 189). Sector G confessed 'our failure as a Church to combat the prevailing national mood of insularity, to identify with the poor in our midst and to work vigorously for a more peaceful world' (ibid.: 290), asserted that membership of the Church was incompatible with membership of the National Front and urged 'the search for credible non-violent alternatives' to war (ibid.: 293).

To many delegates the bishops' message to the Church 'in the light of the National Pastoral Congress', *The Easter People*, published in August 1980, was a considerable disappointment. It is true that it opened with a long theological reflection on 'the sharing Church' which unambiguously recommended the participating, open model of the Church experienced at Liverpool. But when it came to respond in detail to the many specific recommendations of the Congress, the bishops were far more circumspect. On matters of general orientation, such as the value of small groups or the centrality of concern for the poor and the powerless, and on matters which did not explicitly require any further decision-making or shift of resources, such as the condemnation of racist organisations, the bishops generally endorsed the Congress recommendations. Decisions on other matters such as seeking full membership of the British Council of Churches or the question of a married clergy were either accepted only with qualifications or postponed for further consideration. Some pastoral requests such as intercommunion in the case of non-Catholic spouses and the admission to the sacraments of the invalidly married were rejected outright. Finally the bishops indicated a number of gaps in the concerns of the Congress resolutions, for example the evangelisation of our own society (Pro Mundi Vita, 1980: 27–8).

This uneven response to the Congress can best be interpreted as an attempt to conciliate a number of quite different audiences. In this sense *The Easter People* was a 'political' document. First, in their theological reflection on 'the sharing Church' they clearly did not repudiate the experience at Liverpool and offered substantial encouragement to those who favoured the full implementation of the pastoral teaching of the Second Vatican Council. These included the bulk of the Congress delegates, even if many of them were deeply disappointed by the lack of response to the specific recommendations relevant to their work especially in the declining inner cities.

The bishops also had to take account of the reaction of the Roman authorities. With the lessons of the Dutch Church (Coleman, 1978) in mind and the Dutch Synod of January 1980 as a warning against excessive independence on the part of the local Church behind them, and the uncertain prospect of the Synod on the Family in Rome in September–October 1980 ahead of them, the questions of contraception, intercommunion and the pastoral care of the divorced and invalidly married clearly had to be handled with great care, if the full power of a traditionalist and centralist Pope was not to be provoked so as to limit the autonomy of the bishops in England and Wales. In the event, the Congress delegates expressed their concerns on these controversial issues with sensitivity and restraint. Subsequently, in their interventions at the Synod on the Family, Cardinal Hume and Archbishop Worlock expressed the concerns which the vast majority of Catholics in these countries had articulated through the Congress delegates. Cardinal Hume referred to the 'special authority in matters concerning marriage' of married couples and argued that it cannot just be said that people for whom 'natural methods of birth control do not seem to them to be the definitive and only solution ... have failed to overcome their human frailty and weakness' since they 'are often good, conscientious and faithful sons and daughters of the Church' (Catholic Information Services, 1980: 6). Archbishop Worlock pleaded for the restoration of full eucharistic communion for the divorced and remarried and pointed out that pre-synodal consultations had not indicated that Catholics would be scandalised by such a healing ministry of consolation. These representations by English Catholics did not call forth a sharp rebuke from Rome, but the authors of *The Easter People* must have been concerned to ensure that the challenge to the traditional teaching of the Church, on the one hand was not suppressed in such a way as to provoke a new and highly public explosion of discontent by the laity, or on the other hand, allowed to get out of hand and provoke the wrath of the Roman authorities.

The bishops in their response to the N.P.C. also had to bear in mind the reaction of the huge mass of relatively passive and uninvolved, as well as the traditional Catholics in the parishes. These Catholics tended to regard the Church in static and unchanging terms and to consider any changes in rituals or routines with suspicion. Traditional Catholics tended to distinguish sharply between Catholicism and other forms of Christianity and to interpret Catholic teaching on social and moral issues in black-and-white terms. It seems at least likely that in their responses, for example on intercommunion or the pastoral care of the divorced or invalidly married or on the question of a married clergy, the bishops would have been concerned to take account of the views of this constituency. In chapter 7 it will be suggested that the religious worlds of the active minority and the passive majority are sharply distinguished and that the delegates to the N.P.C. overwhelmingly represented only the former. In *The Easter People* it is likely that the bishops took account of the need to make progress slowly and not to antagonise or bewilder the vast constituency of the latter group of Catholics.

It is too early to judge the lasting effects of the National Pastoral Congress on the life of English Catholics. A significant outcome might well have been the realisation, analogous to that of the Latin American Churches in the years of reform since the Conference of Latin American Bishops at Medellin in 1968, that reform starts at the grass-roots level and cannot be enforced from the top downwards. Hence the slogan 'roots before fruits' coined by a former pastoral director from the northern seminary at Ushaw. In his final homily at Liverpool, Cardinal Hume concluded by saying: 'The Congress will be over: and work begins' (Anon., 1981: 304). There are some signs of new developments at grass-roots levels in the dioceses. For example there has been a small growth in the justice and peace movement and the religious authorities were at pains to insist that preparations for the Pope's visit would not be allowed to divert attention from the concrete needs in the dioceses, deaneries and parishes. Initially, the visit was portrayed as an occasion for further spiritual and pastoral renewal in the light of the Congress, and as an opportunity 'to report on what has been done in the dioceses and organisations to help on our becoming the Easter People' (ibid.: xvii-xviii).

In the immediate aftermath of the N.P.C. it seemed possible to regard it as a major turning point in the history of the emergence of Roman Catholicism in this country over the past two centuries. The representatives of the active minority gained confidence at the Congress and a new maturity in an identity as co-partners with their bishops, with 'different ministries but shared responsibility' (ibid.: 318). The Congress may also have strengthened the awareness of the bishops of their own proper independence and authority *vis-à-vis* the Roman authorities. For all its great promise, however, the lasting effects of the Congress have been disappointing. Only one-half of the delegates 18 months later, expressed satisfaction with the bishops' response and only one-quarter with the follow-up to the Congress in their own dioceses and Catholic organisations (Hornsby-Smith and Cordingley, 1983: 42). In the event, too, the Pope's visit bore little direct relationship to the Congress in spite of the fact that it had occasioned the initial invitation.

2.6 THE POPE'S VISIT

If the Church in England and Wales is truly to emerge from the defensive ghetto which is its historical heritage, then it will be necessary for it to shed the ultramontanist tendencies of past years. The remark of one bishop that 'the local Churches have yet to take on Rome' suggests that such tendencies may well have become attenuated in the post-Vatican years. However, any such strains towards independence must necessarily take account of the firm leadership style of Pope John Paul II and his conservative and traditionalist teachings on sexual morality and stress on popular piety. It is these which aroused apprehension among some active 'progressive' Catholics before his visit. They feared that the steady formal legitimation of the Vatican II theology in recent years, with its emphasis on the collegiality of the bishops and the participation of all the 'People of God' in the life of the Church, had so far grown only shallow roots in England and Wales, so that any stern rebuke from a traditionalist pope would have enabled a latent conservatism to manifest itself again in a triumphant reassertion of unquestioning loyalty, obedience and conformity to Rome, even on matters of local pastoral judgement and decision-making.

In the event, none of these fears was realised and the Pope's homilies (John Paul II, 1982) reflected an awareness of and sensitivity to the concerns of English Catholics as they had been articulated in the sector reports from the N.P.C. (Anon., 1981). Nevertheless

in spite of its origins, the organisation of the visit bore very little relationship to the N.P.C. At no time did the seven Sector Presidents who had been influential in the planning and execution of the Congress and the writing of its radical, if tactful, reports formally meet the pope. In fact, in spite of all the talk about the 'Sharing Church', organised laity had no opportunity at all to talk with the pope. Pope John Paul II came to speak *to* the laity, and in the euphoria of the visit only the Catholic Renewal Movement seemed to object at all loudly. In fact, the only people the pope appeared to have the opportunity to *listen* to were representatives of the British Council of Churches at Canterbury. (Hornsby-Smith, Brown and O'Byrne, 1983: 131)

The Pope's visit was also paradoxical in other ways. Catholics appeared to be divided about his leadership style; they were attracted strongly by his warm humanity yet in the main were insistent on making up their own minds on social and moral issues, despite the Pope's teaching, for example on contraception. In general the response of English Catholics to the visit reinforced the interpretation that

there has been an irreversible shift from the view of the pope (or for that matter the parish priest) as having authority as a 'sacred' person to that which recognises the special guiding ministry of the pope (or priest at the local level) to offer religious and moral guidance in situations where, in the last analysis, the individual Catholic makes up his/her own mind ... it seems that English Catholicism has at last come of age and become acceptable to the British people. As one nun put it: 'we can come out now from under the bushes!' (ibid.: 133)

It remains to be seen whether this potentially new status and security of English Catholicism will manifest itself in a confident, challenging and prophetic presence in British society, or rather as an historical relic, cosily absorbed and dissolved as a 'domesticated denomination' in an increasingly secular society, indistinguishable in its religious beliefs and values from other Christian bodies, and in its social and political morality from other citizens. It will be argued later in this book that the bulk of the evidence points to the latter alternative.

2.7 A SOCIAL PORTRAIT OF ENGLISH CATHOLICS

In this chapter we have briefly reviewed the various threads which have been woven together over the past two centuries in the making of contemporary English Catholicism. It has been suggested that in the past two decades, as a result of both social change in post-war Britain and theological change in the Roman Catholic Church on a global scale, the Church in England and Wales has gradually shifted from an institutional model to a more open and participative one. The loss of defensiveness by English Catholics has resulted not only from their social emergence from the inner-city working-class ghetto parishes into the mainstream of British society but also from their slow but steady embracing of the 'People of God' model of the Church with all its implications for priest–lay relationships and lay participation in the life of the Church. It has been argued that the N.P.C. and the subsequent visit of Pope John Paul II marked a key stage in this process and potentially, at least, that they heralded the emergence of a new adult English Catholicism. In this final section we will consider briefly the questions: who are the English Catholics? What are they like? In what ways do they differ from the rest of their fellow countrymen? This social portrait is derived from the Gallup omnibus survey carried out on a national sample of those aged 16 and over in England and Wales in the spring of 1978. The sample was stratified by region and town size with about 100 separate sampling points being used.

The Gallup omnibus survey suggested that in 1978 around 11% of the adult population of England and Wales was Roman Catholic. Including children this indicates that there are 5.4 million English Catholics. A summary of their distinguishing characteristics has been given in figure 2.1. Catholics on average are slightly younger than the general population and appear in proportionately greater numbers in every age group up to 45 than the population generally. Catholics are rather more likely to be single and, compared to the total population, they are less likely to be found in non-manual occupations with a socio-economic status (S.E.S.) in Groups A, B or C in the International Publishing Association (I.P.A.) classification. The tendency to be a relatively young and working-class community is also reflected in lower home-ownership levels and higher Labour voting than the population generally. All the same a slightly higher proportion of Catholics reported a terminal education age (T.E.A.) of 19 or more. The analysis of the immigrant characteristics of Catholics from the 1971 Census returns (table 2.1) suggested that 25% were first-generation immigrants, six times the proportion in the rest of the population.

The Gallup figures suggested that around 40% Catholics attended church at least weekly compared to around 8% of the rest of the population. These figures are comparable to those reported in the 1979 Census of Churches (Anon., 1980a) which showed that adult Catholic attendances were one-third of all weekly adult attendances in England. In a more recent survey, 42% of Roman Catholics reported that they owned a bible and 7% read it at least once a week compared to 63% and 8% respectively for Free Church affiliates (Harrison, 1983: 62–3). In this same survey, 25% of Roman Catho-

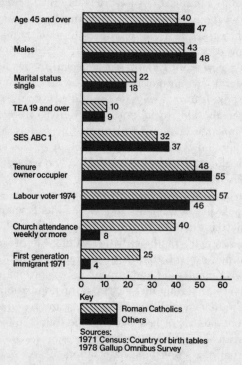

Fig. 2.1 Social characteristics of English Catholics (%)

lics reported attendance at a place of worship once a week or more compared to 7% Church of England affiliates and 33% of Free Church affiliates (ibid.: 66). Within the Catholic community women attended more often than men and the proportion of regular attenders is lowest and the proportion of non-attenders is highest among the young. There is also a clear social-class gradient in church attendance with one-half of professional and managerial Catholics attending weekly compared to just over one-third of Catholic manual workers.

One of the most interesting features of the English Roman Catholic community is the evidence of its geographical movement and distribution over the past 200 years. The origins of this distribution in the recusant tradition and in the mass immigration of the Irish in the nineteenth century are well known. Commenting on the 1851 Census of Religious Attendance, Gay noted that 'with the exception of the London metropolitan region, Catholics are few in number everywhere south of the Bristol to Grimsby line' (Gay, 1971: 94).

Further, within this northern half of the country, a significant concentration of Catholics was to be found in the north-west, and particularly in Lancashire. By the early 1960s, however, the pattern had changed somewhat and Gay pointed to a striking increase over the previous century in the proportion of Catholics living in the south-east. The Gallup omnibus data suggest that by 1978, while the proportion of Catholics in the general population was still greatest in the north-west (21%), two-fifths of English Catholics were now to be found in London and the south-east. These appear to have a somewhat younger age structure than Catholics elsewhere. This probably reflects recent patterns of migration. The proportion of non-manual workers among Catholics in this region is also greater than in other regions. The proportion of Catholics in the central belt from the south-west and Wales to the Midlands and East Anglia continues to be low (7%).

Slightly over 10% of Catholics are converts to Roman Catholicism. Compared to 'born Catholics' they are older, a consequence, perhaps, of the precipitous decline in conversions in the 1960s (Currie, Gilbert and Horsley, 1977). They are more likely to be female than male and more likely than 'born Catholics' to be in non-manual occupations. They have particularly high levels of institutional involvement and compared to 'born Catholics' they are twice as likely to be members of parish organisations. Overall about one Catholic in eight claimed to be a member of a parish organisation. These tended to be disproportionately female, over 35, married and middle class.

This brief portrait of English Catholics suggests that they continue to display many of the characteristics expected of a largely immigrant group and to retain norms of church attendance which sharply distinguish them from the rest of the population. These immigrant roots go back over many generations and there appears to be clear evidence, in their educational and occupational backgrounds and in their geographical dispersion throughout the country, that they have successfully accommodated themselves to British society. It is one purpose of this book to explore the extent to which they can continue to be regarded as a distinctive subculture (Coman, 1977) with a vital community life and identifiable religious belief and moral-value systems. In the following chapter we commence this task by exploring the extent of religious heterogeneity among English Catholics. We have seen that there are good historical reasons for believing that there was considerable heterodoxy of practice and probably belief in the nineteenth and early twentieth centuries. With the advantage of survey data from the late 1970s it is possible to indicate with some precision the nature and extent of heterodoxy among English Catholics more than a decade after the Second Vatican Council.

CHAPTER 3

THE HETEROGENEITY
OF ENGLISH CATHOLICS

3.1 INTRODUCTION

In spite of all the historical and social evidence presented above to the contrary, it has been a commonly held view that the Catholic Church is unusually monolithic in its religious beliefs and practices and that there are high levels of conformity by lay people enforced in a 'priest-ridden' Church. In this chapter we will show that this view of English Catholicism is erroneous.

Using data from the 1978 national survey, a typology of English Catholics will be constructed in terms of variations of religious identity, belief and practice, institutional involvement and sexual morality. These types will be used in all the subsequent analyses to be reported in this book. In the remainder of this chapter several areas of variation between Catholics will be explored. In the first place, considerable variations by sex, age, social class and educational background will be indicated. Secondly, comparisons will be made between those actively involved in the institutional life of the Church and the more passive majority of nominal Catholics. The chapter will conclude with some reflections on the significance of the heterogeneity indicated for the cohesiveness of the English Catholic community.

3.2 A TYPOLOGY OF ENGLISH CATHOLICS

3.2.1 Derivation of typology

In a previous study (Hornsby-Smith, Lee and Turcan, 1982) the extent of heterogeneity among English Catholics was explored by means of secondary analysis of the data from the 1978 survey of Roman Catholics in England and Wales. Six attributes were selected on theoretical grounds and in the light of previous empirical studies of Roman Catholics in this country and in the United States (Fichter, 1954; Greeley, McCready and McCourt, 1976; Lenski, 1963; Stark and Glock, 1968). Single variable indicators were used on pragmatic grounds in order to minimise the loss of data due to the accumulation of missing values where scales are used. In spite of the limitation of single variables, the typology appeared to be relatively robust and substantially unaltered by the employment of alternative indicators. In the choice of indicators, account was taken both of the salience of the variable considered and also the extent to which the variable discriminated between Catholics. The six attributes considered in the derivation of the typology were as follows:

Religious identity: This was measured by the response to the first question asked: 'could you please tell me what is your religious denomination?' A number of those surveyed did not initially identify themselves as Roman Catholics though in response to a subsequent question they reported that they had been baptised as one.

Religious belief: That is the 'expectations that the religious person will hold a certain theological outlook, that he will acknowledge the truth of the tenets of the religion' (Stark and Glock, 1968: 14). As an indicator of doctrinal orthodoxy the response to the following state-ment was chosen: 'at the consecration the bread and wine are really changed into the Body and Blood of Christ'. Those answering 'certainly true' from four alternatives offered were deemed to hold orthodox belief.

Religious practice: This 'includes acts of worship and devotion, the things people *do* to carry out their religious commitment' (ibid.: 15). Stark and Glock include both formal, public ritual and personal, private devotion under this heading. In the study of religious practice in Detroit the frequency of attendance at corporate worship services was used as an indicator of associational involvement (Lenski, 1963). In this present study we have used the frequency of reported Mass attendance. The official norm for Catholics is attendance on Sundays and a specified number of 'holidays of obligation'. Three levels of reported attendance were considered: weekly or more, at least once a year but less than once weekly; and less than once a year, or on special occasions only, or never.

Institutional involvement: Our earlier research in four English parishes had shown that a significant cleavage existed between grass-roots Catholics and 'activists' involved in the wide variety of parish organisations. Similarly, in his study of three urban parishes in the United States in the early 1950s, Fichter (1954) coined the term 'nuclear' parishioners for those Catholics who both received communion weekly and belonged to parish societies. The preliminary analyses of the 1978 survey had also demonstrated that members of parish organisations differed in many respects from those who were not, whether or not they were regular Mass attenders. The 13% of Catholics who claimed to be members of parish organisations were therefore considered to have a high institutional involvement.

Sexual morality: Earlier analysis of the data from the 1978 survey indicated that very considerable divergence from the official norms of the Church was expressed by Catholics, especially in the areas of personal morality such as contraception, divorce, abortion, premarital sexual relations and euthanasia, and that this divergence was not eliminated by controlling for Mass attendance frequency. In addition, orthodoxy in doctrinal matters was not clearly associated with orthodoxy in terms of sexual morality. In the United States, Greeley, McCready and McCourt (1976) also reported 'a comprehensive shift in Catholic sexual values' in recent years.

In order to simplify the analysis and minimise the loss of cases because of incomplete data, the indicator chosen to measure orthodox sexual morality was the response to the statement: 'a married couple who feel they have as many children as they want are not doing anything wrong when they use artificial methods of birth control'. Those who disagreed with this statement were classified as holding a 'traditional' view of sexual morality. All others were classified as holding a 'non-traditional' view of sexual morality.

For the purposes of constructing a typology of Catholics it is perhaps important to note that this indicator has significance not only in measuring the extent to which the traditional teaching of the Church on sexual morality continues to be accepted, but also attitudes towards the legitimacy of the authority of the Church in these areas. Thus, it is of interest to measure the degree to which continued practice and commitment in terms of Mass attendance frequency and doctrinal orthodoxy were associated with attitudes which are non-traditional in the area of sexual morality.

This-worldly involvement: This final dimension clearly derives from the Weberian analysis of the various ways in which salvation may be pursued (Weber, 1966) and, in particular, the contrast between the 'this-worldly asceticism' of puritanism with the 'world-rejecting asceticism' of Catholic monasticism (see, e.g., Greeley, 1963; Green, 1959; Lawlor, 1965; Robertson, 1970). Historically there appears to be evidence that English Catholics in particular have wished to maintain a low profile politically in a predominantly Protestant and sometimes hostile society. Generally they have only emerged as a political force in defence of what they have regarded as their vital community interests, notably the continuation of a viable separate Catholic schools system, or, less effectively, on behalf of what they have regarded as a key moral position, such as their opposition to legalised abortion. In recent years, however, the Roman Catholic Church has become concerned with the issues of international social and economic inequalities and injustice (Abbott, 1966: 183–316). In England and Wales the bishops have recently intervened on such controversial issues as unemployment (*The Tablet*, 6 December 1980), the nuclear deterrent (ibid., 13 December 1980) and the British Nationality Bill (ibid., 31 January 1981). It therefore seems important to explore variations in the extent to which English Catholics consider their religious faith to have relevance for their behaviour in the social, political and economic spheres. The indicator used in the present analysis was agreement with the statement: 'the Church should take active steps to promote social justice even if it means getting involved in politics'. In the event this indicator was found to be insufficiently discriminating for typological purposes and this sixth attribute has not therefore been included in the final typology, which is summarised in figure 3.1.

The typology accounted for 92% of Catholics and can therefore be regarded as reasonably comprehensive. According to the survey only 2% of Catholics were non-identifiers but it seems likely that because of sampling biases this is a considerable underestimation of the true magnitude. On the basis of field work with random samples of Catholics in our study of four English parishes it was estimated that perhaps as many as one in six of one-time or baptised Catholics no

Characteristic	A	B	C	D	E	F	G	H	J	Non-identifiers
Identity: Roman Catholic	+	+	+	+	+	+	+	+	+	−
Belief: orthodox (O)	+	+	+	+	−	+	−	+	+	−
Practice: Mass attendance (A)	+	+	+	+	+	±	±	−	−	−
Institutional involvement (IV)	+	+	−	−	−	−	−	−	−	−
Sexual morality: Traditional (T)	+	−	+	−	−	−	−	−	−	−
Distribution of types (%)	3	6	6	16	5	12	12	9	21	2

Attendance categories: + = weekly or more; ± = at least once a year but less than weekly (intermediate); − = less than once a year, or special occasions only, or never.

Fig.3.1 Defining characteristics and distribution of types of English Catholics (N=1,035)

longer identified themselves as such and this estimate is similar to that found in a series of studies of denominational 'switchers' in the United States in the 1960s (Stark and Glock, 1968: 195) and in the 1970s (Newport, 1979: 528–52; Kluegel, 1980: 26–39; Roof and Hadaway 1979: 363–79). A longitudinal study of people born in 1946 has suggested that, for this post-war cohort, as many as 31% of those who were Roman Catholics in childhood have switched to other religious allegiances by the age of 26 (Wadsworth and Freeman, 1983: 424).

3.2.2 Description of types

The social, demographic and religious characteristics of the ten types of Catholic have been reported previously (Hornsby-Smith, Lee and Turcan, 1982: 445–8). However, a brief portrait of each of the types, which will be considered in the subsequent analyses reported in this book, can now be given.

Involved traditionalists (type A): This is a group of elderly, mainly middle-class Catholics. One-fifth of them are converts and two-fifths are the children of Irish immigrants compared to one-sixth found for Catholics generally. They retain strong communal attachments; four-fifths of them have married Catholics and a similar proportion reports that half or more of their friends are Catholics. They are attached to the traditional patterns of Catholic worship and three-quarters of them attend Mass more than weekly. More than any other type they are unhappy with recent liturgical changes and they are hostile to intercommunion with non-Catholics. Their evaluation of priests is higher than that of any other type. They prefer a traditional model of the 'sacred' priesthood and say they would not accept married priests. They appear to approximate to Fichter's type of nuclear parishioner (1954: 22).

Involved non-traditionalists (type B): In many respects these Catholics are similar to the previous type. Their level of religious commitment is high: one-third of them attend Mass more than weekly and two-fifths of them have attended house Masses and ecumenical services. Their non-traditionalism on birth control has parallels in their relative openness to intercommunion and to married priests. This type consists in the main of middle-class women in early middle age, mainly married to other Catholics and finding their friends within the Catholic community. They include a high proportion of converts. In Fichter's typology they represent a modified version of the nuclear parishioner.

Non-involved traditionalists (type C): These Catholics approximate to Fichter's modal parishioner. They differ from the involved traditionalists chiefly in their social class and immigrant background. They are mainly elderly, lower-working-class males and over two-fifths live in council housing. Nearly one-third of them are first-generation Irish immigrants whereas type A Catholics are disproportionately the children of such immigrants. A higher proportion of this group is married to a Catholic spouse than in any other type. Their communal attachment to the Church is relatively high and two-fifths of them attend Mass more than weekly. Otherwise their religious attitudes and behaviour are very similar to those of the involved traditionalists.

Orthodox attenders (type D): This type can also be considered to be a subcategory of Fichter's modal parishioner. They are slightly older and more middle class and are more likely to have had a Catholic schooling than the average Catholic. They are less likely to be a convert or have a non-Catholic spouse. In their religious characteristics they are slightly more conformist than the average Catholic but they participate in new styles of religious worship and express an openness to change not only on religious matters, such as intercommunion and married clergy, but also on sexual matters, such as birth control and divorce.

Heterodox attenders (type E): This is a young, largely middle-class male group with a higher proportion of those with further education than any other group. Like types C and D this can be considered to be a subcategory of Fichter's modal parishioner. One in ten attends Mass more than weekly and three in ten have attended house Masses. However, their religious attitudes indicate a considerable openness to religious innovation. Only two-thirds consider papal infallibility to be true and abortion to be wrong. Half would approve intercommunion, four-fifths would accept married priests and over two-thirds would allow Catholics to divorce. This type appears to be transitional in many respects from orthodox practice to non-conformity in terms of the major dimensions of religious belief and practice.

Orthodox irregulars (type F): This type can be considered to be a subcategory of Fichter's marginal parishioner (Fichter, 1954: 22, 59–60). It is largely a young, female, lower-working-class group with strong remnants of orthodox belief retained from a largely Catholic schooling. Mass attendance, sacramental practice and prayer levels are all sharply lower than in the previous types though like the heterodox attenders they appear to be transitional in their openness to religious innovation in matters such as abortion, divorce, married priests and intercommunion.

Heterodox irregulars (type G): In terms of both practice and belief this type can also be considered to be a subcategory of Fichter's marginal parishioner. It is younger and slightly more highly educated than the average and has a sharply lower communal involvement than previous groups in terms of Catholic spouses and friendships. This type prays less frequently and has had little contact with new developments in the Catholic Church since the Second Vatican Council. It appears to share transitional characteristics with types E and F. This type gave the lowest support of any to the view that the Church should be prepared to get involved in politics. The explanation for this is not clear but it may be that this group in particular does not regard the Roman Catholic Church as capable of providing satisfactory 'rewards' or 'compensators' (Stark and Bainbridge, 1980a).

Orthodox non-attenders (type H): These Catholics retain beliefs in the central doctrines of the Church but they have not attended Mass for over a year. In this sense they can be regarded as dormant Catholics (Fichter, 1954: 22, 60–1). They are largely middle-aged women living in council housing who have had no further education. They are overwhelmingly in religiously mixed marriages and have relatively few Catholic friends yet they retain a strong attachment to the parish. They appear to have a strong local orientation (Merton, 1957). Their religious beliefs, practices and attitudes are very similar to those of the heterodox irregulars.

Heterodox non-attenders (type J): This is the largest type and comprises over one-fifth of all Catholics but unlike the previous group, this type is the youngest group, two-thirds being under the age of 35. There are fewer converts in this group than in any other and the fact that fewer of them had a Catholic schooling than any other type suggests that their Catholicism may never have been more than nominal. They are less likely to be Irish immigrants than in any other type and under one-third of them have married a Catholic spouse or have mainly Catholic friends. They have a low attachment to their parish and they do not rate their priests highly. Only one-quarter pray daily or believe in papal infallibility. Nearly all would allow Catholics to divorce and priests to marry and under one-half consider abortion to be wrong.

Non-identifiers: These are predominantly male and less likely to be Irish than any other type. Their communal involvement is very slight; only one-quarter have married other Catholics and they have a much lower proportion of Catholic friends than any other type. Nearly half live in council housing. Under half of them attended Catholic schools so that, as with the previous type, their Catholicism may never have been more than nominal. Their alienation from religion is almost complete and only a tiny proportion prays daily. All would accept a married priesthood and almost all would agree with divorce and abortion. All reject papal infallibility.

In the remainder of this chapter variations in the distribution of the derived Catholic types will be used to explore further the extent of heterogeneity in the English Catholic community. For this purpose the ten Catholic types have been collapsed into four: the involved orthodox attenders (types A and B), the non-involved orthodox attenders (types C and D), the irregular attenders (types F and G) and the non-practising (types H, J and the non-identifiers). In the first place there will be a consideration of the variations within the Catholic community between the sexes, generations, social classes and those with different educational experiences. Secondly, the wide gap between the religious worlds of the 'active' Catholic and the average, identifying Catholic will be demonstrated using three different data sources. Apart from the typology, 14 scales were constructed in order to summarise some of the findings. The details of these scales have been given in appendix 1 and supplementary tables using them have been reported in appendix 2. This chapter will conclude with some reflections on the implications of the data for the cohesiveness of the Catholic community.

3.3 DEMOGRAPHIC AND SOCIAL FACTORS

In this section we will look at variations in the religious variables when considering sex, age, social class and terminal education age as independent variables. In appendix 2 a summary of the variations in a selection of social and demographic characteristics with variations in these independent variables has been given in table A1, while table A2 summarises the variations in the religious types and scale-scores with variations in the same independent variables. In both cases the data are those from the 1978 national survey (Hornsby-Smith and Lee, 1979) but comparisons with the lay delegates to the National Pastoral Congress (Hornsby-Smith and Cordingley, 1983) have also been given. Apparent inconsistencies in the averages considering different independent variables are normally due to the presence of missing values. In general, levels of significance have not been reported because it would be misleading to do so. So many comparisons have been made in the analyses reported that a number of 'significant' findings would in any case have arisen by chance. On the other hand, in commenting on the results in the text, particular attention has been paid to those differences which did reach very high levels of statistical significance (in several instances $p < 0.0001$) and also variations which did not reach the 5% level of significance. What is more relevant for our purposes here, however, is the consistency of the patterns which do emerge, and it is these patterns which have been the primary focus of our attention.

3.3.1 Sex differences

The general consideration of the relationship between the sex of respondents and their religious beliefs and moral attitudes led to the conclusion that crude sex differences are not of great consequence for English Catholics but that women other than housewives are more likely than the other groups to diverge from the official teaching of the Church on such issues as birth control, divorce, belief in hell and eternal punishment, the significance of missing Sunday Mass and the infallibility of the Pope. This finding was not altogether what one might have expected from a review of the literature.

In their outline of sex differences in religious behaviour Argyle and Beit-Hallahmi confidently reported that 'the differences between men and women in their religious behaviour and beliefs are consider-able ... women are more religious on every criterion' (Argyle and Beit-Hallahmi, 1975: 71). On the basis of a review of survey data in Britain and the United States, they showed that women had higher levels of church membership, attendance at worship and reported daily prayer, religious beliefs and mystical experiences. In a study of religious experiences in the mid-1970s in Britain, there were similar findings (Hay, 1982: 119–20), although David Martin observed, on the basis of a Bible Society survey in 1979, that the differences between men and women were 'not all that marked' (Martin, 1980: 13). Perhaps the most likely explanations of such sex differences are those which suggest that 'Church-related religiosity is strongest ... on the margins of modern industrial society, both in terms of marginal classes ... and marginal individuals (such as those elimi-nated from the work process)' (Berger, 1973: 114). Luckmann, for example, hypothesises that 'the degree of involvement in the work processes of modern industrial society correlates negatively with the degree of involvement in church-oriented religion' (Luckmann, 1970: 30). Thus he notes that the church-orientation of working women is closer to that of men than that of housewives.

Our initial examination of the data from the 1978 survey of English Catholics indicated that sex differences were of little consequence when compared to age and social-class variations and there were no separate tabulations by sex (Hornsby-Smith and Lee, 1979). Indeed 5 of 15 analyses carried out failed to reach the 5% level of probability. In terms of their social and demographic characteristics (table A1) men and women appeared to be very similar except that fewer women in the national sample were single and a higher proportion of them were converts to Roman Catholicism. However, when the self-identified housewives were distinguished from other females, some distinct differences did emerge. The latter category consisted in the main of young, single girls in slightly higher occupational groups than the housewives. Fewer of them were Irish-born but more were the children of Irish parents, more had attended Catholic schools and very few of them were converts.

The data also indicated that while the proportion of orthodox attenders was the same, women were more likely to be 'involved', that is, members of parish organisations, and more likely to be irregular in Mass attendance than non-practising. More detailed examination of the Catholic types showed that women were more likely than men to hold orthodox beliefs. Women who did not define themselves as housewives were much less likely than the other categories to be involved orthodox attenders.

In the analyses summarised in appendix 2 (table A2) no statistically significant differences in the scores of the three categories of sex were obtained on the scales of adult religious behaviour, new-style activism, liturgical traditionalism, sexual orthodoxy and lay participation. On the other hand, women scored more highly on doctrinal orthodoxy, church commitment, the evaluation of priests and papal authority. It might be noted that all of these scales reflect involvement in the institutional church. Woman were less likely than men to score highly on the world-justice orientation or new-style ministry, both of which reflected radical departures from the traditional parochial model of the Church.

When the scores for women who were not housewives were examined it was clear that there was a strong tendency to heterodoxy or departure from the traditional patterns in the Church. Thus these women scored much lower than the other two groups on doctrinal and sexual orthodoxy, prayer, their evaluation of priests, their stress on papal authority and conformity to institutional identity. They rated the salience of religious sanctions much less than the other groups and in this sense reflected the loss of 'the fear of hell' (Lodge,

1980: 113–27) much more than men or housewives. It might be noted that they were the most likely to have participated in new styles of activism and gave the strongest support to new styles of ministry. Their low score on lay participation is somewhat puzzling and can probably best be interpreted more in terms of their frustration with the institutional Church rather than as a rejection of lay participation. In general terms, therefore, the evidence from Roman Catholics in England and Wales in the late 1970s provides support for the Luckmann hypothesis.

3.3.2 Age differences

In their review of the evidence of the effect of age on religious beliefs and behaviour Argyle and Beit-Hallahmi (1975: 58–70) refer to three distinct models: the 'traditional' model of declining activity from adolescence to the age of around 30 followed by a continuous increase with aging; the 'stability' model with no changes with age; and the 'disengagement' model with continuous decline with age. With our cross-sectional data it was not possible easily to distinguish between (a) aging effects, (b) life-cycle effects, according to which religious behaviour varies in particular with such key events as marriage, the birth and rearing of children, career development events, death of parents and spouse, or (c) generational or cohort effects which may be attributed to particular historical events such as the two world wars or the economic depression or post-war affluence. Without some longitudinal data collected over several decades, it is not possible to distinguish between conflicting explanations. What we can say, however, is that for English Catholics, the differences of religious beliefs and practices and social and moral attitudes between five different age groups were most striking.

The five age groups considered corresponded roughly to distinct stages in the life cycle: the young single adult (15–24), the young marrieds (25–34), the established marrieds (35–49), the middle aged (50–64) and the elderly (65 and over). There appeared to be an over-representation of men in the first age group and of women in the second. There were indications (table A1) that for those born after the late 1920s the post-war changes in educational opportunities and occupational structures were reflected in longer educational experiences and higher occupational status. Post-war affluence and the declining salience of the parish for entertainment and social interaction with expanded leisure opportunities also appeared to be reflected in the lower levels of communal association. Again, the decline of Irish immigration after the 1960s (Hornsby-Smith, 1978b) was indicated by the declining proportion of first-generation Irish while there was still a substantial proportion of second-generation Irish in the youngest age group. The sharp decline of adult converts since the 1960s was also reflected in the lower proportions in the two youngest age groups.

Of the 15 analyses reported in table A2 only that of lay participation failed to reach the level of statistical significance. The types of Catholics and ten of the scales all varied systematically with age while the scores on new-style activism, sexual orthodoxy and world-justice orientation were all at a minimum in the 25–34 age group as suggested by the 'traditional' model referred to by Argyle and Beit-Hallahmi. But in general, while it was not possible with cross-sectional data to disentangle aging, cohort and life-cycle effects (Hornsby-Smith and Lee, 1979: 57–8, 129–32): 'the dominant trend of the results ... is that Catholics are more likely to be critical of the institutional Church or of its authorities or of its official teachings or regulations the younger they are' (ibid.: 130–1). This is consistent with the results of a national British longitudinal study of a cohort born in 1946 which showed that there was a decline of Roman Catholic affiliation from 9.2% in childhood to 7.0% at the age of 26 mainly due to a change to no belief (Wadsworth and Freeman, 1983: 423).

3.3.3 Social-class variations

For the purposes of investigating the effect of social-class factors, respondents were grouped into four main categories: AB (professional and managerial), C1 (lower non-manual), C2 (skilled manual) and DE (semi-skilled and unskilled manual). In general the relationship between religion and social class in Great Britain differs somewhat from that in the United States. In both countries there is a positive association between social class and church attendance but, unlike the United States, in Great Britain there is also a positive association with religious beliefs. This difference has been attributed to differences in the patterns of secularisation in the two countries and the significance of the different historical developments of working-class political movements (Argyle and Beit-Hallahmi, 1975: 166). In the recent analysis of religious experience in Britain a positive association with both social class and educational experiences has also been found (Hay, 1982: 122).

In the national survey of English Catholics it was reported that while

social class differences in religious belief and behaviour are not as significant as might have been expected ... there is evidence of a tendency for the higher social classes to be more involved in the associational life of the Church than the lower social classes. (Hornsby-Smith and Lee, 1979: 126–7)

Before considering the evidence for this conclusion in more detail it should be noted that three-quarters of the C1 respondents were women (with higher than average proportions of young, single and second-generation Irish) while three-quarters of the C2 respondents were men. The DE respondents included a higher than average proportion of first-generation Irish while the proportion of those whose full-time education was completed after the age of 18 in the AB category was four times the average for all respondents (table A1).

Of the 15 analyses undertaken (table A2) only 6 reached the level of significance. The distribution of types indicated the tendency for AB respondents to have higher levels of belief, practice and parish involvement than the other classes. This institutional involvement was reflected in their higher levels of not only liturgical traditionalism but also new-style activism and new-style ministries than all other classes. At the other end of the social class scale DE respondents were not only more likely than other classes to be non-practising in terms of Mass attendance but also more traditional in terms of their stress on sexual orthodoxy, papal authority, the salience of religious sanctions and conformity to institutional identity and their opposition to new-style ministries. In many respects the C2 respondents, mainly male skilled manual workers, were most 'secularised' in the sense of dissociation from church-oriented religion. They reported lowest levels of adult religious practice and prayer, concern with institutional identity, religious sanctions, papal authority or sexual orthodoxy. Their relative alienation from the institutional Church was also reflected in their low support for new-style activism. In the case of this social class, it appears that the response to religious alienation was one of dissociation rather than innovation.

Two observations on these findings might be made at this point. The first is the need to reappraise the supposed ability of the Roman

Catholic Church in England and Wales to maintain a strong working-class allegiance even though other denominations have typically 'lost the working class'. Tentatively it has been suggested that the Roman Catholic Church in England and Wales

is disproportionately attractive for the middle classes and that reforms stemming from the Vatican Council, the increased participation of the laity from liturgical reading to membership of parish councils or national commissions and so on, favour the educated and articulate middle class. This last group is happier with the changes which have emanated from the Vatican Council, more involved in associational activity and is more approving of the Church's belief and value systems. By contrast, working class Catholics are less happy with recent changes, suspicious of the shift of emphasis from ritual to participation, defensive about their loss of a privatised autonomy, and suspicious of proposed new forms of ministry, possibly because they represent new and alternative sources of authority to which they will be expected to respond. (Hornsby-Smith and Lee, 1979: 127–8.)

For the moment we will note that some systematic social-class variations do exist among English Catholics. These will be explored further in the analysis of lay elites in chapter 7. In addition, the impact of Irish immigration on English Catholicism will be considered in chapter 6. One possibility is that English Catholicism appeared to be attractive to some sections of the working class only as long as there was a continuing infusion of Irish working-class immigrants. With the ending of this influx, the real situation has become more apparent; as with other denominations, church-oriented religion does not meet the religious needs of working-class Catholics.

The second observation which can be made about our findings is that occupational differences are difficult to disentangle from those associated with differences of educational experiences. Thus in *Roman Catholic Opinion* it was reported that while on some variables there were clear social-class gradients, on others there was a sharp cleavage between the professional and managerial group and all other groups, which probably reflected the greater salience of their educational experiences and expectations. These will be examined further in the following section. On other variables, particularly political and socio-economic issues, the cleavage corresponded more closely to the distinction between manual and non-manual work (ibid.: 128).

3.3.4 Educational differences

In order to investigate further the separate effects of educational experiences, four categories were distinguished in terms of the age of completion of full-time education. A summary of the characteristics of these four categories has been given in table A1. Further analysis shows that half of those who reported a T.E.A. of under 15 were in the DE social class and that three-fifths of them were aged 50 or over. On the other hand, half of those with a T.E.A. of 19 or over were in the AB social class and nearly three-fifths of them were under 35. The modal types corresponded to late-middle-aged unskilled, young-middle-aged skilled manual, young female white-collar, and the young professional or managerial worker, respectively. Broadly speaking the data indicate that the two measures of communal association, Catholic schooling and Catholic friendship networks, both decrease with further education and higher social class.

The effect of the interrelationship between age, social class and terminal education age could be seen in the analysis of Catholic types and scale scores (table A2). In many instances the results followed a U-pattern and it is the T.E.A. of 15 or 16 which appeared distinctive. Thus, only one-quarter of this group are orthodox attenders compared to two-fifths of the three other categories. They scored lowest not only on traditional measures of institutional involvement such as religious practice, church commitment, sexual orthodoxy, papal authority and the salience of religious sanctions but also on measures of institutional innovation such as new-style activism. It is noticeable that those with the most education rated their priests much less highly than other groups though this reflected both their youth and high social class. This group scored highest not only in terms of church commitment but also in terms of actual or potential institutional innovation, for example, new-style activism and new-style ministries. In contrast those with the least educational experiences were the most traditional, in terms of their sexual orthodoxy, their favourable evaluation of priests, their stress on papal authority and the salience of religious sanctions and in their conformity to institutional identity.

It is clear that the interrelationships between educational experiences, social class and age of respondent are complex and their effects cannot easily be distinguished. In the case of church commitment, middle-class men scored more highly than working-class men and older men more highly than younger men at each T.E.A. Older middle-class and highly educated men were twice as likely as men in general to score highly on this scale. On the other hand, men under 35, whether middle or working class, who left school at the age of 15 or 16 were much less likely than any other group to score highly on this variable. This group was also much less likely than any other group to score highly on the scale of new-style activism which could be said to represent legitimate innovation with official encouragement. In this case the interactions between social class and age with terminal education age were complex and varied and it was not possible to identify a consistent pattern. A low score on the scale of sexual orthodoxy represents a measure of illegitimate innovation in that it would not be sanctioned by the official leadership of the Church. In this case the pattern was clearer in that while the scores were again lowest among those men under the age of 35 who had left school at 15 or 16, there were also strong age differences at each T.E.A. while overall class differences were slight.

Thus in all three cases considered, institutional conformity and both legitimate and illegitimate innovation, particularly low scores were recorded by young men under the age of 35 who had left school at the age of 15 or 16, irrespective of their social class. Unexpectedly, therefore, there does not appear to be any simple relationship between educational experiences and religious attitudes and practice. What does appear to be indicated is that those respondents born in the two decades after the Second World War and leaving school in the 1960s and 1970s at the age of 15 or 16, were particularly disaffected with institutional Catholicism. It remains to explore the reasons why this was the case. For the moment it may be noted that there appear to be separate age, social class and education experience effects on our various dependent variables but that in the case of educational experiences, the relationship is not a simple one but is U-shaped with a minimum corresponding to early school leaving in the 1960s and 1970s.

In the study of the religious affiliation of the national cohort born in 1946 it was reported that change of affiliation, especially change from belief to no belief, by the age of 26 was most strongly associated with the educational level achieved. The apparent inconsistency with the present results may reflect the fact that those who had been Roman Catholics in childhood but no longer identified themselves as such were underrepresented in the national sample of Roman

Catholics. Whereas in the cohort study 31% of Roman Catholics had changed their affiliation by the age of 26, including 26% to no faith or denomination (Wadsworth and Freeman, 1983: 424), only 2% of the national sample of Roman Catholics were non-identifiers. Taking the two studies together it seems possible that while change of affiliation, including disaffiliation, may be strongly associated with educational level achieved and especially with university education, for those Catholics who do retain their affiliation, relatively high rates of institutional involvement persist alongside pressures for institutional innovation.

3.4 VARIATIONS BY INSTITUTIONAL INVOLVEMENT

Apart from the variations in the religious outcomes with differences in the social and demographic characteristics of English Catholics, very large variations were also found among those with different levels of institutional involvement. In sum, the evidence indicates massive heterogeneity of belief and practice amongst English Catholics with increasing divergences from official norms or orthodoxy the less attached, both communally and associationally (Lenski, 1963: 22–4), Catholics are to institutional Catholicism.

For the purpose of comparison, three levels of involvement have been considered. Members of parish organisations have been compared to other Catholics attached to a parish and those who reported that they were not attached to a parish. The characteristics of Catholics with these three levels of involvement have been summarised in table A1 where comparisons have also been made with the lay delegates to the National Pastoral Congress. There it can be seen that members of organisations are disproportionately middle-aged or elderly married women from the higher social classes. Over one-fifth of them are converts compared to half that proportion among Catholics generally and they are much more likely than the other two groups to make their friendships primarily with other Catholics.

Only one of the 15 comparisons made (table A2) did not reach the level of statistical significance, viz. the score on the scale of lay participation. But on all the other dependent measures, considerable and consistent differences emerged. The three categories were sharply distinguished not only in terms of doctrinal orthodoxy and Mass attendance but on all the other religious variables. Non-attached Catholics were twice as likely to record high scores on the scale of new-style ministries and more likely to stress the importance of lay participation, though in the latter case the differences were not statistically significant. They were also least likely to favour liturgical traditionalism. On all the other measures there was a sharp gradient from the non-attached Catholics to the members of parish organisations.

It is not the purpose here to evaluate the 'correctness' of the religious beliefs and behaviour of these different categories of Catholics but simply to note the evidence that there do appear to be three quite distinct religious styles which are disproportionately attractive to different groups of Catholics. When comparisons were extended to the lay delegates to the N.P.C. who disproportionately represented the educated middle class, it was shown that

in terms of belief . . . and practice, parish elites were similar to the Congress delegates. On questions relating to the liturgy, ordinary delegates were much more progressive but on the birth control issue much more traditional than members of parish organisations. (Hornsby-Smith and Cordingley, 1983: 31)

In further analyses it was shown that Congress officials were more progressive in a number of respects than ordinary delegates (see chapter 7).

In the study of four Catholic parishes in the mid-1970s, comparisons were made between parish activists and random samples of both Catholic and non-Catholic electors. Here it was found that statistically significant differences between the Catholic and non-Catholic electors emerged only in the case of a measure of sexual morality, the salience of a rational humanistic orientation to sexual matters being weaker for the Catholic electors. Much more striking was the extent of the divergence between the Catholic activists and the randomly selected Catholic electors. Not only were the activists much more likely than the Catholic electors to stress the official norms of sexual morality but they were also much more likely than both Catholic and non-Catholic electors to emphasise the salience of religious leadership and also to express a social liberalism orientation on such social and political issues as race relations, taxation policy, and the treatment of murderers (Hornsby-Smith, 1978c: 13).

3.5 CONCLUDING REFLECTIONS

In sum, it has been possible to demonstrate wide variations in beliefs and practices among English Catholics. Only in the matter of regional differences was it not possible to demonstrate a high level of heterogeneity (Hornsby-Smith and Turcan, 1981).

It is not the task of the sociologist to indulge in speculative futurology (Goldthorpe, 1978; Noble, 1982: 251). All the same, the patterned distribution of religious beliefs and practices does suggest that the institutional Church is relatively attractive to older Catholics with relatively high social status and educational experiences. On the other hand, it appears to alienate young Catholics, women who are not housewives and post-war early school leavers. To the extent that there are significant generational, gender, social class, educational or other social (e.g. ethnic group) cleavages then it cannot be suggested that English Catholics constitute a homogeneous socio-religious community. One possible implication of the present heterogeneity among English Catholics was suggested in the study of the delegates to the N.P.C.

There is no evidence at all of the widespread conflict anticipated by some commentators as a result of post-war social mobility, the reforms of the Vatican Council or the furore caused by the publication of *Humanae Vitae*. What appears to be much more likely is a growing divergence between the educated, activist, leadership groups ... and the mass of relatively passive, nominal Catholics, largely unconcerned about the renewal processes initiated and encouraged by activists in the Church. The response to this process seems likely to be a growing alienation on the part of the traditional working class mass of Catholics in the inner cities. Its expression is unlikely to be an articulate or explosive reaction so much as a quiet opting out of institutional involvement leaving a core of activists talking to each other in an institution increasingly manifesting exclusivist, sect-like characteristics. There seems to be a danger that the 'Church of sinners', mainly working class, might become a sect of mainly middle class activists. (Hornsby-Smith and Cordingley, 1983: 33–4)

This theme will be explored further in chapter 7 but for the moment it is worth noting the caution that changes in the Church are more likely to have arisen from changing ideas and beliefs in the wider society and as a result of the dramatically changed demographic structure of industrial societies than as a result of the conflicts within the Catholic community (Brothers, 1984). What does seem beyond dispute is that it can no longer be claimed that English Catholics comprise a homogeneous socio-religious community with uniform beliefs and practices. Having established this we will turn in the next chapter to the question which initiated the present series of researches, viz. the extent of social and geographical mobility among English Catholics and the implications for their religious beliefs and practices.

CHAPTER 4

THE IMPACT OF SOCIAL
AND GEOGRAPHICAL MOBILITY

4.1 THEME AND HYPOTHESES

In the Introduction it was noted that the starting point for our programme of research into the changing nature of English Catholicism was the hypothesis that as a result of post-war social and educational changes in Britain, the English Catholic community, with its largely low-status Irish immigrant social origins, was likely to have experienced to a significant degree a social 'mobility momentum' (Bode, 1970) relative to the rest of the population. In the first place this was likely to be reflected in the growth of a sizeable first-generation 'new Catholic middle class' in professional, managerial and administrative occupations as a result of the expanded educational opportunities created in the post-war period. Secondly, it was also likely to be reflected in geographical movement not only from the old centres of traditional Catholic concentration in the north-west to the new areas of economic growth especially in London and the south-east and in the Midlands, but also from the inner-city parishes to the new suburban estates.

In England and Wales, the Oxford Mobility Study of men surveyed in the early 1970s had shown that there was evidence of considerable intergenerational mobility with no decline of intra-generational mobility over several decades. Given the expansion of the 'service' class in recent years it was perhaps not unexpected to find little evidence of strategies of exclusion, though some evidence of strategies of solidarism among the working class was reported (Goldthorpe, 1980: 38–67). In an analysis of the relationship between social mobility experiences and participation in voluntary associations there was little evidence that social mobility was radically dissociative or that it led to social marginality and isolation. Rather, mobile individuals tended to shift towards the prevailing norms of their class of destination and occupy an intermediate position between their classes of origin and destination (ibid.: 175–216). In the present study it will be shown that the effects of social mobility on the religious practices and beliefs of English Catholics are variable and generally slight. They appear to be disruptive of orthodox beliefs, reflect the class of origin in the case of religious practices and the class of destination for other variables.

In his early study, Sorokin suggested that there were conflicting effects of social and cultural mobility on human behaviour. On the one hand, mobility favoured innovation, cosmopolitanism and the intensification of the exchange of ideas; on the other hand, it tended to diminish intimacy and facilitate the disintegration of morals. It also favoured an increase of individualism and superficiality (Sorokin, 1959: 508–41). In the context of religious behaviour we might therefore expect the privatisation of religious beliefs and behaviour among the upwardly mobile. Tumin has drawn attention to the consequences of social mobility including the 'loss of social criticism', 'the diffusion of insecurity', 'the invasion of the family and religious institutions by criteria deriving from the market place', and the polarisation of views between 'a bitter conservatism' among older generations and 'a vituperative contempt for traditions' among the upwardly mobile (Tumin, 1957). Hopper (1971) has suggested that any 'pathogenic' consequences of mobility, and in particular inter-personal isolation, loss of support and difficulties in working out a personal value system, depend largely on the nature of the mobility routes and mechanisms of initial selection and rejection in the education system. Blau (1956) regarded mobile people as 'marginal' and suggested that their mobility inhibited their social integration. On the other hand, Bell (1968) demonstrated the ability of the geographically mobile to be socially integrated with each other in a suburban estate in Wales. The study of geographical mobility or migration has generally been considered in terms of processes of assimilation to the host community (Jansen, 1969; Price, 1969). Gordon (1964) identified seven distinct processes and hypothesised that cultural assimilation was likely to occur before structural assimilation. Zimmer (1970) in a study of a mid-western U.S. community in the early 1950s suggested that the initial limiting influences of migration on community participation were only temporary. However, in a later study in an English midland city, Musgrove (1963) found that immigrants generally compensated for the disruptive effects of both social and geographical mobility by being overrepresented among the leadership of voluntary associations.

In general terms there are grounds for believing that the experiences of both social and geographical mobility can be seriously disruptive, leaving the mobile individual marginal to both the community of origin and of destination. Nevertheless, a wide range of strategies for coping is available. On the one hand, mobile people may withdraw from community involvement. In this case their religious beliefs may be rejected and practices decline or their religion may become increasingly privatised. On the other hand, they may compensate for their marginality and be overrepresented among the more committed members of the parish community, for example in terms of Mass attendance and leadership of parish organisations. In this chapter we will attempt to distinguish between these alternatives as well as test the 'mobility momentum' and 'suburbanisation' hypotheses in the light of our survey data.

4.2 MOBILITY MEASURES

4.2.1 Social mobility

In our parish, national, and N.P.C. delegate surveys, respondents were asked about their own, their father's, their spouse's and their spouse's father's occupations using a battery of questions adapted from the Oxford Social Mobility study. This enabled us to estimate social class in two ways. First, using the Registrar General's six categories (splitting social class III into manual and non-manual) (Office of Population Censuses and Surveys, 1970) and secondly, using the 65-point Hope–Goldthorpe scale (Goldthorpe and Hope, 1974). For the purposes of calculating social mobility experiences, we have compared the occupational gradings of fathers and respondents in the case of male and unmarried female respondents, and the occupational gradings of fathers and spouses, in the case of married female respondents. For female respondents there is currently some dispute about the classification of social class and hence the estimating of social mobility (see e.g., Dale, Gilbert and Arber, 1985; Goldthorpe, 1983; Murgatroyd, 1982). We have here followed John

Goldthorpe's position 'in defence of the conventional view'. (For a discussion of the effects of different assumptions in the calculation of social mobility see Hornsby-Smith and Cordingley, 1983: 36, fn 4.)

With these assumptions we derived three different measures of social mobility. Using the Registrar General's six categories, we have calculated the proportions of our respondents upwardly or down-wardly mobile or immobile, and also the average mobility movement in terms of these six categories. This makes the questionable assumption that the Registrar General's categories constitute an equal interval scale but nevertheless the measure may be considered to have some comparative value. Our third measure is the average mobility movement using the Hope–Goldthorpe scale which has more of the characteristics of an interval scale. In order to explore the relationship between the social mobility experiences of Roman Catholics, as an independent variable, and their religious practices, beliefs and attitudes, as dependent variables, four categories of mobility experience were distinguished by dichotomising occu-pations into manual and non-manual categories. These were:

1 The stable middle class (both respondent or spouse and father in non-manual occupations). Blau (1956) refers to this category as the 'stationary highs'.
2 The upwardly mobile.
3 The downwardly mobile.
4 The stable working class (both respondents or spouse and father in manual occupations). Blau refers to this category as the 'stationary lows'.

In our three main surveys, intergenerational mobility movements were calculated not only in terms of the 6×6 matrix but also in terms of the collapsed 2×2 matrix. In the case of the survey of the lay members of the bishops' commissions, social mobility data in terms of the Registrar General's sixfold classification were also obtained but for those Catholics interviewed at the papal events, we only collected data on current occupational status; for these respondents, therefore, no social mobility data are available.

4.2.2 Geographical mobility

The measurement of geographical mobility was more complex. In our parish surveys respondents were asked not only about their own and their parents' countries of birth but also, for the British Isles, their county or major town of birth. These data were then collapsed into four categories:

1 Local region: for the two Preston parishes this was taken to be Lancashire and the North-West while for the two London parishes it was taken to be London and the Home Counties.
2 Rest of Great Britain.
3 Ireland.
4 Elsewhere.

In the case of the national survey, country-of-birth data, distinguishing between England and Scotland and Wales was collected for respondents and both parents. Thus, while it was possible to identify first- and second-generation immigrants, we were only able to identify those who had been internally mobile between Scotland and Wales and England but not between the regions as we had done in the parish study. Because the number of immigrants was small, the data have been collapsed to distinguish respondents born in England (as 'core') and Scotland and Wales (as 'periphery', as suggested for example by Hechter (1975)), Ireland (combining Northern Ireland and the Irish Republic because of the limited numbers), and elsewhere (including both eastern and southern Europe, combined because of the small numbers). In all cases estimates of first- and second-generation migrants can be made from the parental country-of-birth returns.

Similar analyses were carried out with the N.P.C. delegate survey though in this case the three countries of Great Britain have been grouped together so that no estimates can be made of internal migration. These two surveys therefore yielded the following types of geographical mobility:

1 English (respondent and both parents born in England).
2 Second-generation British (respondent born in England and at least one parent born in Scotland or Wales, the other parent may have been born in England).
3 First-generation British (respondent born in Scotland or Wales, parents born in Great Britain).
4 Second-generation Irish (respondent born in Great Britain; one parent born in Ireland).
5 Second-generation mixed (respondent born in Great Britain; one parent born in Ireland, the second parent born outside the British Isles).

6 Second-generation other migrant (respondent born in Great Britain; at least one parent born outside the British Isles; the second parent born outside Ireland).

7 First-generation Irish (respondent born in Ireland).

8 First-generation other migrant (respondent born outside the British Isles).

In the N.P.C. study the first three categories have been collapsed together. In the national survey only two cases were found in the second-generation mixed category (both with Irish mothers and 'other' fathers). In the analyses which follow, they have been included with the second-generation other category. In the surveys of the lay members of the bishops' commissions and the sample of Catholics attending the papal events only limited country-of-birth data are available.

4.3 THE SOCIAL MOBILITY OF ENGLISH CATHOLICS

4.3.1 Mobility momentum?

Only in the case of our parish surveys do we have directly compar-able data for the rest of the population and which therefore enable us to address the question as to whether or not English Catholics have experienced a 'mobility momentum' relative to the rest of the population (Bode, 1970). Comparisons between Catholic electors and other electors in each of our four research parishes showed that in none of the parishes did the differences in social mobility reach the 5% level of statistical significance (Hornsby-Smith, Lee and Reilly, 1984), so that the hypothesis of 'mobility momentum' must be rejected.

In table 4.1 the weighted averages for the four parishes have been summarised. It can be seen that for these four parishes the non-Catholic electors appeared to be rather more upwardly mobile on average than the Catholic electors. The lower social origins of Catholics are reflected in the smaller proportions in the stable middle class and correspondingly larger proportions in the stable working class. As for the individual parishes, there is no support for the mobility momentum thesis; on the contrary, fewer Catholics are upwardly mobile and more are downwardly mobile than among the rest of the population in these parishes. On the other hand, among

Table 4.1 *Social mobility experiences by associational involvement and religious identification (four parishes, weighted averages, 1974–7)*

Social mobility measure	R.C. activists	R.C. electors	Other electors
A. Registrar General's classification			
(a) 6 categories:			
upwardly mobile, %	61	40	42
immobile, %	21	33	36
downwardly mobile, %	18	27	22
Av. mobility	+0.90	+0.26	+0.41
(b) 2 categories:			
stable middle class, %	31	24	36
upwardly mobile, %	42	22	24
downwardly mobile %	7	13	10
stable working class, %	20	40	31
Av. mobility	+0.35	+0.08	+0.14
B. Hope–Goldthorpe classification (65 categories)			
Av. mobility	+11.0	+2.9	+3.8
N = 100%	71	178	1,106

the group of Roman Catholic activists in these four parishes, over two-fifths are upwardly mobile across the manual–non-manual division compared to under one-quarter of electors generally. This group also experienced lower rates of downward mobility so that the mean mobility movement, using either the two-class or six-class classifications, is well over twice that of the population generally in these four parishes. We will return to the consideration of Catholic elites in chapter 7. Here we will simply note that parish activists differ markedly from Catholics generally in terms of their social mobility experiences and current social class.

4.3.2 The national pattern

As has been mentioned previously, the four parishes in Preston and London cannot be said to be representative of the country as a whole, although they do reflect wide regional and social-class differences. Overall the Catholic densities in the four parishes ranged from 8% to 33% and averaged 17% compared to the national average of 11%. The 1978 national survey of Roman Catholics in England and Wales enabled estimates to be made of the extent of social mobility among a representative sample of Catholics, though of course this survey did not obtain comparable data from non-Catholics.

Table 4.2 summarises the results of these analyses from the 1978 survey, when the intergenerational mobility matrix was collapsed by dichotomising between non-manual and manual (middle- and working-class) occupations. A mean mobility movement in terms of these two categories has been calculated. The results indicate that there appeared to be a great deal more upward mobility in the four parishes of the earlier study than among Catholics generally. In the national sample 15% were classified as stable middle class, 17% upwardly mobile, 15% downwardly mobile, and 53% stable working class, with a net upward mobility of 0.02 classes. The results confirm those in the four parishes that members of Catholic parish organisations (about one in eight of self-identified Catholics) were more likely to be in the stable middle class and had a higher average upward mobility movement. The data also suggest that converts have experienced much higher upward mobility rates than Catholics generally.

In order to explore the influence of migration experiences, separate estimates were made by respondents' country of birth. Because earlier analyses had suggested that migrant Scots and Welsh Catholics had experienced substantial levels of downward mobility (Hornsby-Smith and Lee, 1979: 40, 176), separate estimates were made for them and for Catholics born in Ireland. Other immigrants have been considered together since their numbers were too small for separate analyses by country of birth. The results indicate that migration experiences generally tend to depress or retard upward social mobility, though in the case of Irish-born Catholics, the effect appears to be limited. Data on parents' country of birth also enable us to measure the social mobility of the children of immigrant parents. In the case of the children of Irish-born parents, the evidence suggests that their mobility experiences approximate to those of English-born Catholics when considering the non-manual–manual occupational division. This does not appear to be the case for the children of parents born outside the British Isles (western Europe, e.g. Spain and Italy; eastern Europe, e.g. Poland; and elsewhere, e.g. the West Indies) who continue to experience high levels of downward social mobility.

An attempt was made to compare these figures with the data from

Table 4.2 *Social mobility experiences of English Catholics by associational involvement, religious origins, country of birth and immigrant generation*

Independent variable	N (= 100%)	Collapsed 2 categories				
		Stable Middle %	Upward %	Downward %	Stable working %	Mean movt.
All Catholics	1033	15	17	15	53	+0.02
Assoc. involvement						
Organ. Member	130	19	16	12	52	+0.04
Parish Attached	579	14	16	16	54	+0.00
Not Attached	324	15	18	15	52	+0.02
Relig. origin						
Born R.C.	828	17	17	15	51	+0.02
Convert	100	16	23	7	54	+0.16
Country of birth						
England	665	16	19	11	53	+0.09
Scotland & Wales	58	10	21	22	47	−0.02
Ireland (1st gen.)	143	16	15	15	54	+0.01
Elsewhere (1st gen.)	59	29	9	31	32	−0.22
Immigrant gen.						
Irish parents (2nd gen.)	136	15	18	9	59	+0.09
Elsewhere parents (2nd gen.)	35	31	11	34	23	−0.23

Source: National Survey, 1978.

the Oxford Mobility Study. Using the observed cell values reported for 9,434 males aged 25 to 64 in 1972 (Goldthorpe, 1980: 105) and making the simplifying assumption of a dichotomy between the middle class (Goldthorpe's classes i to iv) and working class (Goldthorpe's classes v to vii) in terms of his definitions (ibid.: 39–42; Heath, 1981: 53), the four types of crude social mobility experiences were 22% stable middle class, 22% upwardly mobile, 12% downwardly mobile and 44% stable working class. The average mobility movement in terms of this dichotomy was +0.09 classes. Slightly higher estimates resulted from using alternative matrices from the same study: +0.12 in Goldthorpe (1980: 44) and +0.10 in Heath (1981: 54). In the London Work and Leisure Study of 1970, Richardson's mobility matrix yielded an average mobility of +0.09 (1977: 44).

In order to approximate the Oxford measures, separate estimates of Catholic mobility for males only have been given in table 4.3. While these data showed that on average Catholics had experienced much lower levels of social mobility than the population as a whole, those born in Great Britain had experienced a significant mobility momentum. They had much higher rates of upward mobility than immigrants but converts continued to be more upwardly mobile than born Catholics. Catholic men born in Scotland and Wales appeared to be more upwardly mobile than Catholic men born in England. The male children of Irish-born parents were less likely to be downwardly mobile than Irish-born males but their mean mobility movement was still lower than that for Catholic males born in Great Britain. Although the numbers were small there was some evidence that second-generation males with parents born outside the British Isles continued to be downwardly mobile, though not as rapidly as their fathers.

4.3.3 Associational involvement

In the analysis of social mobility experiences in the four-parishes study it was noted that whereas there were no significant differences between Catholic and other electors, the 'activists' in the Catholic parishes had significantly different mobility experiences when compared to their co-religionists. Whichever measures were used they experienced much more upward and much less downward mobility and more of them were likely to be members of the stable middle class (table 4.1).

In the national survey, three different levels of associational involvement were distinguished. Members of parish organisations were compared to other Catholics attached to a parish and to Catholics who reported that they were not attached to a parish. The social mobility experiences of these three types of Catholics have been reported in table 4.2. The national data confirm the findings from the earlier study in four parishes, in that organisation members are more upwardly mobile on average than other Catholics, though the differences between the three groups were not statistically significant.

Apart from these three types of associational involvement, data from our other surveys enable us to extend the analysis to various elite groups. Hornsby-Smith and Cordingley (1983: 30–2) reported on the mobility experiences of the lay leaders at the N.P.C. Overall, and

Table 4.3 *Social mobility experiences of English Catholics by country of birth, religious origins and immigrant generation (males only)*

Independent variable	N = 100%	Stable middle	Upwardly mobile	Down- wardly mobile	Stable working	Mean mobility (2 categories)
All males aged 25–64 in England & Wales in 1972 (Oxford mobility study)	9434	22	22	12	44	+0.09
All Catholics	397	17	18	12	52	+0.05
Country of birth:						
England	276	18	20	9	53	+0.11
Scotland and Wales	26	15	27	12	46	+0.15
Ireland	64	11	16	13	61	+0.03
Elsewhere	24	21	8	42	29	−0.33
Religious origins:						
Born R.C.	362	17	17	13	53	+0.04
Convert	35	23	23	9	46	+0.14
Immigrant generation:						
Irish Parents (Second generation)	71	15	16	7	63	+0.08
Elsewhere Parents (Second generation)	18	33	11	33	22	−0.22

Source: National Survey, 1978.

in terms of the Registrar General's six social classes, lay delegates on average were 1.17 classes higher than their fathers compared to only 0.08 for Catholics generally. In terms of the four mobility experiences half the lay delegates were stable middle class and over one third upwardly mobile from the manual working class. Only 4% were downwardly mobile from the middle class and only 8% stable working class compared to over half of Catholics generally. (ibid.: 8–9)

Among the N.P.C. lay delegates three leadership levels were distinguished: officials (members of the Congress committee, sector presidents and topic chairpersons), discussion-group leaders and ordinary delegates. When social class was dichotomised the corresponding mean movements for those three groups were +0.38, +0.25 and +0.31, respectively.

Finally, in our early study of the lay members of the bishops' commissions and other advisory bodies in the mid-1970s we reported that they comprised three different groups:

firstly, one-third are first generation middle class, the bulk of whom have immigrant (mainly Irish) origins; secondly, one-half come from established middle class backgrounds and again the bulk have immigrant (mainly Irish) origins; thirdly, one-fifth were converts to Roman Catholicism and were generally indigenous English. Taken together, it can be seen that well over two-thirds of this sample of lay influentials in the formal structures of advice and consultation in the Roman Catholic Church in this country reported some immigrant origins. (Hornsby-Smith, 1975:9)

It was also reported that:

only about one-third came from recognizably working class backgrounds ... Nearly two-thirds of the male members were upwardly mobile (in terms of the Registrar General's six social classes) ... Only five (of 67) males had experienced downward social mobility ... overall the male lay members had risen an average of 1.15 social classes on a six-point scale. What upward mobility there was seemed to be clearly related to educational achievement. Three-quarters of the members had had some form of further or higher education and over half were university graduates. The pattern was similar when considering the 24 male members from working class homes only; three-quarters had received some form of further or higher education though the proportion of graduates was only two-fifths. (ibid.: 8)

When the occupational statuses of the male respondents and their fathers were dichotomised, the mean upward mobility was +0.36 units, four times the national average.

In sum, the evidence is consistent that, while in general Catholics have experienced rather less upward mobility than the population as a whole, the higher the level of leadership attained, the greater the amount of intergenerational social mobility experienced. Conversely, the greater the amount of upward social mobility experienced, the higher is the leadership level attained in the institutional structures of lay participation in the Roman Catholic Church in England and Wales. In this sense it is meaningful to refer to the 'new Catholic middle class', upwardly mobile as a result of educational achievement and over-represented among the new advisory structures set up in the Church following the reforms of the Second Vatican Council.

4.3.4 The social mobility of Irish immigrants

The country-of-birth data enabled us to make separate estimates of the social mobility experiences of those Catholics with immigrant origins. The significance of immigration for the Catholic community in England and Wales was indicated in chapter 2. Analyses using census returns suggested that something like one-quarter of English Catholics had been born outside Great Britain (Hornsby-Smith, 1986). Of the many different immigrant groups the largest is the Irish with around 672,000 Irish-born Catholics and an additional 640,000 British-born children of Irish parents. This is the only single group present in sufficient numbers in the national survey for separate analysis. The social mobility experiences of first- and second-generation immigrant Irish Catholics have been reported in table 4.2. When the occupational categories are collapsed to focus on mobility across the manual–non-manual division, it can be seen that first-generation Irish Catholics cross this boundary at a similar rate to Catholics generally, though much less frequently than Catholics born in England. Second-generation Irish, however, are much more likely to be upwardly mobile at rates similar to Catholics born in England.

The comparisons summarised in table 4.3, for males only, modify the picture somewhat. These data suggest that there is a larger proportion of stable working-class males among the Irish-born Catholics than among any of the other groups considered. Whereas Catholic men born outside the British Isles experience on average a substantial amount of downward mobility in both the first and second generations, Irish Catholic men experience on average a small amount of upward mobility in the first generation (though much less than that experienced by Catholic men born in Great Britain) and by the second generation are approaching the mean upward mobility movement of Catholic men born in England.

Further analyses of the social mobility experiences of the second-generation Irish immigrants revealed some intriguing differences:

When one distinguishes between those, both of whose parents are Irish, those with an Irish mother and those with an Irish father, striking differences in mobility experiences appear. More than two-fifths of those with two Irish parents experience downward mobility and, overall, this group shows a mean mobility movement of −0.13 units (considering the Registrar General's six-fold classification). Respondents with an Irish father but a mother who is not Irish experience no net mobility movement and just under half are immobile in comparison with their fathers. Respondents with an Irish mother but a father who is not Irish, on the other hand, experience very high levels of upward mobility (+0.28 on average) and only one-quarter of them are downwardly mobile. (While) care is necessary in interpreting these data because the cell sizes are relatively small ... it appears ... that Irish mothers are more successful than Irish fathers in promoting the upward social mobility of their British born children. (Hornsby-Smith and Lee, 1979: 41, 177)

The situation is clearly complex and those findings were not supported by subsequent analyses based on General Household Survey (G.H.S.) data. However, while in general it appears that by the second generation the Irish Catholic in England has converged towards his British-born co-religionist, there are also suggestions in the data that the processes of assimilation for Irish males and females may be somewhat different. These differences will be explored further in chapter 6.

4.4 THE GEOGRAPHICAL MOBILITY OF ENGLISH CATHOLICS

In the weighted sample of four parishes in London and Preston, one-quarter of the Catholic electors had been born outside Great Britain (13% in Ireland, 11% elsewhere) compared to only 9% among other electors (1% in Ireland, 8% elsewhere). In the sample as a whole, 64% of Catholics compared to 68% of other electors had originated in the local region (Lancashire and the North-West for the Preston parishes and London and the Home Counties for the London parishes). The balance of 11% Catholics and 23% other electors had come from the rest of Great Britain. Broadly speaking, Catholics had higher rates of immigration from outside Great Britain and lower rates for internal migration within the countries of Great Britain. This indicates the major importance of immigration for the Catholic community and its relative stability within the country.

On the other hand, when each parish was considered separately some notable differences in the patterns of geographical mobility emerged.

In the first place there has been very little geographical mobility by the Preston Catholics compared to the Catholics in the two London parishes. Many Catholics in the Preston suburban parish had simply moved from another parish in Preston and few had immigrated from outside the county of Lancashire. By contrast half the Catholics in the London commuter parish and two-thirds in the London inner city parish had not been born in the local region. Both of these parishes contained significant proportions of Irish-born Catholics and in the inner city parish in addition, over one quarter of

Catholics had been born elsewhere, usually Europe or the New Commonwealth countries ... the Lancashire Catholics were far less and the London
Catholics far more geographically mobile than the rest of the population in
the same areas ... It may be that these differences reflect new patterns of
migration in the post-war years with London rather than the North-West as
the destination of both Irish and other immigrants. (Hornsby-Smith, Lee
and Reilly, 1984)

The national survey showed that just over one half of English
Catholics had been born in England of English-born parents. A
further 7% were internally migrant British, over one or two generations, from either Scotland or Wales. There were 15% first-
generation Irish and a further 15% second-generation Irish. The
remaining 10% were either first- or second-generation immigrants
from outside the British Isles.

The relationship between social mobility and internal migration
has been summarised in table 4.4. It seems that Catholics born in
Scotland and Wales and moving to England were much less likely to
be in the working class but also much more likely to be downwardly
mobile than Catholics generally. In the second generation, however,
they seem to have a higher mean mobility movement than the
indigenous English, though this result should be treated with caution
because of the small numbers involved. The results of external
migration to England and Wales from both Ireland and other
countries outside the British Isles have already been noted in tables
4.2 and 4.3. The latter group, over two generations, contained a

Table 4.4 *Social mobility experiences of English Catholics by geographical
mobility*

Social mobility experiences	English (over two generations)	Second-generation British	First-generation British	All Catholics
Stable middle	14	13	12	15
Upwardly mobile	18	22	20	17
Downwardly mobile	13	12	25	15
Stable working	55	53	43	53
Mean mobility Movement	+0.05	+0.10	−0.05	+0.02
N = 100%	555	27	44	1036

Source: National Survey, 1978.

much larger proportion than Catholics generally of both the stable middle class and the downwardly mobile and the smallest proportions of those in the stable working class. The net effect was high levels of downward mobility over two generations. The numbers in our samples were too small for detailed analysis but when considering Catholics with different immigrant origins separately, it appeared that only Catholics with at least one parent born in eastern Europe had experienced a net upward social mobility. First-generation eastern Europeans as well as both first- and second-generation western Europeans and those with origins elsewhere had all experienced net downward social mobility.

4.5 RELIGION AND MOBILITY

In the United States, Herberg (1960) has suggested that religious commitment provided an important element of continuity for first-generation immigrants. The second generation, however, tended to reject this aspect of ethnic identification in the process of adjusting themselves to their new environment, but the third generation realised that this was not necessary and that religion provided an important differentiating aspect of identification. In a recent study, however, Wuthnow and Christiano (1979) showed that there was little evidence of the Hansen–Herberg three-generation thesis in the United States. 'First generation Catholic immigrants were less likely than were second generation immigrants (but equally likely as third generation immigrants) to attend church regularly.' In this present study we do not have separate data for third-generation immigrants because in our pilot work in the four parishes we discovered that few of our respondents knew about their grandparents' main occupations or place of birth and we omitted these questions in subsequent fieldwork. We are therefore only able to compare the first- and second-generation immigrants with the indigenous population. In general terms it appears that there is a large measure of convergence of religious beliefs and practices to those of the indigenous population by the second generation, at least among the Irish Catholics.

In his Detroit study, Lenski (1963: 115–18) suggested that social mobility had different consequences for white Catholics and white Protestants. For Catholics upward mobility was associated with higher Mass attendance and this was regarded as reflecting conformity to the standards of new peers rather than the continuing influence of childhood socialisation. More recently Greeley (1977: 50–68) has shown that while ethnic Catholics in the United States have done well in terms of their relative educational and economic mobilities, they have done less well occupationally.

In one of the few British studies, Nelson and Clews (1973) found a negative relationship between geographical mobility and religious orthodoxy and suggested that there was a contrast between a British attachment to a local congregation and the American commitment to the wider religious community: Protestant, Catholic or Jew. It might be doubted that the localism of the British applies to Roman Catholics, for whom a denominational attachment is likely to have some salience, and it is unfortunate that these researchers failed to control for denominational attachment, social class or education. In a recent American study it was reported that geographical mobility had only a limited impact on church attendance and 'may be a less important predictor of church attendance than interpersonal ties' (Welch and Baltzell, 1984: 86–7). In general, the results of this study supported 'the integration–disruption hypothesis' and suggested that geographical mobility inhibited church attendance indirectly through disrupting an individual's network of social ties and bonds of community attachment.

Finally, the implications of social mobility for personal identity have been explored by Luckmann and Berger (1964). They pointed to the problems of status inconsistency for mobile individuals and suggested that the 'mobility ethos' has a quasi-religious character in that 'it can serve as an overarching integrative representation' (ibid.: 340). A wide range of patterns of adaptation is possible from total withdrawal to organised crime. Typically there is a retreat into 'privatisation', 'sexualism' and 'familism', and into compensatory activity in voluntary associations. In this mobility ethos one of the functions of the churches is 'social maintenance and repair services for this precarious private universe' in 'a world of radical subjectivism' (ibid.: 342–3). Elsewhere Luckmann has suggested that 'the prevalent mobility ethos can be considered a specific expression of the theme of self-realisation' and is linked to individualistic and manipulative attitudes. He further hypothesised that the downwardly mobile will be particularly likely to retrench in the private sphere (Luckmann, 1970: 110–11). The identification of a privatised religion among English Catholics will be considered in a subsequent publication.

In the parishes study, contrary to our original suppositions, variations in social mobility experiences were not related significantly with religious practices, beliefs and attitudes. For example, attitudes towards sexual morality were not significantly affected by social mobility experiences, but there did seem to be an effect due to the parish itself, which may have reflected differences in parish climate. Catholic residents in the suburban and commuter parishes, where around two-thirds of the Catholics were upwardly mobile, appeared to be somewhat more traditional in terms of sexual morality than those in the two inner-city parishes where between two-fifths and two-thirds of the Catholics were in the stable working class. Attitudes to authority, on the other hand, were found to be associated in a limited way with social mobility experiences of Catholics insofar as the stable middle class was rather less likely to be accepting of authority (Hornsby-Smith, Lee and Reilly, 1984).

The relatively limited effect of both social and geographical mobility experiences on a wide range of religious variables can be seen in the data summarised in tables A3 and A4 (see appendix 2). Using the religious types derived in the previous chapter and the scales described in appendix 1, it might be noted in table A3 that significant variations with social mobility occur only in the case of doctrinal orthodoxy, adult religious behaviour, new-style activism and liturgical traditionalism. Geographical (mainly immigrant) mobility is significantly associated with only five variables: doctrinal orthodoxy, adult religious behaviour, prayer, sexual orthodoxy and the weight attached to papal authority.

Scores on the doctrinal orthodoxy scale are highest among the socially stable middle and working classes and lowest among the downwardly mobile. Among the various migrant groups the first-generation Irish have the highest scores and second-generation British (i.e. the children of internal migrants) the lowest scores. Adult religious behaviour is much higher among the stable middle class than the other three groups. Irish immigrants also score highest and internal migrants lowest on this scale. The stable middle class also score more highly than other groups on the prayer scale which again is given the highest emphasis by first-generation Irish immigrants. Significantly low scores on this scale are recorded both by the children of internal migrants and by those migrants born outside Europe.

The relatively high levels of institutional involvement of the stable middle class are reflected paradoxically in their much higher scores than the other social mobility groups on both liturgical traditionalism (disapproving of recent changes in the styles of worship in the Church) and on new-style activism (favouring recent innovations such as house Masses and ecumenical services). In contrast, the stable working class report the lowest scores on both these scales.

An indication of the traditional nature of their religion brought by Irish-born Catholics is the fact that they score highest on the scales of sexual orthodoxy and papal authority. In contrast, the lowest scores on these two scales were recorded by the children of both internal migrants and immigrants from outside the British Isles.

Although few of the variations between those with different social mobility experiences are large enough to be statistically significant, a number of general trends can be identified. On 11 of the 15 measures, the stable middle class have recorded the highest scores. They are clearly the most institutionally involved in terms of orthodoxy of belief, religious practice, organisational involvement (both traditional and innovatory), social and personal morality, and awareness of papal authority and a concern about religious sanctions. The evidence summarised here supports the view that the institutional Church is most effective in attracting the stable or established middle-class Catholics.

In contrast, the remaining three groups are remarkably similar. Evidence from the national survey for the emergence of a committed and involved 'new Catholic middle class' is not strong. Their innovatory potential is reflected in the fact that they scored higher than the other groups on the scale of new-style ministries. They were also the least orthodox group in terms of sexual morality and they had the highest proportion of the non-practising Catholics.

On 10 of the 15 measures, the lowest scores were recorded by the downwardly mobile. While few of these reached the level of statistical significance, the general pattern of the results is perhaps indicative of the potentially alienating implications of downward social mobility and to that extent there is support for the disruption hypothesis. It seems possible that both the upwardly and downwardly mobile jettison some elements of the religious culture of their class of origin. In the case of the downwardly mobile there seems to be some loss of both practice and belief though not sexual orthodoxy. In contrast, the upwardly mobile have in large measures jettisoned the conformity to the institutional identity which is strongest among the stable working class, and, more than all the other groups, have rejected the sexual orthodoxy of the Church.

The pattern of religious belief and practice of the indigenous English Catholics is given in the first column of results in table A4. In considering the religious characteristics of internal immigrants it is somewhat surprising to note that Catholics born in Scotland and Wales and now living in England have a relatively weak involvement in the institutional Church. One might have predicted on the basis of the integration hypothesis that mobility would be associated with high levels of social and religious commitment. In fact the opposite appears to be the case. It appears that those most likely to be geographically mobile within Great Britain have attenuated their links with institutional Catholicism. This is shown by the high levels of the non-practising Catholic types among both the first- and second-generation British. Yet there may be signs of the emergence of new styles of religious commitment. The internal migrants, for example, emphasised the importance of new styles of religious activism more than any other migrant group, while the children of such migrants, although having the largest proportion of non-practising of any group, also stressed the importance of church commitment and new styles of ministry more than any other group. Since they rated priests lower than any other group it would seem possible that while some previous experiences had led them to be highly critical of the institutional Church, they would nevertheless favour new developments within the Church. This, of course, is speculative and must be evaluated in the light of the fact that second-generation British Catholics also scored lowest on the scale of new-style activism.

The pattern of responses of the Irish Catholics indicated a large measure of assimilation to the norms of English Catholicism by the second generation. It seems that first-generation Irish Catholics retained many of the traditional aspects of Irish Catholicism. On 9 of the 15 measures they recorded the highest scores. They had the highest levels of religious practice, doctrinal and sexual orthodoxy, liturgical traditionalism, the highest scores on the scales of papal authority and awareness of religious sanctions, and laid the greatest stress on conformity to institutional identity. Conversely they were least likely to emphasise a world-justice orientation or support new styles of ministry. In general terms they reflected to a large extent the characteristics of a pre-Vatican institutional model of the Church. By the second generation, however, there were signs of a considerable degree of convergence to the norms of English Catholicism. There was evidence of assimilation to local Church norms, for example in doctrinal and sexual orthodoxy, liturgical traditionalism, attitudes to priests and new styles of ministry, and so on. There was also an increase in the proportion of non-practising Catholics in this second generation but this was balanced by a high proportion of the involved orthodox attenders. It seems possible that if the first-generation Irish Catholic tends to remain near the periphery of institutional parish life, their children are disproportionately found among the core membership of parish organisations.

In the case of immigrants from outside the British Isles the patterns are not so clear cut and it seems more likely that there is a growing alienation from the institutional Church over the two generations than simply a process of assimilation to the norms of English Catholicism. In the first place, whereas Irish Catholics come to England from a tradition of relatively high levels of religious practice, the other immigrant groups appear more likely to bring with them a norm of non-practice. Over two-thirds of the first generation are non- or irregularly-practising and the proportion rises to four-fifths by the second generation. In some respects the pattern parallels that of the Irish; for example there is a decline of doctrinal and sexual orthodoxy and stress on papal authority by the second generation. On the other hand, the scores on the prayer and evaluation of priests scales are both higher than among the first generation. The numbers involved in these analyses are too small for detailed consideration but they do suggest that the Catholic Church in England and Wales has not been particularly successful in encouraging the commitment of the very large numbers of immigrant Catholics.

4.6 SUMMARY AND CONCLUSIONS

It is necessary to be cautious in using cross-sectional data obtained in single surveys at one point in time to draw conclusions about processes taking place over time. Thus while it might be plausible to regard the high levels of conformity to the institutional norms of religious beliefs and practices among the stable middle class as evidence for the embourgeoisement of English Catholics, such a conclusion would be incautious without the consideration of other evidence, including life histories.

The findings we have reviewed in this chapter lead to the conclusion that whereas for English Catholics generally there is no evidence of a mobility momentum relative to the rest of the population, when the controls for country of birth are introduced into the analysis, it can be seen that those Catholics born in Great Britain had indeed experienced higher rates of net upward mobility. Irish Catholics appeared to converge towards the English norm by the second generation but immigrants from outside the British Isles experienced considerable downward mobility in both the first and second generations. It has also been shown that the higher the level of lay leadership attained within the institutional Church, the greater the amount of intergenerational mobility experienced. This evidence is consistent with Musgrove's explanation in terms of the compensatory functions of leadership in voluntary associations for the disruptive effects of both social and geographical mobility.

Our data suggest that the effects of social mobility on religious practice and belief are generally slight and not as significant as had originally been anticipated. In general they support Goldthorpe's finding that there is little evidence that social mobility is radically dissociative or leads to serious social marginality and isolation. Rather there is a shift, on the part of mobile individuals, towards the prevailing norms of their class of destination. Support for Luckmann's thesis that downward mobility is particularly conducive to a privatised religion was not strong in our data. Rather, it seems more likely that both the upwardly and downwardly mobile jettison some aspects of the religious beliefs and practices of their class of origin.

In sum, the evidence we have reviewed in this chapter suggests that there has been a process of occupational embourgeoisement but only on the part of those English Catholics who are not either immigrants or the children of immigrants. There is also evidence that there has been a significant diffusion of the Catholic population away from Lancashire and the north-west. To some extent, therefore, it can be said that the pre-war Church of the Irish working classes in the industrial north has become the post-Vatican English 'melting pot' Church in the surburban areas, particularly around London and the south-east (Spencer, 1973). Evidence for the assimilation of Irish immigrants will be given in chapter 6. First, however, in order to analyse more effectively the issues of social and religious intermarriage, it is necessary to construct a typology of Catholic marriage types in chapter 5.

CHAPTER 5

CATHOLIC MARRIAGE
AND FAMILY LIFE

———— ❧ ————

5.1 INTRODUCTION

For many people what peculiarly defines English Roman Catholics is their obsession with matters of sex. In particular, the extended agonising and controversy among Catholics over birth control, especially after the publication of Pope Paul VI's encyclical *Humanae Vitae* (1968), has been variously interpreted in Britain with astonishment and incredulity. The official position of Catholics has been considered by many to be distinctly odd but clearly related to the wider issue of religious (and especially papal) authority. On this some commentators have even judged the position of Catholic apologists to have been hypocritical (Scott, 1967).

Apart from the question of contraception, the ferocity of the opposition of Catholic spokespersons on the matter of abortion is well known. While for many people abortion is often regarded as a type of contraception, in general Catholics see it as a distinct moral issue and one which they regard with particular abhorrence. Among Catholic lay leaders, the 1967 Abortion Act is generally considered to have been a political defeat of major proportions and lasting consequences. Catholics have been disproportionately active in the two main anti-abortion pressure groups in Britain: the Society for the Protection of the Unborn Child (S.P.U.C.) and LIFE (Scarisbrick, 1971). However, the failure of attempts to reform the Abortion Act can be attributed in part to the failure adequately to coordinate the anti-abortion lobby, for example at the time of the Corrie Bill in 1980, and to irreconcilable differences between the 'political pragmatists' who wished to limit legalised abortion and minimise the consequences of the 1967 Act, on the one hand, and the 'moral fundamentalists' whose opposition to abortion was absolute and uncompromising (Marsh and Chambers, 1981).

The Catholic obsession with sex is a recurring theme in the writings of Catholic authors. In the early post-war years Graham Greene explored Catholic attitudes to adultery and sin in *The End of the Affair* (1962). More recently David Lodge has reflected the obsessions of the first generation of university-educated 'new Catholic middle class' at different stages of their life cycles in *The Picturegoers* (1962), *The British Museum is Falling Down* (1983) and *How Far Can You Go?* (1980). Among Catholics it often seemed as if concepts of sin were simply defined in terms of violations of the sixth and ninth commandments and as if the other eight commandments were somehow essentially of lesser significance. Associated with this obsession with 'the sins of the flesh' was a strong emphasis on the permanence and inviolability of the marriage contract, strong opposition to divorce, and among official apologists, an ideology of the happy Catholic family with an explicit espousal of a differentiated domestic division of labour. The woman's place was very definitely seen as being in the home and this view was regarded as being not only natural but also legitimated by rather narrow interpretations of the role of the Holy Family of Nazareth.

In the public mind, therefore, Catholics in England and Wales were often defined in terms of the ferocity with which they opposed contraception, abortion and divorce, and propounded a sexual ethic manifestly at variance with the changing behavioural norms of British society. Some interpreted these beliefs as the major defining characteristics of a distinctive Catholic subculture (Coman, 1977). In a fortress-like, defensive Church these distinct norms were further reinforced by a strong emphasis on religious endogamy, underpinned by a formidable array of religious and social sanctions against 'mixed' marriages, and by an insistence that the children of such marriages should be brought up in the Roman Catholic Faith (Canon Law Society, 1983: 189–205). In general, therefore, Catholics were frequently associated with a clear and inflexible sexual ethic and especially an abhorrence of contraception and abortion, a belief in the unbreakable nature of the marriage contract and a firm opposition to divorce, underpinned by a socio-religious ideology of the happy family and a rigid set of social and religious controls and sanctions imposed by powerful religious authorities reinforced by a 'creeping infallibility'.

As long as the Church in this country manifested the characteristics of a fortress, by erecting strong defenses against the influences of the wider society, minimising contact with extraneous influences by discouraging marriage with non-Catholics (for example by means of less solemn and aesthetically unattractive marriage ceremonies or the insistence that children be baptised and brought up as Catholics), and by reinforcing the salience of the Catholic belief and value systems by means of a pervasive Catholic social and religious environment and a nexus of Catholic schools and parishes, then deviant attitudes and beliefs on sexual and marital matters largely remained unspoken and unrecognised. This was further emphasised where the agents of social control such as priests and teachers had considerable power and scope and were buttressed by an ideology which stressed the hierarchical nature of the Church and the infallible authority of its religious leadership. In this chapter we will review evidence that by the end of the 1970s, however, among Roman Catholics in England and Wales there was substantial divergence from the traditional and official norms of the Church and a breakdown of the fortress model with its distinctive subculture. This is apparent in the accelerating increase in the proportions not only of 'mixed' marriages but also of canonically invalid marriages. Current trends, if continued, as seems most likely, suggest that there will be serious long-term consequences in terms of the lack of religious commitment of the children of such marriages and hence of the number and characteristics of affiliated Catholics.

In chapter 3 it was shown that there is a considerable amount of religious heterodoxy, in terms of both practice and belief, among English Catholics. This heterodoxy is also apparent in the five marriage types which will be distinguished in this present chapter. Considerable variations were found in the religious beliefs and practices of non-mixed marriages depending on whether or not the respondent or spouse was a convert, and between valid and invalid mixed marriages. Processes of disaffiliation have been explored by relating the time of apostasy with that of marriage in an attempt to discover the causal sequence and determine whether exogamy leads to apostasy or vice versa. A separate section also summarises the evidence relating to Catholic attitudes to marriage and family life at the end of the 1970s. The discussion of Catholic separation and

divorce that follows raises the question, which will be considered
further in chapter 9, as to whether Catholic community life is
supportive of the marital bond rather than of married people. In sum,
the evidence reviewed in this chapter leads clearly to the conclusion
that there has been a significant change in the nature of the Church in
this country in the post-war years. In particular, not only do
Catholics demonstrate a much higher degree of heterodoxy in their
attitudes to sexual and marital morality than has hitherto been
assumed, but there has also been a very substantial breakdown of the
social and religious constraints to intermarriage. These social and
religious changes are in a dialectical relationship with the dominant
forms of religious authority, a relationship which will be examined
further in a subsequent publication.

5.2 A TYPOLOGY OF CATHOLIC MARRIAGES

5.2.1 Catholic endogamy and canonical validity

Since 1958, regular ecclesiastical statistics on Catholic marriages
have been collected by the Catholic Education Council. Three types
of marriages are recorded by parish priests: ordinary marriages,
convalidations (or the canonical validation of legal marriages, for
example in Register Offices, which were not previously recognised by
the Church) and authorised marriages but not held in a Catholic
Church. In each case, records distinguish marriages where both
parties are Catholic from those where only one party is a Catholic
(i.e. the religiously 'mixed' marriages). The statistics show that in
1983 the total number of marriages between two Catholics registered
by the parish clergy had declined to only 40% of the peak in 1961. On
the other hand, the total number of mixed marriages continued to
rise steadily throughout the 1960s to a peak in 1970 but the number
had fallen subsequently by one-third in 1983. The total number of
marriages recorded by parish priests (equivalent to 'valid' marriages) rose to a steady level of around 46,000 annually from 1960 to
1970 but has since fallen to only 60% of this level in 1983. The net
effect has been an increase in the proportion of mixed marriages
recorded from under one-half in 1958 to two-thirds a quarter of a
century later.

However, these figures do not take into account those marriages
involving at least one Catholic partner which are canonically invalid

in the sense that they have not been solemnised by a priest. The 1978 survey reported in *Roman Catholic Opinion* for the first time provided some relevant data on the scale of invalid marriages. It was reported that:

slightly more than half of married Catholics are validly married to other Catholics, about one quarter are validly married to non-Catholics, three per cent are invalidly married to a Catholic partner, while slightly less than one fifth are in an invalid mixed marriage. (Hornsby-Smith and Lee, 1979: 107–8)

When the figures are broken down by the year of marriage (table 5.1) it is clear that there has been a remarkable shift in the distribution of marriage types since the 1950s, so that for the cohort of self-identifying Roman Catholics in England and Wales married between 1970 and 1977, as many as 36% were in invalid marriages and the proportion of Catholics in mixed marriages had risen to 67%. These figures indicate that four-fifths of marriages in the 1970s involving at least one Catholic partner were religiously mixed and that over two-fifths of them were invalid. Thus the dramatic decline in the number of Catholic marriages recorded by the Catholic Education Council (C.E.C.) since 1970 (C.E.C., 1984) appears to reflect a significant increase in the propensity of English Catholics to marry outside the Church.

The evidence suggests that men are no more likely to enter an invalid marriage than women, although when valid marriages only are considered, women are much more likely to marry-out than men. There are no social class differences in the contraction of invalid marriages but those in non-manual occupations are more likely to marry a non-Catholic spouse in a Catholic ceremony than those in manual occupations. Irish-born Catholics are more likely than other groups to contract valid non-mixed marriages and are least likely to contract invalid marriages (Hornsby-Smith and Lee, 1979: 109–10).

Social background data indicate that as expected:

exogamous and more especially invalid marriages are more likely to occur where the involvement of self or significant others in Catholic practice or with Catholic institutions or community life is attenuated. (ibid.: 112)

Thus the offspring of a mixed marriage or of a marriage where the level of parental religiosity was low were more likely themselves to enter a mixed or invalid marriage than those where both parents were Roman Catholics or where the level of parental religiosity was

Table 5.1 *Distribution of Catholics by marriage type and year of
marriage (%)*

	Year of marriage					
Marriage type	Up to 1939	1940–9	1950–9	1960–9	1970–7	All R.C.s
Valid non-mixed	68.5	64.6	68.5	51.6	30.2	52.8
Valid mixed	22.2	19.5	20.8	28.3	33.5	25.7
Invalid non-mixed	3.7	3.7	1.5	1.2	3.2	3.0
Invalid Mixed	5.6	12.2	9.2	18.9	33.0	18.6
Weighted N = 100%	55	84	134	254	185	813

Source: Hornsby-Smith and Lee, 1979: 232.

high. Again, the greater the proportion of education in Catholic
schools, the greater the likelihood that respondents had entered a
valid non-mixed marriage and the less likely they were to have
entered an invalid mixed marriage. The density of Catholic friendships during adolescence was also relevant; the evidence suggested
that it was the availability of Catholic partners (as indicated by the
density of Catholic friendships at the age of 17) which was particularly important for the encouragement of in-marriage (ibid.:
114).

5.2.2 The elaboration of marriage types

Since conversion to Roman Catholicism has often been associated
with marriage to a Catholic, the above typology of marriage types has
been elaborated to take account of this. Lazerwitz, for example,
reported the general finding on intermarriage and conversion or
religious 'switching' that most conversions to Catholicism (and to
Protestantism) in the United States were the result of intermarriages
(1971: 42). In the following discussion, 'mixed' marriages will be
taken to refer to religious intermarriage. It should also be noted that
the term 'convert' generally refers to a denominational 'switcher'
(within the Christian faith) or to a switcher from no religion to
Roman Catholicism. In our national sample under 1% of the convert
respondents had held a non-Christian faith prior to becoming a
Roman Catholic.

   In a study of interfaith marriages in Detroit, Besanceney (1965) noted the importance of distinguishing between marriages where the partners continued to be religiously mixed and those where one partner was converted to the religion of the other partner. However, the classification of married couples simply by their present religious preference failed to distinguish those marriages where the partners had been socialised in different religious traditions. In this present study, therefore, the non-mixed marriages have been subdivided according to whether the respondents and their spouses were born Catholics or converts. These marriages were not further subdivided by canonical validity because 95% of non-mixed marriages were valid (Hornsby-Smith and Lee, 1979: 232) and the number of invalid non-mixed marriages was too small for separate analysis. The first three types in our modified typology are therefore:

1 Born-Roman Catholic respondents with born-Catholic spouses (BB)
2 Convert respondents with born-Catholic spouses (CB)
3 Born-Roman Catholic respondents with convert spouses (BC)

Thus although Types CB and BC both include one born-Catholic partner and a convert partner, their religious socialisation experiences will have differed and, following Besanceney, it is important to distinguish their current religious beliefs, practices and attitudes. There were only a handful of convert respondents with convert spouses in the national survey and they therefore have not been considered in the subsequent analyses.

In the case of respondents in religiously mixed marriages the key distinction, made in the early analyses in *Roman Catholic Opinion*, was between those in canonically valid and invalid marriages. This provided the basis for the definition of the two remaining marriage types:

4 Born-Roman Catholic respondents with a non-Roman Catholic spouse in a valid marriage (VM)
5 Born-Roman Catholic respondents with a non-Catholic spouse in an invalid marriage (IM)

In the analyses which follow, comparisons have been made with all respondents who can be classified in terms of these five types.

5.2.3 Variations of religious practice and belief

In making comparisons between respondents in the five marriage types, a relevant consideration is the attachment to religious norms which prescribe and proscribe marital choices and so inhibit or encourage the rate of heterogamous marriages (Marcson, 1950). Thus we might hypothesise, for example, that committed Catholics who depart from the norm of endogamous mate selection will compensate by a higher than average rate of religious practice and orthodoxy of belief. Specifically we might expect high rates of approved religious involvement from those whose spouse has married-in and converted and also from converts as compensation for their marginality. Conversely, those who have married-out without conversion of their spouses, and who have to that extent demonstrated a relative unconcern for in-group social and religious sanctions, are likely to show relatively low rates of religious involvement. This is particularly likely to be the case for those who have so attenuated their links with the Catholic community that they have contracted an invalid marriage. The data from the national survey enable us to test these hypotheses.

First, though, it is necessary to note some social and demographic variations between the five marriage types. The two types with the largest proportions in the over-50s age group are those with convert spouses (BC) and converts (CB) and there is a progressive fall in age through the BB, VM, and IM types which is entirely consistent with the rapid decline in the number of converts in England and Wales from a peak of 16,250 in 1959 to only one-third of that figure in the early 1980s (C.E.C., 1984) and the evidence of an increase in both mixed and invalid marriages since the 1950s. Converts, and those in valid mixed marriages, were more likely to be women than respondents in the other groups. Nearly one-third of the BB respondents (both partners born Catholics) were first-generation Irish immigrants with a higher than average proportion in lower-working-class occupations. On the other hand, born-Catholic respondents with convert spouses (type BC) were disproportionately second-generation Irish and skilled working class. Convert respondents were disproportionately middle class, had no Irish origins over two generations, had rarely attended Catholic schools and reported few Catholic friends in adolescence. As predicted above, they appeared to compensate for their marginality by having the strongest attachment to their parish and were twice as likely as married Catholics generally to belong to parish organisations (Turcan and Hornsby-Smith, 1981).

A summary of the religious practices and beliefs of each of the five marriage types has been given in table A5. The differences between the marriage types of all 15 comparisons were statistically highly significant. On only one measure, the importance of lay participation in the Church, did endogamous Catholics (type BB) score higher than all other marriage types. On eight of the scales and also in terms of orthodox belief and weekly Mass attendance, born Catholics with a convert spouse (type BC) scored higher than the other types. These Catholics also recorded by far the lowest proportions on non-practice. They were much more traditionalist in their religious orientations than the other groups as can be judged from the fact that they scored lowest not only on the importance of lay participation in the Church but also on the scale of new-style ministries.

The validity of distinguishing between marriages where the respondent was a convert (type CB) and those where the respondent's spouse was a convert (type BC) was indicated by the differences between the two types. Convert Catholics were much more likely to be members of parish organisations and were much less traditional in their orientations than type BC Catholics. For example, they scored much lower on the scales of liturgical traditionalism or papal authority than born Catholics who were married either to another Catholic or to a convert spouse. They also scored highest not only on the Church commitment and evaluation of priests scales but also on new-style activism and world-justice orientation.

The scores of Catholics with non-Catholic spouses followed the predicted patterns with significantly lower levels of practice, orthodoxy and involvement. On the other hand, they recorded higher scores on the scale of new-style ministries than any of the all-Catholic marriages. Those in invalid marriages consistently recorded lower scores on practice and belief scales but were even more strongly in favour of new-style ministries than those in valid mixed marriages.

In every respect, therefore, the variations between the five marriage types conformed to the predictions made at the beginning of this section. If born Catholics with born-Catholic spouses are regarded as the norm in a socio-religious community which values religious endogamy, then those who still value attachment to that community and marry a spouse who switches into the community, demonstrate their commitment by higher levels of conformity to the traditional institutional norms of practice and belief. Similarly, those who have themselves converted into the community compensate for their marginality by also manifesting higher levels of practice and belief. Unlike the previous group, however, converts are not only more involved in parish organisations but are also more open to religious innovations such as new models of priesthood and a greater concern for the issues of social justice. Those Catholics who deviate from the norms of in-group marriage also report much lower levels of practice, belief and involvement, and this is particularly the case for those who have not only married-out but also failed to conform to the canonical disciplines regarding intermarriage.

Other tabulations, not reproduced here, support the interpretation that Catholics in type BC marriages are the most traditionalist. Of these, four-fifths had heard of the Second Vatican Council compared to under three-quarters of converts and three-fifths of born Catholics with born-Catholic spouses. As many as one-third of them thought there had been too many changes in the Church recently. They appeared to be attached to a fortress model of the 'one, true' Church, accepted papal infallibility without reservation and strongly emphasised the education of Catholics in separate Catholic schools. Their religion could in many respects be described as fundamentalist. In contrast, the modal type of born Catholic married to another born Catholic seemed to have a relatively passive and adapting religious style.

5.3 INTERMARRIAGE AND RELIGIOSITY

In this section we will consider the nature and extent of the relationship between the type of marriage contracted and (a) indices of religious practice and (b) attitudes to ecumenism. In particular, using the data from the national survey, it was possible to test the predictions that heterogeneous marriages were likely to have resulted in a decline of religious practice but more favourable attitudes towards ecumenism.

5.3.1 Intermarriage and religious practice

The relationship between the type of marriage and various measures of religious practice were reviewed in outline in *Roman Catholic Opinion*. From the survey responses it was possible to estimate whether or not cessation of Mass attendance on a weekly or regular basis took place before or after marriage. Overall, two-thirds of the non-attenders had ceased to practise before their marriage. Of those who currently reported non-attendance, about one-half of those in valid marriages, whether religiously mixed or not, had stopped attending Mass regularly before their marriage compared to over 90% of those who had entered an invalid mixed marriage. Of those currently non-attending who had ceased to practise before marriage, one-half had entered an invalid marriage compared to only one in seven of those who had only stopped practising at or after their marriage. Those in mixed, and especially in invalid mixed marriages, were likely to have fewer children and fewer of them were baptised or likely to be educated at a Catholic school (Hornsby-Smith and Lee, 1979: 114–17, 237–41) so that the long-term consequences of such marriages for the English Catholic community seemed likely to be considerable.

These figures are relevant for the evaluation of the extent to which mixed marriages 'cause' processes of disaffiliation including cessation of Mass attendance, membership leakage or switching, and declining commitment to the norms of the Roman Catholic community, or whether there is a selective mating process which results in those who are already weak in religious adherence being more predisposed to marry-out and contract mixed or invalid marriages. In a panel study in the United States, for example, Haerle has reported that:

the acknowledged lower rates of regular church attendance of the inter-married Catholics appear less a consequence of contracting an interfaith union as such as they are a consequence of that complex of background factors which is associated with, and predisposes one to contract, an interfaith marriage ... A good part of the admittedly lower church attendance record of the intermarried is due to a continuation of the irregular attendance habits established in the engagement stage. (Haerle, 1969: 215–16)

In the case of English Catholics some relevant data have been reported in tables 5.2 and 5.3. In the first of these tables it can be seen that three-quarters of those in type BC marriages are still attending Mass regularly. Between three-fifths and two-thirds of those in other all-Catholic marriages do so and the proportion drops to half of those in valid mixed marriages. Only around one-fifth of Catholics in these four marriage types reported that they had stopped attending Mass before the age of 20. In sharp contrast, three-fifths of those who contracted an invalid marriage had ceased to practise their religion by the age of 20. This suggests strongly that those who had already attenuated their religious attendance habits were predisposed to

Table 5.2 *Age of cessation of weekly or regular Mass attendance by type of marriage (%)*

Age of cessation	Type of Marriage					All types
	BB	CB	BC	VM	IM	
Never attended	4	16	1	1	10	5
1–12	3	6	0	2	11	4
13–19	13	2	9	16	41	17
20–29	6	2	3	17	19	11
30 and over	8	15	12	15	5	10
Still attending	66	60	75	50	13	53
N = 100%	304	73	73	204	143	796

Source: National Survey, 1978.

Table 5.3 *Marriage type by frequency of Mass attendance and time of lapsation (%)*

Marriage type	Non-attending			Irregular attenders			Regular attenders	All
	Before marriage	After marriage	Other	Before marriage	After marriage	Other		
BB	21	21	31	30	45	49	47	38
CB	2	2	14	0	24	8	13	9
BC	1	10	4	3	3	10	15	9
VM	22	54	8	38	25	26	23	26
IM	54	13	43	29	3	7	3	18
N = 100%	128	65	72	60	34	136	303	798

Source: National Survey, 1978.

break the marriage norms of the Church and that the habits established before marriage continued to be reflected in their present religious practice. In the case of those invalidly married only one in eight claimed to be still attending Mass regularly.

These patterns are indicated clearly in table 5.3. Whereas two-thirds of those no longer attending had contracted a mixed marriage, only two-fifths of the irregular attenders and one-quarter of the regular attenders had done so. Conversely only one-quarter of the non-attending Catholics were in a type BB marriage compared to nearly one-half of the regular attenders. The proportion of marriages with at least one convert was three times as great among regular attenders as among the non-attenders. Within both the non-attending and irregularly attending categories there is a highly significant relationship between cessation of practice before marriage and contracting an invalid marriage, and contracting a valid mixed marriage and cessation of practice at a later date. Taken together the two sets of data appear to be consistent with Haerle's study in the United States.

Finally, the type of religious commitment has been found to be significantly related to the marriage type. Towler (1974: 166–72) has distinguished three main types of commitment: *local*, where the integrity and identity of the local parish or congregation are important; *party*, where the commitment is to the denomination and its symbols of religious belonging; and *pragmatic*, where the attachment to a congregation or denomination is provisional and qualified. Using the national survey data these three types of commitment were operationalised in ways which will be considered further in section 9.5. Briefly, it was found that over one-half of born Catholics with a convert spouse (type BC) had party or local commitments compared to one-quarter of all married Catholics (table 5.4).

Table 5.4 *Type of religious commitment by marriage type (%)*

Type of commitment	Type of Marriage					All
	BB	CB	BC	VM	IM	types
Party	14	9	24	10	4	12
Local	13	20	28	15	2	14
Pragmatic	13	13	9	9	18	12
Other none	60	58	39	66	77	62
N = 100%	305	73	73	204	144	799

Source: National Survey, 1978.

Not surprisingly, nearly one-fifth of the invalid marrieds had only a pragmatic religious commitment, a much higher proportion than for any of the other marriage types.

5.3.2 Intermarriage and ecumenism

In his well-known essay on intermarriage, Merton has written about the social functions of endogamy which:

is a device which serves to maintain social prerogatives and immunities within a social group. It helps prevent the diffusion of power, authority and preferred status to persons who are not affiliated with a dominant group. It serves further to accentuate and symbolize the 'reality' of the group by setting it off against other discriminable social units. Endogamy serves as an isolation and exclusion device, with the function of increasing group solidarity and supporting the social structure by helping to fix social distances which obtain between groups ... It appears that notable increases in group consciousness and solidarity involve a tightening of endogamous prescriptions ... outbursts of moral indignation are defensive devices which stabilize the existing organisation of interpersonal relations and groups. (Merton, 1972: 22)

Merton's theory is very relevant for our analysis of the growth of religious intermarriage among English Catholics since 1960. Before then, strong social disapproval (including ostracism by close family and kin) and religious sanctions (for example, low-key ceremonies without flowers or music or other symbols of joy) served to reinforce group solidarity in a fortress Church, maintain a privileged view of salvation and prevent the diffusion of religious authority from the Roman Catholic clergy to those of other denominations or none. Just as increases in group consciousness involve the tightening of endogamy so, conversely, a decline in the sense of its socio-religious distinctiveness, resulting from processes of social mobility and assimilation on the one hand, and from the theological reformulations about membership and ecumenism emanating from the Second Vatican Council, on the other hand, entails a weakening of both prescriptions and proscriptions in the rules governing the choice of a spouse.

Estimates of communal involvement over time which demonstrate the steady erosion of the fortress model of the Church have been summarised in table 9.1. Of particular relevance here is the reduction in the proportion of Catholics marrying other Catholics from over 70% in the late 1930s to around 30% by the late 1970s. Saunders has shown that: 'attitudinal opposition to interfaith marriage will be highest among members of exclusive churches and lowest among members of ecumenically oriented churches' (Saunders, 1976: 109). It follows that the easing of relations between the Christian Churches in recent years and the attenuation of its exclusivist claims to salvation by the Roman Catholic Church is likely to have been reflected in a decline in both institutional and individual opposition to interfaith marriage. In practical terms the significant increase of religiously mixed marriages since the 1950s is likely to have as its correlate a substantial easing in ecumenical attitudes and contacts.

At the personal, as opposed to the institutional level, we might have expected to find that those Catholics in mixed and, more especially invalid, marriages would espouse more favourable attitudes to ecumenism and related issues. It might therefore have been predicted that they would be less likely to support separate Catholic schools and more likely to stress lay participation in the Church. They would also be more likely to be critical of the doctrine of papal infallibility, to favour intercommunion and be less traditional in their attitudes to married or women priests. Conversely, it might have been anticipated that converts would be more likely to stress the distinctiveness of the religious community they had joined and hence be less favourably disposed towards ecumenism.

The results from the national survey, summarised in table 5.5 do not entirely support all these predictions. Far from those in mixed and invalid marriages being most active in attending ecumenical services, the reverse is the case. It seems that ecumenical practices very largely reflect religious practices within the institutional Church. While one-third of convert respondents and one-quarter of born Catholics with convert spouses have attended such services within the past two years, only a small proportion of those in mixed marriages, whether valid or not, have done so. Behaviour, however, is one thing; attitudes are another, and it can be seen that they generally follow the expected pattern. Those in mixed marriages, and especially invalid marriages, are more likely than the two groups of born Catholics to approve of intercommunion or accept married or women priests, and less likely to believe the doctrine of papal infallibility or send their children to Catholic schools. Although converts are more likely than born Catholics with a convert spouse to have attended an ecumenical service, those in the latter group consistently support a more exclusivist interpretation of the Church and are more traditional in their acceptance of institutional norms than any of the other marriage types. Thus the fact that they rate Christian unity more highly than any of the other groups suggests that they still espouse an earlier model of Christian unity in terms of 'returning to the fold' and the submission of 'our separated brethren' to the primacy of Peter (Hornsby-Smith, 1983b). Their relatively high levels of attendance at ecumenical services and the conversion of

Table 5.5 *Attendance at ecumenical service within two years and ecumenical attitudes by type of marriage (%)*

Ecumenical Practice and attitudes	Type of Marriage					All types
	BB	CB	BC	VM	IM	
Ecumenical Service, % attended	15	33	24	9	5	14
Christian Unity, % extremely imp.	55	55	67	55	50	55
Intercommunion, % approve	44	53	27	54	65	49
Jesus handed leadership to Peter & Popes, % cert. true	70	71	82	63	35	63
Under certain conditions, the Pope is infallible, % cert. true	53	44	72	42	16	45
Married priests, % accept	52	62	29	68	85	61
Women priests, % accept	21	23	14	27	45	26
Sends children to Catholic school, % very imp.	42	37	65	29	19	36
Catholics should be educated in sep. schools, % agree	41	43	73	38	27	41
Christian Unity orientation						
Ambivalent	28	22	18	30	39	29
Inclusive	25	39	14	36	52	33
Exclusive	32	28	55	19	5	25
Invitational	15	11	13	16	5	13
N (= 100% max.)	305	73	73	204	144	799

Source: National Survey, 1978.

their spouses are consistent with this interpretation and with the position outlined earlier in section 5.2.3.

Table 5.5 also reports the results of an analysis of orientations to Christian Unity which were identified on the basis of dichotomised scores on the papacy scale (which measured the extent of support for the traditional teaching on the leadership of the Church and papal infallibility) and on intercommunion (indicating an openness to full participation in the central act of worship to non-members) (see figure 5.1). Brief characteristics of those with the four orientations are given below:

		Stress on papacy	
		Low	High
Approval of	High	Inclusive	Invitational
intercommunion	Low	Ambivalent	Exclusive

Fig. 5.1 Unity orientations of English Catholics

Ambivalent: About one-third of all Catholics expressed an ambivalent attitude to Christian Unity in that while they underemphasised the role of the papacy they also disapproved of intercommunion. Over half of the youngest age group and a disproportionate number of Catholics from inactive parishes were found in this category. Those with this orientation scored less than average on various measures of religious practice and doctrinal and sexual orthodoxy. They were rarely active in parish organisations and were relatively critical of priests. They rarely attended ecumenical services. Among married Catholics, two-fifths of the invalidly married (IM) but under one-fifth of the born Catholics with convert spouses (BC) indicated this orientation.

Inclusive: Around one-third of all Catholics expressed a low emphasis on the papacy but favoured intercommunion and were deemed to have an inclusive orientation. They were likely to include a disproportionate number of young adults in the 25–34 age range. One half of those in invalid marriages (IM) and two-fifths of converts (CB) expressed this orientation. Like the previous group, those Catholics with this orientation scored less than average on the various measures of religious practice and orthodoxy. They were not involved in parish organisations, were critical of priests and rarely attended ecumenical services.

Exclusive: Of all Catholics, one-quarter put a strong emphasis on the papacy and did not favour intercommunion. These were said to have an exclusive orientation to Christian Unity. They were found disproportionately in the older age group, especially the over-65s, and included a disproportionate number of both first and second generation Irish and born Catholics. They were found especially in active parishes, were most active in parish organisations and scored highest on all the religious belief and practice variables. While they tended to be fairly traditional in liturgical matters they were more likely than any of the other groups to have attended an ecumenical service. Well over one-half of born Catholics with convert spouses (BC) selected this orientation which is consistent with their general traditionalism in religious matters. At the other extreme only about 5% of those in invalid marriages selected this orientation.

Invitational: Rather more than one in ten of all Catholics put a strong emphasis both on the papacy and on intercommunion and have been defined as having an invitational orientation. They were disproportionately found in the 50–64 age range among those Catholics in active parishes who had a high proportion of Catholic friends. Unlike the previous group they were not traditional in liturgical matters or in terms of new styles of ministry and they had only an average involvement in parish organisations. Nevertheless the likelihood that they had attended an ecumenical service was only a little less than that of the previous group. Although they tended to have heterodox views on sexual matters they were otherwise orthodox Mass attenders. Those in valid mixed marriages (VM) and born Catholics with born Catholic spouses (BB) were three times as likely as those in invalid marriages (IM) to register this orientation.

Further consideration of the data suggested that the most significant cleavage in terms of nearly every indicator of religious commitment was between those scoring high or low on the papacy scale. Those Catholics with high levels of institutional involvement, that is the parish activists who were most likely to be involved in ecumenical services, were also most likely to have an exclusive orientation towards Christian Unity. By contrast the average weekly Mass attender was most likely to have an invitational orientation. In general terms decline of practice and more particularly increase of doctrinal and sexual heterodoxy was likely to be related to inclusive or ambivalent orientations.

5.3.3 A note on interchurch marriages

In the previous analyses religiously mixed marriages have simply been divided into the canonically valid and invalid. It might be argued that this simply reflects the traditional official disapproval of mixed marriage, fails to take into account the religious heterogeneity of such marriages in terms of practice and belief, and ignores the changing ecumenical climate since the Second Vatican Council. Thus Fr John Coventry, S.J., the chairman of the Association of Interchurch Families, has written:

> To call any marriage which is not one between two Catholics 'a mixed marriage' simply lumps together all those who are not Catholics, as if they were all the same. But there is an enormous difference between a Catholic marrying another Christian and all other mixed marriages. (Coventry, n.d.:3)

The Association of Interchurch Families was formed in 1969 in order to promote the ecumenical potentialities of marriages between committed Catholics and committed Christians of other traditions. In a recently published appeal to the Churches they have reported on their experiences of eucharistic sharing which has increased greatly in recent years. Only a dozen of the 80 respondents to a survey of couples replied that they had never received communion together (Reardon and Finch, 1983: 23–4). The Association has commented that:

> inevitably interchurch families go ahead of their Churches as a whole in their actions; this may be untidy, and uncomfortable at times, but it is surely right. In the ecumenical movement the Churches are called to commit themselves to one another in love, but they are not yet willing to do it. But this is just what church families *are* trying to do. (Reardon and Reardon, n.d.: 5)

In the national survey and parish data there were no direct measures of such membership. However, an approximation was attempted using the national survey by considering separately those mixed marriages where the Catholic partner was a regular weekly Mass attender and the non-Catholic spouse attended Mass at least monthly. Only eight cases meeting these conditions were identified. It is interesting to note that these Catholic respondents scored more highly than married Catholics generally on measures of doctrinal orthodoxy and religious practice and they were much less likely to approve of either married priests or women priests. Further research would be necessary to explore the religious beliefs and practices of Catholics in interchurch marriages in greater detail.

5.4 CONTRACEPTION, ABORTION AND DIVORCE

In this section some of the recent evidence relating to the attitudes of English Catholics to different aspects of marriage and family life and, in particular, to their views on the controversial issues of contraception, abortion and divorce, will be reviewed. In the surveys in the four parishes we have comparable data for Catholic and non-Catholic electors as well as parish activists. The national survey data will summarise the views of a representative sample of English Catholics at the end of the 1970s. Both these surveys indicated that the attitudes of active Catholics differed markedly from Catholics generally and this will be demonstrated in particular from the follow-up survey of delegates to the N.P.C.

In the first of a planned annual series of studies which aimed to chart changes in British social values during the 1980s, a number of attitudes to sexual relationships, divorce, abortion and contraception have been compared for different religious groups in Great Britain. In general terms it was reported that people with a religious affiliation were less tolerant of homosexual relationships, divorce and legal abortion. When considering seven different circumstances in which abortion might be legalised, Roman Catholics were more resistant than other religious groups.

Interestingly, however, even among Roman Catholics, around a quarter support legal abortion for each of the reasons of preference, and at least 70 per cent support it if the mother's health is endangered or if the pregnancy has resulted from rape. (Jowell and Airey, 1984: 141. See also 136–43, 154–6)

On the whole, in the tabulations so far available, Roman Catholics appeared to differ little from the general population in their attitudes to premarital or extramarital sexual relationships by either the husband or the wife.

In general terms these recent findings confirm the results of opinion poll data relating not only to the general population but also to professional groups such as doctors and nurses, that while Catholics generally expressed more restrictive attitudes towards abortion than other groups, nevertheless a substantial minority reported that

Table 5.6 *Attitudes of Catholic and non-Catholic electors on marital and sexual matters, % agreement (Four Parishes, weighted average)*

Item	Attitude	R.C. activists	R.C. electors	Other electors
5	Divorce should be readily available where one partner considers the marriage has broken down.	8	45	53
9	It is a good thing that abortion is available legally for those women who want one.	9	39	73
12	World overpopulation is the biggest moral problem of our time.	26	49	60
29	Pornography is a major evil in our society.[a]	93	57	45
39	A husband or wife should always be able to get a divorce if their partner commits adultery.	11	48	49
44	Religious leaders should speak out on questions of sexual morality.[a]	87	59	44
	N = 100% (unweighted)	84	266	1,164

[a] Data for three parishes only; question not asked in the London commuter parish.

'they do not have a conscientious objection to termination of pregnancy in virtually all cases' (Cheetham, 1976).

5.4.1 Catholic and non-Catholic electors

It was reported above in section 3.4 that significant differences between Catholic and non-Catholic electors in the study of four parishes only emerged in the attitudes related to sexual morality 'with the salience of a rational humanistic orientation to sexual matters being weaker for the Catholic group' (Hornsby-Smith, 1978c: 13). For the four parishes considered, weighted averages of the levels of agreement with six questions on marital and sexual matters have been given in table 5.6 for Catholic activists and electors and non-Catholic electors. It can be seen that on divorce, overpopulation (a proxy for attitudes to contraception; at this early stage of our research the S.S.R.C. advised us not to address the question of birth control directly), pornography and the salience of religious leadership on sexual matters, non-Catholic electors were up to one-third more likely to agree with a 'liberal' position than Catholic electors. On the matter of abortion, however, the Catholic position was more clearly distinct; non-Catholic electors were nearly twice as likely as Catholic electors to approve of legal abortion. Comparisons between Catholic electors and parish activists showed clearly that the latter were far more orthodox in their responses to all six questions, particularly on the matters of divorce and abortion where under one in ten agreed with a 'liberal' position.

5.4.2 The national survey

The attitudes of the nationally representative sample of English Catholics on a wide range of social and moral issues were reported in *Roman Catholic Opinion* (Hornsby-Smith and Lee, 1979: 52–3, 192). Overall, three-quarters of the respondents (but three-fifths of weekly Mass attenders and over four-fifths of the under 25s) agreed with the statement 'a married couple who feel they have as many children as they want are not doing anything wrong when they use artificial methods of birth control'. On two separate statements on divorce, one suggesting that 'two people in love do not do anything wrong when they marry even though one of them has been divorced' and the other that 'Catholics should be allowed to divorce' there was agreement from nearly two-thirds of English Catholics in spite of the strong and traditional prohibitions. On the other hand, two-thirds of Catholics agreed with the statement 'except where the life of the mother is at risk, abortion is wrong' (though one-quarter disagreed). A majority of Catholics thought that 'the Church can never, in practice, approve the homosexual act' but only 44% agreed with the statement 'if a person in his right mind is suffering from a painful disease which can't be cured and he wants to die, termination of life should be permitted'. Finally, only one-third of Catholics considered 'it is wrong for an engaged couple to have sexual intercourse before they are married'. On all these items the under 25s and those who had not attended Mass for over a year were consistently more critical of the official teaching than older age groups but social class differences varied. Lower-working-class respondents were more favourable towards divorce than professional and managerial respondents but were less likely to take a 'liberal' position on contraception or homosexuality.

5.4.3 Congress delegates

A number of attitude questions used in the *Roman Catholic Opinion* study were also asked in the survey of delegates to the N.P.C. The results showed that:

on social and moral issues ... the Congress delegates were far more orthodox or traditional than Roman Catholics generally, for example in their attitudes to divorce, contraception, premarital sex, euthanasia, abortion ... On contraception and divorce priests and female religious were more orthodox than lay delegates but there were no differences between the three delegate groups (priests, religious and laity) on abortion and euthanasia. Occupational differences were generally not significant ... though teacher delegates were unexpectedly more orthodox on divorce ... than other groups. Sex differences were slight ... though housewives were more traditional on divorce ... than other women who were much less likely to condemn premarital sex. (Hornsby-Smith and Cordingley, 1983: 13, 49–51)

5.4.4 Catholic practice: contraception and abortion

In his study of changing Catholic attitudes to and practice of contraception, Spencer reported that the Lewis–Faning study of 1947–8 for the Royal Commission on Population and the Population Investigation Committee's Marriage Survey of 1959–60 as well as a number of other studies had all found evidence that the practice of contraception was widespread. He reported that

the review of British Catholics' attitudes towards, and practice of, fertility control shows clearly that Catholics use various contraceptive measures on a large scale, that they are doing so increasingly but still lag behind their fellow citizens in this respect. (Spencer, 1966b)

In the study of the family intentions of a large probability sample of women in England and Wales who had been married once only and were under the age of 45 in 1967, it was reported that the 'safe period' was used more frequently by Catholic couples (31% where both partners were Catholics, 17% where the wife only was a Catholic and 15% where the husband only was a Catholic compared to 11% of all groups). However, a greater proportion of Catholics (39%) used withdrawal as a contraceptive technique (Woolf, 1971: 4–5, 83, 86). In a follow-up study five years later it was reported that

when a method of contraception was used by couples in which only one partner was Catholic, it was more likely to be a reliable method if the Catholic partner was the wife rather than the husband ... The use of less reliable methods of contraception, or none at all, was proportionately greater for couples in which both husband and wife were Catholic ... (Woolf and Pegden, 1976: 116, 133)

Similarly, in her study of family size and family spacing in England and Wales in 1973, Cartwright reported that

The differences between Catholic and other mothers in their current use of birth control methods were relatively small. Rather more of the Catholics were not using any method of birth control, 18% compared with 9%, more of them relied on the safe period, 4% against 1%; and fewer of their husbands had been sterilized, 1% compared with 4%. There were the significant differences in their current use of the pill, coil, withdrawal, and female sterilization ... Fewer Catholics had ever taken the pill – 57% against 68% (Protestants), and fewer had used the sheath – 58% against 72%. (Cartwright, 1976: 45–6)

The same study also reported that the proportion of mothers who had considered abortion when they found they were unintentionally pregnant did not vary to any significant extent with the mothers' religion (Cartwright, 1976: 69–71). In sum, the evidence seems to indicate clearly that Catholic practice, like Catholic attitudes, while still significantly different from that of the population as a whole, has nevertheless in recent years converged rapidly towards the national norms.

5.4.5 Marital breakdown among Catholics

The national survey of Roman Catholics reported that the proportion of Catholics who were currently divorced was similar to that estimated for the population as a whole by the Office of Population Censuses and Surveys (O.P.C.S.) This finding was supported by the study of the recently divorced undertaken at the Marriage Research Centre (Thornes and Collard, 1979: 53) so that 'it seems possible to suggest that, overall, Catholics are not any less prone to divorce than members of the population at large' (Hornsby-Smith and Lee, 1979: 117). A comparison of those ever divorced with those never divorced showed that women and lower-social-class respondents were disproportionately found among the divorced who were also rather more likely to have had an unhappy childhood and to report that they had not been close to either parent (Hornsby-Smith and Lee, 1979: 242–4).

A recent American study has indicated that intermarriage represents both the greatest single source of conversion to Catholicism and the greatest source of disidentification (Hoge, 1981: 72). The relevance of this for English Catholicism can be seen in our data. Only two-fifths of Catholics were in marriages where both partners were born Catholics. One-fifth were in marriages where at least one partner was a convert and over two-fifths were in mixed marriages. The proportion of ever divorced or separated was 6% among all-Catholic marriages but 12% among those in mixed marriages.

Further analyses of these data in terms of the marriage type of the respondent indicates, however, that while 5% of the four valid marriage types had ever been divorced or separated, one-quarter of those in invalid marriages had been. Expressed differently, whereas under one in six Catholics ever married were in invalid marriages (IM), three-fifths of the divorced and remarried and nearly one-third of the divorced and separated groups were. These results strongly suggest that the widely reported finding that mixed or interfaith marriages are more likely to break down (Bumpass and Sweet, 1972) needs to be qualified. In the case of these English Catholics in the late 1970s, marital breakdown was concentrated among those in invalid marriages; those in valid mixed marriages were no more likely to experience breakdown than those in the three types of religiously homogeneous marriage (BB, CB and BC).

In a recent study of the data from the national survey, the relationship between three demographic variables (age, sex and terminal education age) and four socio-religious background variables (the religiosity of both parents, the happiness of the respondent's childhood and their involvement in the Catholic subculture at this time), the time of any lapsation from religious practice relative to marriage, the type of marriage entered and marital breakdown were explored further. The results showed that marital breakdown among English Catholics was chiefly influenced by early lapsation from the practice norms of the Church and by the type of marriage entered, which was itself significantly associated with the timing of any lapsation. In sum, early lapsation was related to invalid marriage which in turn was related to higher marital breakdown. There did not appear to be any direct relationships between marital breakdown and either the demographic or socio-religious background variables.

Both the timing of any lapsation relative to marriage and the type of marriage entered were also strongly related to all the socio-religious outcome variables considered: the respondent's type of Catholicism, communal involvement, religious commitment and unity orientation (Hornsby-Smith, Turcan and Rajan, 1985).

One sign of the growing concern for the scale of marital breakdown among Catholics and the need to promote the pastoral care of divorced Catholics has been the recent proliferation of groups affiliated to the Association of Separated and Divorced Catholics, which was started in Manchester in 1981 with the support of the Bishop of Salford. Another indicator is the programme to provide support at the parish level for marriages, especially in the early years. This programme was started by a group of priests mainly in the south-east of England in 1980. It remains to be seen what effects these initiatives will have on the rates of marital breakdown among Catholics. What they do show, however, is a greater degree of openness in recognising the scale of the phenomenon and a greater willingness by the institutional Church to search for pastoral responses which meet the needs of the people concerned while continuing to stress the traditional Christian belief in life-long marriage.

It may be that when considering such developments within the Catholic community, the distinction needs to be made between support primarily for (a) the maintenance of the marital bond and (b) the individuals concerned in vulnerable or disintegrating marital relationships. The distinction is important. To stress the former would be to endeavour to maintain the institutional norms of permanent marriage and to suppress the formal and overt recognition of marital breakdown, while the latter would put the primary emphasis on pastoral support for the individual in a situation of marital breakdown, regardless of whether or not such breakdown became overt and formally acknowledged by divorce or separation. Clearly a great deal of research needs to be undertaken on this matter; at the time of writing such research is still very much in its infancy.

5.5 CONCLUSION

In this chapter we have reviewed some empirical evidence relating to the patterns of marriage formation and breakdown and sexual morality norms of the English Catholic community in the last quarter of the twentieth century. In every respect the evidence leads to the conclusion that by the end of the 1970s there had been a breakdown in the defences surrounding the Catholic community so that it no longer made sense to regard it as having a distinctive subculture protected by endogamous marriage, its own norms of sexual and familial morality internalised through the interlinked nexus of social-ising agencies of family, school and parish, led by a powerful clergy with recognised authority and an imposing array of social and religious sanctions to enforce compliance. The social changes since the Second World War dissolved many of the barriers to social interaction with the rest of the population and led to a convergence on social and moral issues, and the religious changes legitimated by the Second Vatican Council led gradually to a decline in the hostility between different socio-religious groups. The net effect can be seen in the evidence we have reviewed of a considerable degree of hetero-geneity in terms of religious attitudes, sexual morality and marital behaviour, a significant increase in the proportions of both mixed and invalid marriages, especially since the 1960s, and a corresponding decline in the rates of religious practice and an increase in the divorce rates.

As has been mentioned in chapter 2, between one-fifth and one-quarter of English Catholics are either first- or second-generation Irish immigrants. In the following chapter, the inter-action between their patterns of social and geographical mobility and their patterns of marriage formation will be considered and the contribution which intermarriage makes to religious and social assimilation to the norms of British society evaluated.

CHAPTER 6

THE ASSIMILATION OF IRISH CATHOLICS

———— ❧ ————

6.1 INTRODUCTION

The significance to the Catholic Church in Britain of Irish immigration cannot be overestimated. The rapid growth in the size of the English Catholic population in the century following the restoration of the hierarchy in 1850 is largely due to the influx of successive waves of mostly working-class Irish migrants coming in search of greater economic security particularly in the industrial towns in the north of England (Gwynn, 1950; Hickey, 1967; Lees, 1979: 164–212; Ling, 1973; McLeod, 1974: 72–80; 1981: 128–31; Norman, 1984: 216–20). For well over a century the Irish have been the largest immigrant community in Britain. Given this fact and the continuing conflict in Northern Ireland, it is extraordinary that there has been no major study of the Irish in Britain since John Jackson wrote his book over two decades ago (Jackson, 1963).

One of the consequences of the continuous influx of Irish immigrants has been the over-optimistic assumption that the Catholic Church in England and Wales has uniquely been able to retain the allegiance of working-class adherents (Holmes, 1978: 163; Norman, 1984: 6). With the decline of Irish immigration since the 1950s as a result of changes in the Irish economy attendant upon the accession of the Irish Republic to the European Economic Community (E.E.C.), any such association seems more likely to have been spurious and dependent upon the continuation of large-scale migration of mainly working-class Irish which suppressed or postponed high rates of 'leakage' or apostasy.

In this chapter, therefore, we will review evidence relating to the assimilation of Irish Catholics in England and Wales. Two aspects of this process have already been considered. In chapter 4 evidence relating to the social and geographical mobility of Irish Catholics over two generations was presented. In table 4.2 it was reported that while the mean upward social mobility of Irish-born Catholics was similar to that for Catholics in England and Wales generally, it was much lower than that for Catholics born in England. Considering movement across the manual–non-manual division only, the evidence from the national survey suggested that by the second generation, Irish Catholics were experiencing net upward mobility at rates similar to those for Catholics born in England. The data in table 4.3 showed that Catholic men born in Ireland experienced a much lower amount of net upward mobility in the first generation than Catholic men born in Great Britain but that by the second generation their mean upward social mobility movements had converged towards those experienced by their British-born co-religionists. Further evidence on the social mobility of Irish immigrants is presented in section 6.3.

The situation, however, is clearly complex and as reported in *Roman Catholic Opinion* (Hornsby-Smith and Lee, 1979) there appeared to be some evidence that, for second-generation Irish Catholics, it was having an Irish mother which was important in promoting the upward social mobility of their British-born children. It seems likely that patterns of marriage formation and both religious and ethnic intermarriage effect the processes of religious and social assimilation to the norms of British society. In order to explore these matters further, use will be made of the classification of marriage types developed in chapter 5.

Secondly, the religious characteristics of Irish Catholics will also be investigated in order to determine the extent to which it can be said that Irish Catholics assimilate to English Catholicism in terms of patterns of belief, moral attitudes and religious practice over two generations. More generally, this chapter will consider the case of Irish Catholics in England and Wales as a case study of the processes of structural and cultural integration and assimilation. But first we will review, on the basis of recent census returns, the scale of Irish immigration in recent decades and official estimates of the size of the Irish community in England and Wales.

6.2 TRENDS IN IRISH IMMIGRATION

It is estimated that something of the order of 95% of the population of the Irish Republic are Roman Catholics and around 33% or more of the population in Northern Ireland. Clearly, then, Irish immigration having had such a numerical impact on the English Catholic community, was likely also to have strongly influenced the character of the Church in Britain as it emerged from the post-reformation nadir over the past two centuries.

The country-of-birth data from the censuses over the past 130 years indicate the scale of this Irish immigration (table 6.1). In 1851 nearly 3% of the population had been born in Ireland. In all four post-war censuses the proportion has been around 1.5%, approaching 2% in 1961 at the time of peak immigration from Ireland. In 1981 there were over three-quarters of a million people resident in England and Wales who had been born in Ireland. Although this represents a 12% decline over the 1971 figure, the Irish remained the biggest single immigrant community in these countries with over 1.6% of the population. In 1981 just over one-quarter of these immigrants had come from Northern Ireland, a proportion which has risen steadily from 18% in 1911 and 1931.

The changing pattern of Irish immigration in the post-war period is indicated by the census returns which show that in 1981 3.6% of the people in Greater London had been born in Ireland compared to only 2.0% in the West Midlands Region and 1.8% in the North-West Region. Apart from the evidence that post-war patterns of migration have resulted in a greater concentration of first-generation Irish in London compared to the historical concentrations in the north-west, there is evidence in both 1971 and 1981 of a striking gradient of Irish-born people from relatively high concentrations in inner-city areas to lower than average proportions in the surrounding rural areas. In the most recent figures for 1981, the proportion of Irish-born people was 3.6% in Greater London, 1.7% in the Outer Metropolitan Area and 1.3% in the Outer South-East. These figures all illustrate the twin patterns of migration in the post-war years: (a) from the north-west to the south-east and especially Greater London, with a concentration in inner-city areas, for example, supportive parishes organised around the ethnic community (Rex and Moore, 1967), and (b) outward geographical mobility from inner-city areas to the suburban estates, only occurring at a later stage of the migration

Table 6.1 *Irish-born residents in England and Wales, 1851–1981*

Country of birth	1851	1871	1891	1911	1931	1951	1961	1971	1981
All countries, $\times 10^6$	17.9	22.7	29.0	36.1	40.0	43.8	46.1	48.8	48.5
Northern Ireland, $\times 10^3$				69	70	135	188	216	209
Irish Republic (incl. part not stated) $\times 10^3$				307	311	492	683	676	580
All Ireland, $\times 10^3$	520	567	458	375	381	627	870	892	789
Proportions per 10^5 population Northern Ireland				190	175	308	407	443	431
Irish Republic (incl. part not stated				851	779	1125	1482	1386	1196
All Ireland	2899	2493	1580	1041	954	1433	1889	1829	1627

Source: 1961 Census, country of birth tables, table 7; 1971 and 1981 censuses.

process and probably associated with successful establishment in the labour market, some upward social mobility and assimilation to British society.

One of the tabulations from the 1981 Census indicates the age structure and regional destinations of those who have migrated to Britain within the past year. The first point to note here is that only 3.2% of the quarter of a million recent migrants came from Ireland and they were much more likely than other migrants to be in the 20–44 age range. Only 11% of those from the Irish Republic were children under the age of 16 compared to 24% of all recent migrants. Interestingly, as many as three-fifths of the Irish migrants were registered in the south-east regions; only 7% were going to the depressed west Midlands and 9% to the traditional areas of the north-west. There were significant differences, too, between the two groups of Irish migrants. Of those from the Irish Republic, 45% were resident in Greater London, three times the proportion of those from Northern Ireland.

The net effect of the ending of mass Irish immigration since the

1950s and 1960s is likely to have been a gradual reduction in the proportion of Catholics who are first-generation Irish immigrants. Estimates based on census country-of-birth data, and assuming that Roman Catholic concentrations among the different immigrant groups are the same as those in the sending countries, suggest that in 1971 12.5% of English Catholics had been born in Ireland (one-half of all immigrant Catholics) but that by 1981 this proportion had declined to 11.0%, only 47% of all Catholic immigrants. Unfortunately, the 1981 census questionnaire did not ask for details regarding the country of birth of parents so that no accurate estimate of the numbers of second-generation Catholic immigrants is possible at this time. However, some relevant data in the 1971 Census suggest that around 14% of English Catholics were second-generation immigrants from the Irish Republic. At the beginning of the 1970s something like three-fifths of all second-generation immigrant Catholics had originated from the Irish Republic (Hornsby-Smith, 1986).

6.3 PATTERNS OF OCCUPATIONAL ACHIEVEMENT

Apart from the clues about Irish Catholics which can be gleaned from the census returns and the analysis of the country-of-birth tables, another valuable and largely untapped resource is the annual General Household Survey (G.H.S.) of a nationally representative sample of 11,000 households in Great Britain. In a recent study based on the 1979 and 1980 surveys, Hornsby-Smith and Dale (1986) compared 1,224 first- and second-generation immigrants from the Irish Republic and Northern Ireland with a control group of 1,200 'English'. Both samples were confined to those aged 16–49, inclusive, because the G.H.S. asks father's occupation and birthplace only for those aged under 50. The G.H.S. unfortunately does not ask the religious affiliation of respondents but, as has been noted above, Roman Catholics make up 95% of the population of the Irish Republic and around 33% of Northern Ireland.

The social origins of the Irish sample were decidedly more working class but their current distribution between manual and non-manual statuses were similar to those of the English control group. Again, while the educational qualifications of first-generation immigrants were lower than those of the second generation, by the second generation the educational qualifications of Irish men and women from both parts of Ireland exceeded those of the English control group. This suggests a very considerable measure of assimilation in terms of educational achievements by the second generation.

The analysis of the occupational distributions of men and women from the Irish Republic and Northern Ireland separately suggests a complex situation. A comparison between the occupational distributions of fathers of Irish immigrants and fathers of the English control group showed substantial differences. However, the occupational distributions of the immigrant groups themselves indicated that, although there were differences between them, they resembled that of the English control group more closely than their fathers had resembled the fathers of the English. This suggests that by the second generation the Irish immigrants are generally able to assimilate into the English occupational structure without any noticeable tendency to cluster into particular groups of occupations.

Another indication of occupational assimilation is the ability to achieve upward social mobility. If immigrant groups are at no disadvantage within the host country, then they might be expected to experience similar rates of mobility to those of the host population. To test this the occupations of fathers were compared with those of respondents in order to establish mobility rates. Because of the different occupational distributions of men and women their social mobility experiences were considered separately.

The results showed that first-generation males from both the Irish Republic and Northern Ireland came from lower social origins and experienced lower net rates of upward mobility than the English control group. It seems, however, that the experiences of second-generation males from the two parts of Ireland are quite different. Whereas those from the Irish Republic appeared to experience a considerable upward 'mobility momentum' (Bode, 1970), those from Northern Ireland appeared to have become much more firmly entrenched in the working class. It might be noted here that, to the extent that one can generalise from the religious differences of the two Irish samples, there is no evidence that a protestant ethic is likely to be conducive to worldly advancement, or conversely, that a Catholic identification is likely to inhibit upward social mobility. These findings are in line with those reported in the United States (Greeley, 1963, 1977; Weber, 1930).

The social mobility experiences of Irish women are quite different. Using women's own social class, the evidence suggests that the net experiences of upward social mobility of both the Irish first-generation samples were the same as those for the English control group. By the second generation, however, both the Irish groups were experiencing much higher rates of upward social mobility than the English control group. While among the first generation those from the Irish Republic appeared to have a larger proportion in the stable working class, by the second generation differences between the two Irish samples were insignificant.

The extent of occupational assimilation and the degree of upward social mobility of second-generation immigrants might be expected to vary with parentage and with whether both parents or only one were immigrants. It was noted in section 4.3.4 that in the 1978 national survey reported in *Roman Catholic Opinion* (Hornsby-Smith and Lee, 1979), second-generation Irish immigrants with an Irish-born mother and a father who was not Irish reported particularly high rates of net upward social mobility. Conversely, net downward mobility was reported in the case of those second-generation Irish, both of whose parents had been born in Ireland. 'It appears ... that Irish mothers are more successful than Irish fathers in promoting the upward social mobility of their British born children' (Hornsby-Smith and Lee, 1979: 40–1, 177). The G.H.S. study enabled this tentative conclusion to be tested on the basis of much larger and more representative national samples.

In the G.H.S. sample just over nine in ten fathers and mothers had been born in Ireland for the first generation; for the second generation, just under two-thirds of the fathers and just under three-fifths of the mothers had been born in Ireland. The vast majority of 'non-Irish' parents had been born in England. The findings show that for both males and females, there was very little difference in the mean mobility movements between those, both of whose parents were Irish, and those who had either a father or a mother only who was Irish. For first-generation immigrants the numbers were too small for separate analysis but for second-generation Irish immigrants, when the results were elaborated to take account of the marital status of the respondents, considerable doubt was thrown on the assumption that the type of Irish parentage was a key variable in the subsequent social mobility experiences of Irish immigrants in England over two generations.

When finally the effect of educational qualifications in promoting upward social mobility was explored, the evidence indicated that for those with manual origins, the chances of achieving non-manual occupational status increased with the level of educational qualifications obtained. Second-generation Irish immigrants without any qualifications were more likely to be upwardly mobile than those in the first generation or the English control group but otherwise there were few differences in the chances of upward social mobility by immigrant generation for those with some qualifications. In sum, the data showed that the chances of upward mobility across the manual–non-manual division depended more on the level of qualifications attained than on the immigrant generation. This also suggested that there were few barriers to occupational achievement for Irish migrants in England. In general it might safely be concluded from this study that there is a substantial measure of structural assimilation of the Irish in England by the second generation.

6.4 MARRIAGE PATTERNS

What appeared to be a much more significant factor than the type of Irish parentage in the determination of the subsequent social mobility experiences of Irish immigrants to England over two generations was the degree of ethnic endogamy maintained and the extent to which both first- and second-generation Irish immigrants married out. These are important indicators of assimilation to English society. In the G.H.S. study, among the married first-generation immigrants from the Irish Republic, under half the males and two-fifths of the females married Irish-born spouses. For those from Northern Ireland, the proportions were about one-fifth for both sexes. However, by the second generation, only 4% of the males and 7% of the females who were married had a spouse who was born in Ireland.

In a recent study of the 1971 census statistics, Caulfield and Bhat (1981) have reported that 31% of marriages in Great Britain in which at least one partner had been born in the Irish Republic were endogamous, that is, both partners had been born in the Republic. This is equivalent to 47% of first-generation married Irish immigrants to Britain, a figure which is consistent with those from the G.H.S. analysis. Caulfield and Bhat also report that 28% of second-generation Irish residents of Great Britain in 1971 were from endogamous unions where both parents had been born in the Republic. They go on to show, on the basis of the Registrar General's returns of live births of first-generation Irish immigrants to Great Britain, a significant reduction in the endogamous rate from 33.6% couples in 1970 to 24% in 1977 (ibid.: 81–2). The figures, they suggested, 'could be interpreted as a sign of an increasing rate of assimilation of the Irish in Britain' (ibid.: 83).

The G.H.S. study showed that the implications of declining endogamy for social mobility were striking. When the relationship between the country of origin of the spouse and the net mobility movements across the manual–non-manual division was investigated, the results showed clearly that out-marriage was strongly related to higher rates of upward social mobility. In all cases the mean mobility movement was greater where there was a non-Irish spouse. Furthermore, the analyses suggested that not only were Irish women more likely than Irish men to marry out in the first generation, but also that generally Irish women were likely to achieve greater social mobility through their non-Irish husbands than was achieved by Irish men who married non-Irish women.

Further analyses of the 1978 national survey of English Catholics indicated the extent to which these broad patterns of assimilation of Irish immigrants to Britain generally were shared by Irish Catholics. Table 6.2 reports the type of marriage entered into by Irish Catholics in terms of the five-fold classification reported in chapter 5. For Irish Catholic men the proportion of religiously mixed marriages increased from one-fifth in the first generation to one-quarter in the second generation towards the English Catholic norm of two-fifths. The figures for women were more striking: from one-third in the first generation to two-thirds in the second generation exceeding the norm for English Catholics of one-half. The high propensity to contracting invalid marriages on the part of Irish women of both generations might be noted and while significant differences between the two Irish groups and the other English Catholics persisted, there clearly was a distinct convergence towards the indigenous Catholics by the second generation.

In table 6.3 the time of lapsation relative to the time of marriage has been given for all three groups. It can be seen that there were important differences between the sexes. In the case of the men there appeared to be few differences between the first and second generations or convergence towards the English pattern. On the other hand, Irish women appeared to converge rapidly towards the English pattern by the second generation. It seems likely that Irish women,

Table 6.2 *Marriage type by immigrant generation and sex (%)*

MARTYPKT	MALES				FEMALES			
	First-gen. Irish	Second-gen. Irish	Not Irish	All	First-gen. Irish	Second-gen. Irish	Not Irish	All
BB	67	52	35	44	55	27	27	31
CB	0	0	13	8	0	1	15	11
BC	12	22	12	13	10	8	7	7
VM	14	13	20	18	19	47	32	32
IM	7	13	20	16	16	18	19	18
N = 100%	60	45	190	295	69	67	299	435
p		0.0001				0.0000		
V		0.24				0.22		

Source: National Survey, 1978.

Table 6.3 *Time of lapsation relative to marriage by immigrant generation and sex (%)*

LPSTIME	MALES				FEMALES			
	First-Gen. Irish	Second-Gen. Irish	Not Irish	All	First-Gen. Irish	Second-Gen. Irish	Not Irish	All
Before marriage	24	23	28	27	13	35	31	28
At/after marriage	13	10	26	21	11	17	20	18
Still attends	63	67	46	53	77	48	50	54
N = 100%	60	45	203	307	72	68	326	465
p		0.0176				0.0009		
V		0.14				0.14		

Source: National Survey, 1978.

with their greater propensity for out-marriage, in terms of both ethnic membership group and religious identification, and their greater social mobility, were much more prone to a decline of religious practice than Irish men.

The impact of the migration experiences on the marital stability of the Irish can perhaps be judged from the proportions of Irish-born

people recording their marital status as divorced. In 1961 the proportion was 0.4% compared to 0.6% for the population as a whole. By
1971 the proportion had risen to 1.0%, the same as the population
generally and by 1981 the proportion was 4.2%, much higher than
the average of 2.8% for the population generally. Whereas in 1961
and 1971 the rates for those born in the Irish Republic were much
lower than those for Northern Ireland, by 1981 they were identical.
These figures are crude marital status data, useful in pointing to
trends but possibly misleading in some respects. For example, in
their analysis of the 1971 census returns (for Great Britain), Caulfield
and Bhat calculated that when the divorce rates for all residents were
standardised to take into account the different age profiles of the Irish
immigrants and the general population, the propensity to divorce
among first-generation immigrants from the Irish Republic was only
two-thirds that of the general population in the case of the men and
under three-fifths in the case of women (ibid.: 74).

The 1978 national survey of English Catholics yielded no statistically significant differences between first- and second-generation
Irish Catholics and non-Irish Catholics in terms of a propensity to
marital breakdown. There did not appear to be any consistent
patterns which could be discerned and the cell sizes were too small for
adequate analysis.

Finally reference might be made to the evidence summarised by
Caulfield and Bhat which strongly suggested that between the mid-
sixties and the mid-seventies, the contraceptive practices of Catholics, including women born in the Irish Republic, had converged
almost completely with those of women generally in this country
(ibid.: 79). In sum, there is a substantial body of evidence which
supports the view that by the second generation, Irish Catholics have
largely adopted the marital norms of English Catholics generally.
This seems to be a more rapid process in the case of Irish women,
who, in the second generation, have a greater propensity to contract
religiously mixed marriages even than English Catholics while their
conformity to the Mass attendance requirements are almost identical
to those of English Catholics.

6.5 RELIGIOUS OUTCOMES

Given their historical importance to the growth of English Catholicism it is important to trace the changes which take place in the

religious beliefs, moral attitudes and institutional practices as a result of the migration process. There seems to be plenty of evidence that a crude model of the highly religious Irish immigrant rapidly succumbing to the materialism of a secular British society is inadequate (see e.g. Lees, 1979; McRedmond, 1980). The Irish Report of the European Value Systems Study reviews the attitudes, beliefs and church-going of a representative sample of people in the Irish Republic in 1981 (Fogarty, Ryan and Lee, 1984). These indicate substantial levels of deviation from the official norms of the Church on the part of the Catholic respondents and an Irish journalist has recently asked: *Is Irish Catholicism Dying?* (Kirby, 1984). In spite of these clear indications that the secularising tendencies of a modernising society are apparent in Ireland, the Republic is still an overwhelming 'Catholic' country and migrants to England and Wales still have to adjust to a significantly different religious environment.

In an earlier publication some of the evidence available in the late 1970s was reviewed. This included an analysis of surveys of their readerships by the *Catholic Herald* in England and Wales and the *Catholic Standard* in Ireland. While the samples were clearly not representative of the Catholic populations in the two countries, when comparisons were made between first- and second-generation Irish Catholics and English Catholics, it was concluded that 'religious accommodation to the norms and values of English Catholicism appears to be complete and the evidence ... suggests that it occurs very largely in the first generation, that is on the part of Irish-born immigrants. These results appear to suggest that ... there is little evidence of a persistent and distinctive subculture of Irish Catholicism in this country' (Hornsby-Smith, 1978b: 32).

In a second study of random samples of electors in an inner-city parish in London in the mid-1970s it was again possible to compare first- and second-generation Irish immigrants with other British Catholics. Here it was reported that while relatively high rates of religious in-group marriage persisted into the second generation, on most other indicators of attachment to the institutional Church and religious, moral and social beliefs, there appeared to be a decline which was particularly striking among the children of Irish-born parents, that is in the second generation (ibid.: 33).

In an overview of the situation of Irish Catholics in England in the late 1970s it was noted that

Table 6.4 *Catholic type by immigrant generation and sex (%)*

R.C. type (TAG)	MALES				FEMALES			
	First-gen. Irish	Second-gen. Irish	Not Irish	All	First-gen. Irish	Second-gen. Irish	Not Irish	All
Involved orthodox attenders (% A & B)	3	16	10	9	16	15	12	13
Non-involved orthodox attenders (% C & D)	36	28	24	27	28	21	21	22
Irregular attenders (% F & G)	32	14	21	22	32	22	29	28
Non-practising (% H & J plus non-ident.)	19	34	41	35	18	38	35	33
N = 100%	54	44	187	285	63	63	298	423
p		0.0681				0.2864		
V		0.22				0.16		

Source: National Survey, 1978.

in recent years the undesirable jobs in the British economy have increasingly been undertaken by successive waves of coloured immigrants. With the deterioration of the economic climate in Britain there even appears to have been a reversal in the flow of migrants and some net return flow to Ireland. For the previous generations of Irish migrants now settled in Britain the arrival of lower-status immigrants has provided opportunities for promotion and upward social mobility. With these opportunities there has been a significant movement out of the inner-city ghetto areas and into the suburbs and a substantial measure of assimilation into British society. This in turn has contributed to the gradual change in the nature of Roman Catholicism in England which can no longer be depicted as a predominantly Irish, working class, urban phenomenon. (ibid.: 39)

These findings are consistent with the picture of assimilation which emerges from Liam Ryan's survey of 1,432 post-war migrants from the Irish Republic living in the London area in the early 1970s. On the basis of this study it was concluded that

a majority of Irish immigrants in Britain have successfully integrated with

Table 6.5 *Standardised scores on religious outcome scales by Irish immigrant generation and religion of spouse*

Religious outcome	Irish immigrant generation	Religion of spouse	
		R.C.	non-Cath.
Adult religious practice	1st (Irish born)	159	83
	2nd (Irish parent)	175	65
	Other British born	136	65
Doctrinal orthodoxy	1st (Irish born)	130	116
	2nd (Irish parent)	124	90
	Other British born	117	92
Church involvement	1st (Irish born)	134	93
	2nd (Irish parent)	148	80
	Other British born	127	79
New-style activism	1st (Irish born)	117	65
	2nd (Irish parent)	165	85
	Other British born	138	65
Private prayer	1st (Irish born)	117	107
	2nd (Irish parent)	123	95
	Other British born	109	94
Sexual orthodoxy	1st (Irish born)	163	98
	2nd (Irish parent)	218	60
	Other British born	143	62

Note: Second generation are those born in Great Britain with at least one parent born in Ireland. Other British born are those born in Great Britain, neither of whose parents was born in Ireland.
All other British born = 100
Source: Adapted from Hornsby-Smith and Lee, 1979: 200

the host society and ... a sizeable minority have reached the further stage of assimilation ... (one)-third are at various levels of accommodation, that is they have established themselves economically and residentially and conform to the basic social norms of Britain but without becoming fully part of the new society and without losing their Irish identity and Irish cultural traits; ... a further third have achieved integration into British society in that they are involved in the full social, civic, political, religious, and economic life of Britain, have achieved some degree of occupational and residential mobility, but without developing any allegiance to Britain and without loss of Irish cultural identity; a final third are well on the way toward identificational and cultural assimilation with their adopted country. (Ryan, 1973: 231–2)

Finally, we can report some findings from further analyses of the 1978 national survey in *Roman Catholic Opinion*. In table 6.4 the distribution of Catholic types (Hornsby-Smith, Lee and Turcan, 1982) for first- and second-generation Irish Catholics in England and Wales and non-Irish Catholics shows a convergence to English patterns of non-practising by the second generation. This holds for both sexes and might be considered to be substantively important even if, because of the small numbers involved, the variations between the three groups did not reach the levels of statistical significance.

The processes of religious assimilation can be seen more clearly in the standardised scores on six outcome scales reported in table 6.5. These data confirm that this process occurs over two generations but with the important proviso: only where the respondent who was either born in Ireland or who had an Irish parent had married a non-Catholic spouse. Where s/he was married to another Roman Catholic there remained sizeable differences in the scale scores between the second-generation Irish and those Catholics who had been born in Great Britain and who did not have a parent who was Irish.

When the separate effects of family structure and religious endogamy were considered in the case of second-generation Irish Catholics it was reported that for all six scales the scores were higher where both parents were Roman Catholics. Unexpectedly, however, where both parents were Catholics, higher scores were obtained where the respondent's father rather than his/her mother was Irish on all six scales, and on five of the scales the scores were higher where only the father was Irish than where both parents were Irish (Hornsby-Smith and Lee, 1979: 61, 201). However, these findings need to be treated with some caution in the light of the analysis of G.H.S. data which, as reported earlier, did not confirm the importance of the Irish mothers in social-mobility experiences. It seems necessary to conclude that the structure of the Irish family and the patterns of marriage of Irish immigrants, especially religiously mixed Anglo-Irish marriages, are related to the religious attitudes, beliefs and practices of Irish Catholics in England and Wales over two or more generations in ways which are not yet fully understood.

In sum, while the data are sometimes inconsistent between the sexes, and while differences between the three groups, first- and second-generation Irish Catholics and non-Irish Catholics, do not always reach levels of statistical significance, it does seem that by the second generation there has been a general convergence in the

religious beliefs, attitudes and practices of Irish Catholics towards
the norms for English Catholics. In other words the evidence points
to a substantial measure of religious assimilation by the second
generation.

6.6 THE ASSIMILATION OF IRISH CATHOLICS

The importance of the massive waves of Irish immigration over the
past century and a half for the growth and characteristics of
contemporary English Catholicism cannot be underestimated. The
Irish have always been the largest immigrant group and they
continue to be even though, with the slowing of immigration since the
peak years in the 1950s and 1960s when they were sucked in to meet
the insatiable demands of an expanding labour market in the years of
recovery after the Second World War, their proportion in the
population has declined from around 1.9% in 1961 to 1.6% 20 years
later. The bulk of this migration has come from the Irish Republic
though there has been a steady increase in the proportion from
Northern Ireland. (This suggests the continuing peripheral economic
status of Northern Ireland with respect to the core of mainland
Britain while the economy of the Irish Republic has grown in
strength and independence.)

The net effect has been of inestimable value for the Church in
England and Wales. In 1851 the proportion of Irish Catholics was
estimated to be 63% (Hughes, 1950: 43) and as late as 1890 Cardinal
Manning opined that 'eight-tenths of the Catholics in England are
Irish' (Gwynn, 1950: 266). We have seen that by the late 1970s nearly
a quarter of English Catholics were either first- or second-generation
Irish immigrants. If one takes into account earlier generations, there
is little doubt that most English Catholics owe their religious
allegiance at some stage to their Irish ancestry. Thus the size of the
Catholic community has grown from around 900,000 (or 5.0% of the
population) in 1851, at the time of the restoration of the hierarchy
(Currie, Gilbert and Horsley, 1977: 154), to around 5.4 million (or
11.4% of the population) in the late 1970s.

We have noted the extraordinary paucity of data relating to this
largest immigrant community in Britain. In part this reflects the
general perception of their unproblematic assimilation to British
society. Their non-visibility and similar language and cultural
capital have clearly distinguished them from other migrant groups

such as the Polish political exiles and Italian migrant workers who did not share these advantages and the highly visible black migrant workers who experienced high levels of prejudice and discrimination in their adaptation to a relatively hostile society.

In sum, the assimilation of Irish Catholics is not a simple process but is mediated in particular by the patterns of social and religious endogamy or exogamy. While social mobility and assimilation are accelerated by national intermarriage, religious convergence and assimilation to the norms of English Catholicism are accelerated by religious intermarriage. Since the rates of exogamy have been increasing rapidly in the past two decades, the ease and speed of assimilation of Irish Catholics seem likely to increase.

CHAPTER 7

CATHOLIC ELITES

7.1 INTRODUCTION

In earlier chapters it has been suggested that the Second Vatican
Council in Rome in the early 1950s had legitimated a fundamental
shift in the understanding of the nature of the Church and of its
religious mission (Abbott, 1966). In theological terms this shift was
characterised as one from an institutional model of the Church to
servant, herald, community and sacramental models (Dulles, 1976).
In this country Cardinal Hume has referred to a shift from an
embattled fortress Church to a pilgrim Church on the move. Socio-
logically, McSweeney (1980) has regarded the significance of the
changes taking place in the Church as 'the search for relevance' in the
contemporary world. Using an organisational framework suggested
by Burns and Stalker (1966), we have suggested that the shift can be
interpreted as one from a 'mechanistic' model to an 'organic' model
of the Church in terms of its authority relationships and the new
stress on the active participation of all the 'People of God' in a
changing world (Hornsby-Smith and Lee, 1979).

The active participation of the laity was first experienced by most
Catholics at the parish level in the liturgical reforms which emerged
after the Second Vatican Council. In time there was a demand for lay
readers and, later, lay special ministers to speed up the distribution of
Holy Communion at Mass. In some parishes there has been the
development of a multiplicity of lay ministries, of healing, care of the
sick, leadership of prayer groups, and so on (Comerford and Dodd,
1982; O'Sullivan, 1979), all legitimated by the teaching of the

Vatican Council. The unanticipated consequence of these reforms
was the replacement of the potentially classless Catholic activist (e.g.
for flower arrangements or church cleaning rotas) with a more
specialised, educated, articulate laity familiar with public speaking
and leadership roles, disproportionately located among the middle
classes.

The second area where the participation of the laity in the work of
the institutional Church was experienced was in the new structures of
consultation and advice which were to be set up at all levels in the
Church. At the parish level where there had long been a variety of
Catholic organisations, such as the Union of Catholic Mothers and
the Knights of Saint Columba, with their opportunities for lay
initiative and leadership in specified areas of activity, there was the
slow growth of parish councils. Sometimes the membership was
selected by the parish priest but in more recent years many have been
elected, for example at annual parish meetings. While the emergence
of parish councils has been extremely patchy, the development of
advisory commissions at the diocesan level has been even slower. In
the early 1980s not all dioceses had Diocesan Pastoral Councils or
Justice and Peace Commissions. At the national level, however,
probably in dutiful response to the norms expected by the Vatican
authorities in the post-conciliar era, the bishops set up a variety of
commissions and advisory bodies in the late 1960s (Bishops' Conference of England and Wales, 1971). At all these levels, those emerging
in these new participatory structures tended to be people pro-
fessionally experienced in leadership roles and decision-making, with
some sort of relevant expertise and articulateness. Not surprisingly it
will be shown that at all these levels the officials in Catholic
organisations and members of advisory bodies were disproportionately educated and occupationally middle class, and that they
differed significantly from the socio-economic characteristics of
English Catholics generally.

In this chapter, therefore, we will examine some evidence relating
to these Church 'activists' at the parish and national levels. We will
also review some findings from a survey of the delegates to the
National Pastoral Congress of 1980. In particular, we will report on a
study of the 'progressivism' of English Catholics in the light of this
survey and point to its complex and multifaceted nature. In conclusion it will be suggested that there are growing cleavages in the
Church in England and Wales between the predominantly educated

middle class, progressive activists, on the one hand, and the bulk of Mass-attending and relatively passive Catholics, on the other hand.

7.2 PARISH ACTIVISTS

In our study of four parishes in the mid-1970s, randomly selected Catholic electors were compared with a core group of active Catholics identified in each case by the parish priest. Notable differences between them were found. Activists were generally older, had much higher educational, occupational and housing statuses and were likely to have been resident in the parishes for a longer period than the average Catholic. Interestingly, a much larger proportion of the activists had been born in Ireland and it seemed that they included a large number of long-stay or assimilated Irish immigrants who were bringing up their children in this country. By contrast the Irish-born Catholic electors seemed to have migrated more recently. There were higher proportions of both stable middle class and upwardly socially mobile experiences among the activists compared to the average Catholics in these parishes.

There were also striking differences between the activists and randomly selected Catholic electors on religious beliefs, attitudes and practices. Not only were the activists much more likely than the Catholic electors to stress the institutional norms of sexual morality but they were also much more likely to emphasise the salience of religious leadership than either Catholic or non-Catholic electors. Furthermore, the activists were much more likely than the other two groups to express a social liberalism orientation on such social and political issues as race relations, taxation policy and the treatment of murderers. It is important to note that the cleavage between the parish activists and the average Catholic appeared to be greater than that between the average Catholic and the average non-Catholic living in the same area. This suggests that lay participation at the parish level is not so much representative of the laity generally as of a small elite group of institutionally involved and committed Catholics whose views were generally supportive of the norms of institutional Catholicism (Hornsby-Smith, 1978c).

These findings were generally confirmed in the national survey of Roman Catholics in 1978. About one Catholic in eight claimed to be a member of a parish organisation and two-fifths of these belonged to no other organisation. They were disproportionately female, middle aged or elderly, from higher social-class backgrounds, and politically conservative. On the other hand, office holders were more likely to be converts, male, middle-aged and upwardly mobile. Office holders rated their priests more highly than ordinary members who in turn rated them more highly than non-members. Their general religious traditionalism was reflected in the fact that they were more likely than the other categories to consider there had been too many changes in the Church recently (Hornsby-Smith and Lee, 1979: 45–51, 188–91).

7.3 MEMBERS OF THE BISHOPS' ADVISORY COMMISSIONS

In our study of the members of the bishops' commissions in the mid-1970s we found that about two-fifths of the lay members were single, a fact which indicated that a considerable proportion of them were what one informant called 'professional Catholics' who had been active in Catholic organisations all their lives. About two-fifths of the sample were female though the proportion varied from commission to commission. Fewer than one-third of the members were under the age of 40 so that the commissions appeared to be overwhelmingly middle-aged in their membership, in spite of the fact that some of them had broadened their age span by coopting a number of young people.

Lay members of the commissions were also overwhelmingly middle class; we did not come across a single instance of a member who was currently employed in a manual occupation. In all, only about one-quarter came from recognisably working-class backgrounds though the proportion was about one-half in the case of the Laity Commission. One-half of the members were upwardly mobile (in terms of a six-point scale based on the Registrar General's social classes and splitting his social class III into manual and non-manual categories). Half of these were aged 45 or under and so were potential beneficiaries of the 1944 Education Act. What upward mobility there was seemed to be clearly related to educational achievement. Between two-thirds and three-quarters of the members had had some form of higher education and over one-half were university graduates. In general, therefore, there was clear evidence that the 'new Catholic middle class' were well represented on the new formal structures of consultation and advice in the Church.

About one-fifth of the members were converts and there were also indications that conversion had played a significant part in the religious ancestry of a number of other members. The immigrant origins of many English Catholics were also apparent. Around one-half had Irish origins and a further one-quarter had other immigrant origins. This number included several from Europe, but the numbers were boosted by the presence of eight West Indian or African members on the Racial Justice Commission. At least one member was very proud of his recusant roots, but in general there were few signs that an older, indigenous English Catholicism retained any significant influence at least among the formal membership of the bishops' commissions.

Although the formal fact of advisory membership is not the same as the substance of influence over decision-making, our informants in the mid-1970s left us with the strong impression that the Bishops' Conference had been taking increasing note of the advice of the commissions. In so far as this is true, the formal channels of influence representing the rise to power of the new middle classes may be expected to grow in importance in the Church as the older, public-school, upper-class pragmatic Catholicism declines. (On the other hand, representatives of this older, established Catholicism claim to have been influential in recent episcopal appointments, including that of Cardinal Hume.) In contrast there was no evidence of a strong working-class or trade-union influence on the commissions which seemed no more capable of bridging the class barriers or the gap between the articulate and the inarticulate than any other institution in our society.

The religious attitudes of the majority of the commission members could generally be termed 'progressive' (Mansfield and Hornsby-Smith, 1982). Well over half of those interviewed were enthusiastic about the changes emanating from the Second Vatican Council. Some went further and described their disappointment at the apparent lack of interest at the parish level. Only about one in eight of the members could be labelled 'traditionalist' in the sense that they were critical or even cautious about the changes in the Church since the Council. At the other extreme, there was an even smaller number of 'radical' Catholics who felt that much of the radical renewal advocated by the Council had been lost in the clamour over what they saw as the relatively trivial changes which had in fact taken place. Overall, though, it could reasonably be judged that the religious orientations of the lay members of the commissions were far more favourable towards change in the Church than those of the average parishioner in this country.

In an analysis of the work of the commissions, four different outcomes were postulated, depending on the nature of the membership and the definition of the task set (Hornsby-Smith and Mansfield, 1975). When a consultative body had a predominantly representative membership and the task set was of a diffuse kind, the outcome was likely to be a lack of precision or focus, and the making of generalisations. When a commission had a membership which was not primarily representative in nature but expert in some relevant manner, and yet its task-definition was relatively diffuse, the likely outcome was the attempt by professionals to bring some systematic order to their field of concern. In a particular study of the International Justice and Peace Commission, it was shown that the diffuse nature of the task-definition contributed to the high level of conflict on this commission (Mansfield and Hornsby-Smith, 1975). When a commission or advisory body had a predominantly representative membership but also a task which was very specific, it was suggested that there was a tendency for Michels' Iron Law of Oligarchy (Michels, 1949) to operate and for key administrators to be overwhelmingly influential in the pursuit of administrative goals. Finally, when a commission consisted of members who were expert in some relevant way and where the nature of the task to be undertaken was clearly and specifically defined, the likely outcome was the professionalisation of the means for pursuing the task.

The research carried out on members of the bishops' commissions in the mid-1970s led us to suggest the need for three quite different types of structures: expert advisers and 'think tanks', consultative bodies with fully representative membership, and action-oriented organisations with executive powers. In England and Wales, the bishops revised the structures of the Bishops' Conference, abolished the commissions and, in 1983, set up a comprehensive system of departments (Bishops' Conference of England and Wales, 1983). It remains to be seen how effective these new structures will be and whether they will confirm or reduce the influence of the new middle-class progressives who had emerged in the 1970s in the new participative structures in the Church at the national level.

7.4 DELEGATES TO THE NATIONAL PASTORAL CONGRESS

In this section we will review some of the major findings from a survey of the 2,000 delegates to the National Pastoral Congress which was held in Liverpool in May 1980 (Anon., 1981). This was a major event in the history of the Roman Catholic Church in England and Wales and represented a culmination in the process of 'renewal' or adaptation to the demands of the contemporary world 15 years after the ending of the Second Vatican Council. As was indicated in chapter 1, all the delegates other than the bishops were surveyed by postal questionnaire in November–December 1981, 18 months after the Congress. Of the replies obtained, 1,276 were usable and the overall response rate of 65% was regarded as satisfactory, given the limited resources available (Hornsby-Smith and Cordingley, 1983).

The first aim of the survey was to elicit the reactions of the delegates to the Congress, which was a unique opportunity for extended discussion between bishops, clergy, men and women in the religious orders, and lay people about the life, work and needs of the Church in the late twentieth century. Delegates were invited to comment not only on the Congress itself but also on the preparations and consultations which had preceded it, the content of the seven sector reports, and the bishops' response to these reports three months later in *The Easter People* (Anon. 1981: 307–98). They were also asked to comment on the follow up at the local level 18 months after the Congress.

The results of this inquiry were striking. While many delegates referred to the Congress itself as a 'conversion experience', where it had been a great joy to participate in the prayer and work of an open, sharing, listening and celebrating Church, 18 months after the Congress they expressed clearly a feeling of being let down by the bishops. Whereas four-fifths of the delegates or more expressed satisfaction with all aspects of the Congress itself, only one-half were satisfied with the bishops' response and only one-quarter were satisfied with the response to the Congress in their own diocese or organisation. Furthermore, two years later, when Pope John Paul II became the first pope to visit Britain, ostensibly as a direct follow up to the N.P.C., even the sector presidents from the Congress did not meet him. My own early suggestion that the N.P.C. would come to be seen as a major turning point in the emergence of the Church in

Catholic elites

Table 7.1 *Social characteristics of priest, women religious and lay delegates to the National Pastoral Congress*

Social and religious characteristics	Priest delegates	Women religious delegates	Lay delegates	All laity (*Roman Catholic Opinion*)
Sex, % male	100	0	55	44
Age, % under 35	16	6	27	42
Marital Status				
% single	100	100	30	19
Terminal Education				
Age, % 19 or over	95	82	47	12
Qualifications,				
% Degree	45	43	32	2
Irish Immigrants:				
% first generation	20	34	6	15
% second generation	11	2	7	15
Social Class:				
% RG I, Professional	97	25	13	3
% RG II, Intermediate	2	72	55	16
% RG III Man – V				
Manual	1	2	7	52
Communal Association:				
% half or more friends				
R.C.	96	95	74	44
% all Catholic schools	77	79	64	60
% convert	6	17	15	10
N = 100%	176	94	959	1,036

Note: One delegate who responded as a female priest has been excluded.
Source: Hornsby-Smith and Cordingley, 1983: 7.

England and Wales: 'potentially, the *rite de passage* from a childlike passive deference and conformity to a mature and responsible adult Christianity' (Hornsby-Smith, 1982: 259) can be seen in retrospect as premature and unduly optimistic.

The second aim of the survey was to describe the demographic, social and religious characteristics of the delegates in ways which enabled direct comparisons to be made with the findings in *Roman Catholic Opinion* (Hornsby-Smith and Lee, 1979) from the national sample of adult Catholics surveyed in 1978. In particular it was hypothesised that the delegates would be representative of 'activist' Catholics but not of 'grass-roots' Catholics and hence that the Congress manifested a growing cleavage between an active minority and the passive majority of Catholics in England and Wales. It was also thought likely that delegates would disproportionately represent middle-class Catholics with higher educational experiences.

The survey findings, summarised in table 7.1 provided support for these hypotheses. That the delegates were 'middle class and middle-aged' can be seen from the relatively low proportions aged under 35 and their high educational and occupational statuses. Over two-fifths of the priests and women religious and one-third of the lay delegates were graduates and nearly all had had some form of higher education. Over two-thirds of the lay delegates were in the Registrar General's social classes I or II and only 7% were in manual occupations compared to over half among Catholics generally. One-fifth of the priests and one-third of the women religious had been born in Ireland. Among the lay delegates, though, Irish immigrants were underrepresented. Only 6% had been born in Ireland but a further 7% had Irish parents. Generally it seemed that the delegates were overwhelmingly middle-aged or elderly, well educated and occupationally successful. Around one in six of the women religious and lay delegates were converts but relatively few of the priests were. There were indications that for all three groups of delegates the levels of communal association (Lenski, 1963: 23) were higher than average as judged by the proportions who had attended Catholic schools and the extent to which their friendships were found chiefly within the Catholic community.

When considering intergenerational social mobility across the manual–non-manual division, the mean upward mobility movement of lay delegates was 0.33 compared to 0.02 for Catholics generally in the 1978 national survey. In terms of the four possible mobility experiences, half the lay delegates were stable middle class compared to 15% for Catholics generally, and over one-third were upwardly mobile from the manual working class compared to one-sixth among Catholics generally. Only 4% were downwardly mobile (one-quarter of the proportion for Catholics generally) and only 8% stable working class compared to over half for Catholics generally.

Details of the religious beliefs, attitudes and practices of the delegates have been reported elsewhere (Hornsby-Smith and Cordingley, 1983). These showed that around seven delegates in eight favoured a shift of resources towards adult education and urged a clear commitment by the Church 'to speak out more clearly on the grave social injustice of unemployment and to seek ways to help the unemployed'. Over three-quarters of the delegates urged the compassionate consideration by the bishops of the desire of divorced and remarried Catholics 'to share completely in the sacramental life of the Church' and two-thirds thought 'the Church should condemn the possession and use of nuclear weapons' and favoured the reception of Holy Communion under both kinds (i.e. the appearance of both bread and wine) as a norm. Three-fifths considered that the Catholic Church should join the British Council of Churches and nearly half the delegates wanted women to be admitted as permanent deacons.

On social and moral issues the Congress delegates were far more orthodox or traditional than Roman Catholics generally, for example in their attitudes to divorce. On the other hand, they were more progressive on social justice issues. For example, four-fifths thought that 'the Church should take active steps to promote social justice even if it means getting involved in politics' compared to only one-third of Catholics generally. It is also striking that as many as nine delegates in every ten approved of the bishops making public statements on issues of political concern such as unemployment, the nuclear deterrent and the Nationality Bill. Delegates were given two specific examples: the bishops' statement (July 1979) that Britain was irreversibly a multiracial society and their statement (December 1980) on unemployment as a distortion of the divine plan. More than seven delegates in eight approved of both statements, remarkably powerful evidence for this-worldly religious orientations among this sample of Catholic activists.

In terms of belief and practice, delegates were also shown to be quite distinct from Catholics generally. Nearly all attended Mass at least weekly compared to under two-fifths of Catholics generally and over half read the Bible weekly compared to only 7% reported for Catholics generally (Harrison, 1983: 63). On other measures of belief and practice they were much more orthodox. They were also much more likely to have attended ecumenical services and to have been involved in charismatic prayer groups. They were less likely to be traditional in their liturgical attitudes but they were also less likely to approve of intercommunion.

In sum, the picture which emerged from the survey of the delegates to the 1980 N.P.C. was that, compared to Catholics generally, the delegates were very heavily involved in the life of the institutional Church in terms of a wide range of religious practices. On liturgical, social and political issues they were much more progressive but on the issues of personal morality they were much more traditional than other Catholics. This suggested that the 'progressivism' of Catholics in England and Wales was complex and required further analysis. For the moment we might note that in the analyses of the N.P.C. delegates, the differences between priests, women religious and lay delegates or between the sexes or social classes, were all relatively slight. To this extent the delegates were remarkably homogeneous. Furthermore, it seemed to indicate clearly that there was no evidence of a cleavage between priests and lay people, at least among the progressive activist Catholics in the Church in England and Wales at this time.

7.5 THE PROGRESSIVISM OF CATHOLIC ELITES

It has been shown in the preceding sections of this chapter that at every level in the Church in England and Wales activist Catholics differed from the Catholic population generally in their approval of the liturgical, theological and social changes legitimated by the teaching of the Second Vatican Council. They also differed sharply in their adherence to orthodox Catholic moral teachings. In this section we will explore further some evidence on the progressivism of Catholic elites on the basis of the survey of delegates to the N.P.C. This survey aimed to make up for some of the shortcomings of the 1978 national survey of English Catholics by broadening the range of social justice issues considered and also by attempting to explore further measures of a post-Vatican theological orientation.

Bishop Butler has written that in the two decades since the end of the Second Vatican Council 'already a generation is reaching adulthood that has no memory of the pre-conciliar Church, a generation for which compulsory "fish on Friday", the "Tridentine" Latin Mass, and strong hostility to Protestantism are either unknown or seem as odd as the crinoline' (1981: 211). In the main, however, there have been conflicts in the Church between those who have welcomed the changes emanating from the Council (broadly speaking the 'progressives') and those who have resisted them (broadly speaking the 'traditionalists'). Thus 'within the Church two rival models are in subtle conflict. One clings to the old Church – authority, submission, verbal deposit, closedness; the other seeks to renew the Church and fulfill its present promise in leadership, co-operation, living faith, and openness' (O'Dea, 1968: 234; quoted in McSweeney, 1980: 141).

A number of attempts have been made to compare the essential characteristics of the pre-Vatican or traditional and the post-Vatican or progressive Church. Apart from the work of Dulles which we have noted previously, surveys have been undertaken with priests (Pro Mundi Vita, 1973; Reidy and White, 1977) and nuns (Neal, 1970, 1971) to distinguish pre-Vatican from post-Vatican orientations, and analyses of the delegates to the 1967 Third World Congress for the Lay Apostolate (Vaillancourt, 1980) and of the delegates to the 1976 Bicentennial Program 'A Call to Action' in the United States (Varacalli, 1983) have been undertaken. However, there has been no systematic empirical study of the nature of religious progressivism among English Catholics.

For the purpose of our investigations among the delegates to the N.P.C., progressivism has been taken to mean the selection of views regarded as having been promulgated by the Second Vatican Council with its shifts of religious ideology and pastoral emphases which are to an extent distinct from those corresponding views regarded as having been espoused by the official Church in the years before the Council, over the whole range of ecclesiastical concerns, including the areas of doctrine and theology, liturgy, spirituality, pastoral and missionary strategies, personal and social morality, and political involvement.

In order to remedy the shortcomings of the national survey in terms of the range and validity of the measures of progressivism employed, delegates were offered 12 pairs of alternatives to explore different shades of belief and religious meanings. In each case they were invited to indicate which emphasis came closer to their own view. Only between 1% and 4% felt unable to select between the options offered because they regarded both alternatives as being either equally correct or important or equally incorrect. The alternatives offered had been derived from a number of different sources: the Weberian distinctions between submission and mastery and between this-worldly and other-worldly orientations (Weber, 1966), Sister Marie Augusta Neal's treatment of pre-Vatican themes (Neal, 1970, 1971), the survey of members of the Society of the Divine Word which distinguished between pre-Vatican, Vatican and post-Vatican theological orientations (Pro Mundi Vita, 1973), Avery Dulles' analysis of models of the Church (1976), and some aspects of liberation theology (Gutierrez, 1974; Sobrino, 1978; C.E.L.A.M., 1980).

The detailed responses to this question have been summarised in table A6. They

indicate clearly the broadly 'progressive' characteristics of the Congress delegates. Thus they stressed an immanent rather than a transcendent view of God who had created us to master a world which is good and work for its transformation. Religion tended to be this-worldly and could not be divorced from the everyday concerns of politics and from social and economic issues. Even so a large majority of the delegates selected the more 'traditional' position and regarded evil as essentially resulting from personal sin rather than structural sin and saw the primary missionary concern as changing the hearts of individuals. Delegates were progressive in seeing the Church as essentially a community of believers, in regarding the Mass as a community celebration with the Christian minister as being authorised by the People of God to build up the Christian community and in viewing missionary activity more in terms of human development than individual conversion. (Hornsby-Smith and Cordingley, 1983: 19)

A number of other questions on the survey of the delegates were also used in this present analysis. Delegates were first asked whether or not they agreed with eight key recommendations of the Congress, ranging from the liturgical norm for Holy Communion and sacramental practice in the case of divorced and remarried Catholics to the question of official comments on unemployment. The opportunity was also taken to assess the support for a more politically active involvement by the Catholic Church in England and Wales. Thus delegates were asked the six questions on the morality of the nuclear deterrent which the bishops had posed in December 1980. Three further questions explored the stance of the delegates towards the making of public statements by the bishops on politically controversial issues, including those on the multiracial nature of British society and on unemployment. Delegates were also invited to indicate the level of their agreement or disagreement on five-point Likert scales on nine matters of religious, social and moral concern in order to obtain comparable data with those obtained in the national survey. In a similar manner delegates were asked to indicate their level of approval on six recent liturgical changes and their general opinion about recent changes in the Church, Christian Unity, and whether or not they would accept married priests or women priests and approve of women playing a further part in the life of the Church. In sum, there were 49 different variables covering a variety of social, moral, liturgical and theological issues where there has been a shift of emphasis or of attitudes in the Church since the Second Vatican Council.

The analysis of the data appeared to indicate that the patterns of progressivism were complex and that a high score on one aspect did not necessarily entail a high score on other aspects. Fuller details of the early analyses have been reported elsewhere. Briefly, three stages of investigation have been undertaken. First, smallest space analysis plots revealed four aspects: socio-political, moral, liturgical and theological, on which delegates could hold any combination of progressive or traditional views. When single indicators for each aspect were chosen it was possible to construct a scale of progressivism and show that one-quarter of the delegates were progressive on all four aspects (Hornsby-Smith and Cordingley, 1983: 21-2).

A second approach involved the use of factor analysis of all 49 survey attitudes. This analysis suggested six distinct factors: a liberal or permissive orientation to Church rules, opposition to nuclear defence strategies, liturgical progressivism, openness to ministerial innovation, a community emphasis in the Church and an emphasis on this-worldly religion. Again dichotomising each dimension yielded a matrix of 64 cells which were collapsed to give seven types (Hornsby-Smith, Procter, Rajan and Brown, 1985: 10–15).

The third approach involved the use of cluster analysis to group together similar individuals. Using discriminant analysis, seven clusters were identified and interpreted. Six discriminant functions were found to be interpretable: progressive theology of the Church, anti-nuclear-defence stance, progressive morality, progressive liturgical roles, socio-political religious involvement and a community emphasis. The analysis of the mean values of each discriminant function for each cluster and distinguishing those values above or below the mid-point of the range yielded the typology of progressive types given in figure 7.1. The social and religious characteristics of these seven progressive types of delegates have been summarised in table 7.2 (ibid.: 16–25).

It can be seen that cluster 1 differed from all the other types in being 'progressive' on the morality dimension. It was a deviant type in the sense that on this dimension respondents did not conform to the official teaching of the Church. Thus only 2% were 'traditionalists' on the birth-control issue (types A and C) and there was a very high proportion of young graduates and of delegates who were not involved in parish organisations. A lower proportion of this type compared to any other read the Bible or attended Mass daily.

Cluster	Function						Type
	3	1	4	6	5	2	
	Progressive morality	Progressive theology	Progressive liturgy	Commun. emphasis	Socio-pol. Religion	Anti-nuclear	
1	+	+	+	+	+	+	Deviant progressive
7	−	+	+	+	+	+	Pure conforming progressive
5	−	+	+	+	+	−	Conforming progressive (trad. defence policy)
6	−	−	+	+	+	+	Conforming progressive (trad. theology)
4	−	−	−	+	+	+	Communally involved traditionalist
3	−	−	−	−	+	+	Individualistically involved traditionalist
2	−	−	−	−	−	−	Pure traditionalist

(Key: + = Progressive; − = Traditional)
Source: Hornsby-Smith, Procter, Rajan and Brown, 1985: 21.

Fig 7.1 A Typology of Progressive Types (see note p. 156)

The other six types with this sample of English Catholic elites were all conformist on the morality dimension and varied in their progressiveness on the other five dimensions. Cluster 7 was the modal type and had a particularly high proportion of priests and nuns. Among the lay delegates it had the highest concentration of type B Catholics (involved in parish organisations but heterodox on the birth control issue). About one-quarter of cluster 5 progressives were

Table 7.2 *Social and religious characteristics of progressive types (%)*

Characteristic	Progressive type (Classmen)							All
	1 Deviant progressive	7 Pure conforming progressive	5 Conforming progressive (def.)	6 Conforming progressive (theol.)	4 Communally involved traditionalist	3 Individually involved traditionalist	2 Pure traditionalist	
Male priests	6	16	12	15	1	9	12	12
Female religious	2	13	5	8	4	5	0	7
Lay delegates only								
Sex, % Male	54	44	63	61	39	65	70	55
Age, % under 35	40	17	15	19	43	7	0	22
Education, % Graduate	45	35	31	23	6	20	20	28
Convert, %	10	13	23	14	11	21	17	15
*R.C. type**								
Involved traditionalists, % A	1	11	15	53	15	49	50	24
Involved non-traditionalists, % B	56	70	61	32	53	16	30	50
Non-involved traditionalists, % C	1	3	3	9	4	26	7	7
Orthodox attenders, % D	40	15	19	7	28	9	13	19
Attends Mass daily, %	4	11	10	19	6	22	17	12
Reads Bible daily, %	10	21	12	26	10	24	10	18
All delegates (N = 929)	15	28	16	20	9	10	4	100

* The term 'traditionalist' here refers to acceptance of the traditional teaching on birth control. For details of the derivation of this typology see Hornsby-Smith, Lee and Turcan, 1982.
Source: Hornsby-Smith, Procter, Rajan and Brown, 1985: 22.

converts; this cluster was distinguished from pure conformist progressives by their espousal of a traditional nuclear defence policy. Cluster 6, which was the second largest cluster, had the largest proportion of type A Catholics (involved in parish organisations and traditional on the birth-control issue). About a fifth of them attended Mass and one-quarter read their bibles daily. In contrast, a very low proportion of cluster 4 delegates, a high proportion of whom were young women, did so. As with cluster 6, a high proportion of cluster 3 delegates, one-fifth of whom were converts, attended Mass or read their bibles daily. It is noticeable, however, that the proportion who were non-involved traditionalist (type c) Catholics was three times that of any other cluster. Their religion, in other words, appeared to be a highly privatised one of personal devotions. Finally, cluster 2 was the smallest group of delegates who were traditionalist on all six dimensions. It can be seen that a high proportion of them were relatively elderly men and that a relatively high proportion were involved in parish organisations.

The data summarised in table 7.2 provided evidence for the view that there was no simple unidimensional scale of progressivism. There was no clear pattern in the variations of the social and religious characteristics considered from either the deviant progressive cluster 1 or pure conformist progressive cluster 7 delegates to the pure traditionalist cluster 2. A relatively high proportion of priests was found in clusters 6 and 7 and of nuns in cluster 7. Clusters 4 and 7 consisted mainly of women, and clusters 1 and 4 were disproportionately younger and clusters 2 and 3 disproportionately older delegates. Clusters 3 and 5 had high proportions of converts. Traditionalists on the birth-control issue (types A and c) were disproportionately found in clusters 2, 3 and 6 while the highest proportions of those involved in parish organisations (types A and B) were found in clusters 2, 6 and 7. Clusters 3 and 6 had high proportions of delegates who attended Mass or read their bibles daily while clusters 1 and 4 had particularly low proportions.

Clearly the nature of the religious progressivism of this sample of English Catholic elites was extremely complex and not interpretable in terms of some unilinear process such as a general shift over time from an other-worldly to a this-worldly religious orientation or from a personal to a social focus of morality. On the contrary, it is apparent that for this sample of active Catholics, a rejection of the segregation between religion and politics need not necessarily have involved an

acceptance of recent liturgical changes or a community emphasis in
the model of the Church adopted. Similarly, a strong community
emphasis may or may not have been associated with a non-conforming or 'progressive' morality which might have reflected a greater
concern for personal decision-making.

The typology outlined as a result of this study of the delegates to
the N.P.C. (figure 7.1) indicated that only 7 of a possible 64
combinations were relevant for this particular sample of Catholic
elites. There is, however, no reason to believe that this would be the
case for other samples, such as a nationally representative sample of
English Catholics. What we might infer from the delegate study is the
broad outline of the key dimensions of a classification of progressivism among Catholics generally, on the basis of the similarities
between the three analyses reviewed above. These seemed to indicate
three overriding dimensions, each with lower-order elements, as
follows:

1 *Progressive ecclesiology*, including:
   (a) theology of the Church
   (b) orientation to Church rules and authority
   (c) liturgical orientation
   (d) openness to ministerial innovation
   (e) community emphasis
2 *This-worldly involvement*, including:
   (a) socio-political religious involvement
   (b) anti-nuclear-defence stance
3 *Progressive morality*, including:
   (a) emphasis on liberation from sinful structures
   (b) rejection of traditional personal, sexual and marital pros-
        criptions

When each of these three higher level dimensions is dichotomised
there are eight possible combinations of traditionalist-progressive, as
indicated in figure 7.2. In terms of this classification cluster 1 was
type 8 and progressive on all three dimensions, while cluster 2 was
type 1 and traditional on all three dimensions. Cluster 3 was type 2,
progressive only on the involvement dimension and cluster 7 was
type 4 traditional only on the morality dimension. Clusters 4, 5 and 6
were hybrid types according to this classification; clusters 4 and 6
were intermediate between types 2 and 4 and cluster 5 was intermediate between types 3 and 4.

| Involvement | | Ecclesiology | | | |
| | | Traditional | | Progressive | |
		Other worldly	This worldly	Other worldly	This worldly
Morality	Traditional	1	2	3	4
	Progressive	5	6	7	8

Fig. 7.2 A classification of Catholic progressive types

7.6 COMPETING ELITES IN THE CHURCH

The term 'elite' in this chapter has been used very broadly to refer to those people who emerged at the parochial, diocesan and national levels within the Roman Catholic Church in England and Wales as a result of a variety of processes of election or cooption in the years following the Second Vatican Council, as officers, delegates or representatives in the new participatory structures which were intended to signify the new 'People of God' model of the Church. In general terms it is argued that these persons were 'at the head of a specific social organisation which has an internal authority structure' and as such constituted an elite (Giddens, 1973: 120). On the other hand, it is recognised that what Giddens calls the 'mediation of control' or 'the actual (effective) power of policy-formation and decision-making held by the members of particular elite groups' (ibid.: 121) is an important issue which cannot be assumed but which needs to be determined empirically.

The evaluation of the 'power' and 'influence' of the various Catholic elites in the decision-making processes at the three levels in the Church in this country is beyond the scope of this review. At the parish and diocesan levels the situation appears to be very varied and to reflect the authority, style and preoccupations of the local parish priest or bishop. It seems likely that effective power of policy-formation and decision-making by lay elites is extremely rare at these levels but there may be a more diffuse influence on the religious leadership on relatively minor issues such as the maintenance of Church property or the normal age for conferring the sacrament of confirmation. At the level of the national commissions lay advisers frequently felt that their advice was simply politely received but quietly ignored so that no-decision was a typical outcome of recommendations made.

In the case of the N.P.C. it can perhaps be argued that the delegates originally constituted an 'abstract elite' since, in principle, recruitment of delegates was relatively open and their social integration was relatively low. During the course of the Congress their social integration was increased so that they emerged more like a 'solidary elite' (ibid.: 120). Similarly, in the early stages of the Congress the range of issues considered was relatively restricted (in that delegates were substantially isolated from each other in groups and there was a large measure of specialisation to a restricted range of issues) and effective power was diffused among the members of the group. This constituted a 'democratic' order. However, during the course of the Congress, as discussion shifted to topic areas, then sectors, and emerged subsequently in the *Congress Reports*, it is possible to argue that the range of issues considered became broader and effective power consolidated in the hands of the sector presidents, topic chairpersons and discussion group leaders who drafted the major reports. In Giddens' terms, therefore, there was a shift from 'democratic' to 'autocratic' power-holding (ibid.: 122).

In terms of Giddens' overall typology of elite formations and power it can therefore be suggested that the 'leadership groups' which went to the Congress emerged subsequently as a 'power elite' (ibid.: 123), overwhelmingly 'progressive' in its religious ideology and committed to action alternatives in the reforming spirit of the Second Vatican Council.

However, as has already been noted, it seems that in the follow-up to the Congress the progressive elites who had attended the Congress had been resisted by the 'established elites' of parish clergy and traditionalist core groups in parishes and organisations as well as the mass of passive, uninvolved nominal Catholics. While there is no evidence of a major explosion of discontent in the Church at the moment it would appear that there are two competing elites in substantial conflict over the nature of the Church, the implications of the Second Vatican Council, the relationships between religion and politics, and the nature of religious authority. The future of the Church in this country may well depend on the outcome of this struggle.

Table 7.3 *Religious characteristics by leadership type (%)*

Religious characteristics	N.P.C. lay delegates			Roman Catholic Opinion		
	Official	Leader	Delegate	Organ. member	Parish attached	Non-attached
R.C. type						
Orthodox Attenders (A+B+C+D%)	93	97	97	99	39	4
Progressivism						
Scale scores high (3+4%)	85	73	54			
On L,T,S aspects (%)[a]	63	62	40			
Personal moral % agree with birth control)	81	53	48	58	73	91
Liturgical (% approval both kinds)	92	92	83	62	57	60
N = 100%	27	89	824	125	560	317

[a] L = Liturgical progressivism
  T = Theological progressivism
  S = Social moral progressivism
Source: Hornsby-Smith and Cordingley, 1983: 21–2, 31.

A comparison of the data from the survey of N.P.C. delegates and the national survey of adult Catholics may throw some light on the nature of these competing elites at the parish and national levels, though comparable data from Catholics at the parish level are available on only two of the four aspects of progressivism. In table 7.3, six groups have been compared in terms of their religious practice and progressivism. Three groups of lay delegates have been distinguished: officials (members of the Congress committee, sector presidents and topic chairpersons), discussion group leaders and ordinary delegates. From the 1978 national survey, members of parish organisations have been compared to other Catholics attached to a parish and Catholics not attached to a parish. In terms of belief (assumed orthodox in the case of the delegates) and practice, parish elites were similar to the Congress delegates. On questions relating to the liturgy, ordinary delegates were much more progressive but on the birth-control issue much more traditional than members of parish organisations. Thereafter there was a striking filtering out of traditionalist leanings at each of the two levels of the Congress hierarchy. In other words, officials were more progressive than leaders, who were more progressive than members of parish organisations (on liturgical matters, though not on the birth-control issue).

These data are suggestive. It seems that at the parish level the nearer to core membership a Catholic is, the more traditional he or she is on the birth-control issue. From this core group those who were especially traditional on this issue but approving of the new liturgical developments were the most likely to be selected as ordinary delegates. But the Congress leadership itself was much more progressive and it may be that sponsorship processes by the Congress officials were involved in the selection of the more progressive delegates as discussion group leaders. In sum, at the moment it would appear that in the official leadership of the Church the more actively involved progressive elites are in the ascendancy.

This takes us as far as our own research data will go. In order to demonstrate a latent conflict between these progressive elites and the older, more established, 'traditional' elites, further investigation of specific issues would be necessary at all levels in the Church. For the moment the following impressions might be offered. In the parishes, the priests have the power of gatekeepers to open or shut gates, encourage or inhibit innovations and control information through their monopoly over formal channels of communication. On occasion their defensiveness in the face of social and religious change may be buttressed by local lay traditionalists who favour the older model of the priest as a 'man apart' with unchallengeable, traditional authority. Conversely, traditional or convenience Catholics who favour the continuation of 'things as they have always been' in the parishes, might well resist the proposals for liturgical and pastoral changes from progressive priests and their lay allies. There is clearly a need for more case studies of parishes in order to document conflicts between traditionalists and progressives with different religious ideologies and models of the Church.

There has also not yet been a social scientific study of the bishops in England and Wales since the Second Vatican Council. Such a study would include the processes of consultation and decision-making in the appointment of bishops, the role of the Apostolic Delegate, and the power and influence of various lay elites in promoting the cause of their own preferred candidates. Again, there appear to be wide variations between dioceses in the types and extent of lay involvement in the pastoral decision-making processes. Not all dioceses have had Pastoral Councils and, even where they do exist, they are sometimes regarded as 'mere talking-shops'. Until very recently few dioceses had Justice and Peace Commissions. In both parishes and dioceses, a change in the religious leadership has, on occasion, resulted in the abrupt termination of previously established practices. In these cases the lay elites often seem powerless to resist such policy changes and the laity as a whole are, as yet, nowhere near mobilising their 'power of the purse' to influence the distribution of resources within the Church at every level.

Where prophetic elements in the Church regard their work with the poor, deprived and oppressed, in the inner-city areas especially, as hampered by bureaucratic rigidity or a traditional opposition between individual devotion and socio-political involvement, it might tentatively be suggested that they will move towards the periphery of the institutional Church and seek the fulfillment of their religious vocation of commitment to the poor either in ventures which do not depend on the support of the clerical leadership in the Church, or in collaboration with secular groups having similar purposes.

On the other hand, it might be argued that the progressive elites in the Church have developed an extremely effective communications network through an interlocking nexus of largely lay-run organisations such as the Catholic Institute of International Relations (C.I.I.R.), Pax Christi, and, through its educational programmes, the Catholic Fund for Overseas Development (C.A.F.O.D.). As a result of their commitment and competence, those in contact with these organisations have often emerged at the national level, as delegates to the N.P.C. or as members of the bishops' advisory bodies and consultative commissions. A follow-up study of the members of the commissions or the new departmental advisory committees would be likely, therefore, to indicate signs of a continuity of progressive lay advice since the late 1960s, sufficiently consistent to suggest that oligarchic tendencies (Michels, 1949) are evident in the new bureaucratic structures in the Roman Catholic Church in England and Wales today.

Whether or not this represents the victory of the progressive elites depends on the evaluation of their influence on the decision-making processes in the Church in recent years. Thus, while part 1 of *The Easter People* advocated a 'Sharing Church' model (Anon., 1981:

307–28), many progressive delegates at the Congress regarded the bishops' response on specific policy recommendations (Pro Mundi Vita, 1980) as unsatisfactory. On the other hand, in preparation for the Special Synod of 1985, the bishops published an outspoken defence of collegiality (Bishops' Conference of England and Wales, 1985).

A cautious conclusion might be, therefore, that there are competing elites in the decision-making structures in the Church today. Much of the conflict between these elites remains latent and there have been relatively few manifest explosions of discontent. Traditional positions in the Church have been challenged by the new, largely educated, middle-class progressives who appear to have infiltrated the new participatory structures at every level in the Church. At the national level in particular the progressives seem to have established a firm grip but traditional elites appear to have by-passed these structures on occasion by the use of informal influence based on status grounds. Where traditional elites have retained a dominant position, progressives have either been driven to the periphery of the Church or have sought to achieve their goals through secular channels. The outcomes of these conflicts are likely to be important for the type and extent of the influence of the Catholic community on political decision-making in Britain today, which is the subject of the next chapter.

Note:
In a revised version of this analysis, to be published in the *Journal for the Scientific Study of Religion* in 1987, some relabelling of the clusters has been undertaken. Cluster 1 is referred to as 'progressive'; 7 as 'conformist'; 5 as 'pragmatic'; 6 as 'reformist'; 4 as 'communal'; 3 as 'political'; and 2 as 'traditionalist'.

CHAPTER 8

CATHOLICS AND POLITICS

———— ⚜ ————

8.1 INTRODUCTION

It was once observed that there are three interest groups in British
politics whose mobilisation is to be feared: the miners, the Brigade of
Guards and the Catholic bishops. This attributes to the Catholic
community in Britain a political power for which it would be difficult
to find convincing evidence. In this chapter we will attempt to
evaluate the political influence of Roman Catholics in Britain by
considering two particular areas of concern to Catholics: educational
policy and abortion legislation. It will be suggested that the evidence
does not support the fears expressed about the power of the Catholic
bishops.

Politics is concerned with the question of goal-setting in society,
the ideologies which underpin those goals and the strategies for
seeking their attainment by those who have differential power of
resource mobilisation in the pursuit of their own ends. Lasswell thus
regarded politics as the answer to who gets what, when and how
questions (Lasswell, 1958). Lord Butler regarded consensual politics
in a pluralist parliamentary democracy as 'the art of the possible'
(Butler, 1971). We will, therefore, also consider the political voting
patterns of English Catholics as well as their attitudes, relative to the
rest of the population, on a number of controversial issues. Consideration will also be given to variations within the Catholic community
and in particular between the various elites at both the national and
parish levels.

The Church, in spite of its participating People of God ideology, is not a democratic institution. Decision-making generally resides with male clerics and is increasingly contested. This is potentially most likely to occur in the future in the matter of women's role in the Church. Accordingly, a preliminary and tentative statement on the embryonic Catholic feminist movement has also been offered. Finally, some evidence relating to the fledgling justice and peace movement will be reviewed which suggests that there is growing opposition to the domestication of the Catholic Church in this country over the three key areas: relations with Third World countries, domestic issues such a racism and unemployment, and the peace movement.

8.2 ENGLISH CATHOLICS: A POLITICAL FORCE?

8.2.1. The historical legacy

In his rather gloomy evaluation of the state and potential of the Catholic Church in England and Wales as it celebrated the centenary of the restoration of the hierarchy, Bishop Beck observed that:

> it seems to be generally admitted that the influence of the Catholic community in England on public life is by no means commensurate with its size, and there seems to be a good case for arguing that, at least until very recent years, this influence has been throughout the greater part of this century declining. It has been said that the height of Catholic influence was reached about the period when the Liberal Government of 1906 took office. The Irish influence in the House of Commons was then at its strongest and was later to die away almost entirely. Nothing in Catholic public life has replaced it ... Politically, since the withdrawal of the Irish Members, the Catholic influence has, on the whole, been negligible. (Beck, 1950b: 602–3)

This judgement has some confirmation in the fact that the proportion of Catholic M.P.s is only about half their proportion in the population generally and this situation has remained unchanged for decades. There are approximately as many Jewish M.P.s, although the number of Jews is less than a tenth of the Catholic population (Scott, 1967: 38). A number of reasons for this phenomenon might be offered. Most obviously, the defensive mentality forged especially among the Catholic gentry in the penal years following the Reformation and the continuing expressions of anti-Catholic prejudice well into the twentieth century, generated a desire for a low political profile. During this period, 'the price of their survival was exclusion from public, professional and military life ... (but) the retreatist, sect-like tradition of three centuries was ... hard to shake off' (Spencer, 1973: 125–6). In the twentieth century Catholics emphasised their loyalty through service in the diplomatic services and heroism during the two world wars (Mathew, 1955: 272; Scott, 1967: 140).

A second element in the explanation is a general other-worldliness (Lawlor, 1965) or 'anti-world' attitudes (Scott, 1967: 13), again most emphatically expressed by Bishop Beck: 'the "other-worldliness" in a Catholic must always be his dominant if not immediately evident, characteristic' (Beck, 1950b: 604). Later, in his introduction to *The Case for Catholic Schools* (Beck, 1955: 1–2), Beck was to quote with approval the well-known claim that 'death and original sin are the constants in the light of which the Catholic Church surveys humanity. Life is a preparatory stage and its values are secondary ... the quintessential left by a Catholic education is a lasting consciousness of the fact and meaning of death' (Evennett, 1944: 124–6). It is suggested that a profound dualism between religion and politics was a characteristic feature of Catholicism in the years before the Second Vatican Council. In a country where it constituted only a small minority so that political 'pillarisation' with parallel parties, trade unions and welfare organisations was not a viable option, and where the major political conflicts articulated class interests, Catholics seem to have been happy to have allowed pluralist politics take their course and concentrated on the struggle for personal salvation in 'the life hereafter'.

8.2.2 Political impotence

In the late 1950s a Catholic Labour M.P. was quoted as saying: 'There is not much to say about the influence of English Catholics in public life: they exert very little' (Scott, 1967: 78). A proper evaluation of the political power of English Catholics would require a more thorough investigation than we can give it here. All we will attempt is a brief review of the testimony of a number of Catholic parliamentarians and others interviewed by George Scott, and offer the suggestion that any such evaluation might consider two test cases in particular: the extent to which Catholic educational policy claims on the State have been met over the years, and the failure of the anti-abortion lobby to prevent the passage of the 1967 Abortion Act or subsequently to amend it in any major particulars. On the basis of such an inquiry it might be suggested that, in spite of the fears expressed at the beginning of this chapter, the Catholic community on its own has relatively little in the way of political resources, that there is probably no single issue on which Catholics could achieve sufficient unanimity and substantial mobilisation in the 1980s, and that they have little more influence than any other interest group in pluralist Britain.

After reviewing the influence of pro- or anti-Catholic prejudice in political voting in the 1960s, George Scott doubted whether it made more than 100 votes difference at the constituency level. This subjective judgement seems a sound one, as is Scott's further conclusion that any such influence might be more likely in local government. A particularly profitable area of inquiry might well be the development of a Catholic schools policy from the years of expansion in the 1950s and 1960s to the years of contraction in the 1970s and 1980s, particularly in areas such as Liverpool, Manchester and the Inner London Boroughs, where the proportion of Catholics is well above the national average. The evidence also seems to support Scott's further conclusion that the claim that Catholics are 'priest-ridden', and likely to have their political voting patterns influenced from the pulpit 'is not any longer generally tenable' and that 'there is now common agreement among priests and laity that any such attempt would be deeply resented by the Catholic electorate' (ibid.: 61–4).

The struggle for Catholic schools It is a major conclusion of Peter Coman's analysis of Catholic attitudes towards the establishment of the British Welfare State in the early post-war years that

despite acceptance of the welfare goals of social security, greater educational opportunity and better health, there was a pervading fear that the distinctive Catholic subculture would be undermined by the wider society with a different normative system, operating through its political expression in the very powerful twentieth-century state. (Coman, 1977: 67)

The collectivist trend in social policy conflicted with repeated emphasis on the principle of subsidiarity in the papal social encyclicals since Leo XIII's *Rerum Novarum* in 1891. But the proposals for educational reform which were to find their expression in the 1944 Education Act and the reforms proposed in the Beveridge Report of 1942:

threatened the Roman Catholic subculture by endangering the financial viability of its segregated school system and by making possible the eventual spread through National Health Service of practices in the field of sexual and marital conduct incompatible with Catholic moral teaching. (ibid.: 40)

In the event it was the protracted battle over the financial implications of the 1944 Education Act which led to the mobilisation of the Catholic community in defence of the right of a separate schools system and control over the religious curriculum and moral teaching. The net cost to the Catholic community was estimated to have been £50 million with annual interest and loan repayments of around £6 million (Hornsby-Smith, 1978a: 28). A number of dioceses were said to have been near to bankruptcy as a result of the school building programmes in the 1960s and 1970s in a period of unprecedented inflation and high interest rates (Hornsby-Smith, 1978a: 10). In order to ease this burden the government grant available for school building programmes was raised from 50% to 85% in a number of stages as the bitter religious antagonisms of the years up to 1944 gradually declined and there was an 'end of "passionate intensity"' (Murphy, 1971: 121–9) over the issue.

To the extent that the Catholic community won the right to a segregated school system substantially paid for out of public funds and that the dual system is now an established and uncontroversial political fact in England and Wales, it could be argued that they had demonstrated a mighty power of political mobilisation for a struggle which had raged for over a century (ibid., 1971). The cost of the victory was, however, considerable. The battles of the 1950s for an increase in grant and the administrative effort of the massive school building programme itself consumed almost all the available energies in the community and diverted attention from competing claims for the limited financial resources (see, e.g. Scott, 1967: 148–64). It could be said that there was a displacement of goals (Merton, 1957) so that the building of Catholic schools came to be regarded as an end in itself. Until recently little attention was paid to the quality or effectiveness of Catholic schools.

With the decline of the school population and the squeeze on public expenditure since the early 1970s, Catholics have, if anything, suffered disproportionate cuts in schools and colleges of education. Since the peak years in the mid-1970s over 200 Catholic-maintained schools have closed and the number of pupils in them has declined by over 100,000 or 13% (C.E.C., 1985; private communication). In the

1978 national survey only 38% of Catholics thought that 'Catholics should be educated in separate Catholic schools' compared with 46% who did not (Hornsby-Smith and Lee, 1979: 80, 215). There has also been a noticeable concern to shift resources away from schools, for example to adult education (Konstant, 1981), and in the more tolerant or indifferent religious climate of the 1980s, it is very doubtful if the Catholic community could again be mobilised for a major defence of the dual system, or, in Coman's terms, the defence of a specific Catholic subculture.

Defeat over abortion legislation The second test case to evaluate the political power of Catholics concerns recent abortion legislation. There is, perhaps, no single moral issue to which official Catholicism is more strongly opposed. (The extent to which English Catholics deviate from this stance was discussed above in section 5.4.) Any attempt to claim that Catholics constitute a politically powerful interest group in British society must therefore address the issue of their failure to prevent the passage of the 1967 Abortion Act or of the several attempts subsequently to amend it. 'The fact is that in Britain the Catholic Church is astonishingly unorganised for political action or the applying of public pressure' (Scott, 1967: 79).

All the same, the Roman Catholic Church has been regarded as a major opponent of the 1967 Abortion Act and the hierarchies of both Scotland and of England and Wales issued joint statements in 1979–80 at the time of the Corrie Bill to amend it (Marsh and Chambers, 1981: 131, 144). This was the ninth parliamentary attempt and Roman Catholic M.P.s were prominent in all of them. Roman Catholics have also comprised a large part of the memberships of the two main groups in the anti-abortion lobby: the Society for the Protection of the Unborn Child (S.P.U.C.) and LIFE. Marsh and Chambers analyse in detail the failure of the attempts to amend the 1967 Act and point to strategic and tactical weaknesses among the Corrie supporters. For our purposes here it is of interest to note that a major reason 'was the divisions which existed on the anti-abortion side' (Marsh and Chambers, 1981: 162). In particular, the 'fundamentalist' stance of the extra-parliamentary lobby resulted in the failure to determine priorities and seek the appropriate political compromises which might pragmatically have resulted in more restrictive legislation. It might tentatively be suggested that the conflict between a fundamentalist stance on principle and a pragmatic need to compromise in pluralist democratic societies is likely to result in practice in a weak Catholic contribution to political decision-making.

In sum, for historical reasons Catholics have made little contribution to politics in Britain. An other-worldly religious stance, at least in the pre-Vatican era, can be said to have reinforced this weakness. In spite of the size of its constituency, Roman Catholics are by no means homogeneous in their social, moral and political beliefs and attitudes, even on such issues as abortion and the dual system of schooling in Britain. Furthermore as a result of post-war social change they have become widely dispersed throughout British society. The potential, therefore, for mobilising them behind any particular campaign is strictly limited. This is particularly so as the tightly knit Catholic subculture of the early post-war years breaks down.

8.3 SOCIAL, ECONOMIC, POLITICAL AND MORAL ATTITUDES

In previous chapters evidence has been provided not only of the heterodox nature of Catholic beliefs and attitudes (chapter 3) but also of the deep cleavages which exist between the educated, progressive activists on the one hand, and grass-roots Catholics on the other (chapter 7). Further evidence for these conclusions will be provided in this section which will also illustrate the remarkable extent to which Catholic attitudes have converged with those of the general population on a wide range of social, political and moral issues. The results appear to provide further justification for the view that the distinctiveness of a separate Catholic subculture in England and Wales had all but disappeared by the 1980s.

8.3.1 Comparative attitudes at the parish level

In this section we will briefly review some of the findings of the surveys of social, economic, political and moral attitudes of randomly selected samples of Catholic and non-Catholic electors and selected samples of activists in the four parishes investigated in the mid-1970s. Of the four scales constructed from the 27 questions common to all four parishes, statistically significant differences between Catholic and non-Catholic electors emerged only with respect to sexual morality, with the salience of a rational humanistic orientation to sexual matters being weaker for Catholics. These results would seem to indicate that the sort of Catholic subculture in England described by a number of writers (Coman, 1977; Hickey, 1967; Ward, 1965) is not as distinctive as it once was (Hornsby-Smith, Lee and Reilly, 1984). A similar revision of the traditional model of the Catholic in the United States has been reported by Greeley (1977). In both societies predominantly low-status immigrant communities have experienced considerable mobility in recent decades and the attendant processes of structural and cultural assimilation to the dominant patterns in the host society (Hoge, 1986).

What was more striking about the data was the extent of the divergence between Catholic activists at the parish level and the randomly selected Catholic electors. Not only were the activists much more likely than the Catholic electors to stress the institutional norms of sexual morality but they were also likely to emphasise the salience of religious leadership more than the other two groups. They were also much more likely to express liberal views on such social and political issues as race relations, taxation policy and the treatment of murderers (table 8.1). This cleavage between the parish activists and the average Catholic provides further confirmation of the finding in the previous chapter that lay participation at the parish level is not so much representative of the laity generally as of a small, elite group of institutionally involved and committed Catholics whose views are generally supportive of the norms of institutional Catholicism. It might be noted, however, that in 1974-7 when the data were collected both Catholic activists and electors were more supportive of the view that Northern Ireland should be part of the Irish Republic than electors generally in the four parishes.

8.3.2 Grass-roots Catholics and lay elites

In the recent study of British values systems it was reported that religious people tend to have a more conservative political outlook and favour greater respect for authority and the major political institutions. There is an association between belief in God and the political right, although the religiously active are slightly more leftward-leaning in their views (Abrams, Gerard and Timms, 1985: 86, 158). English Catholics appear to be exceptions to the first part of this general pattern. For historical reasons, largely grounded in differences between the political parties with respect to the Irish

Table 8.1 *Selected social, political and moral attitudes by associational involvement and religious identification (Weighted Averages, Four Parishes, % Agreement)*

Attitude	R.C. activists	R.C. electors	Other electors
5 Divorce should be readily available where one partner considers the marriage has broken down.	8	45	53
7 If a person is suffering from a painful illness and wants to die he should be allowed to do so.	18	44	65
9 It is a good thing that abortion is available legally for those women who want one.	9	39	73
11 Northern Ireland should be part of the Irish Republic rather than the United Kingdom.[a]	71	70	58
18 We should be prepared to accept a drop in our standard of living in order to help people in poorer countries to live better.[a]	73	44	36
19 Religious leaders should speak out on race relations issues.[a]	82	59	56
20 There should be special tax advantages to encourage married couples to limit their families to 2 or 3 children.	12	48	52
23 An increase of income tax is better than further cutbacks in the social services.[a]	50	42	43
24 One should pay particular attention to religious leaders.	66	37	19
25 Britain should give up her nuclear weapons as a gesture towards peace.[a]	29	31	26
26 Murderers should be hanged for their crime.[a]	22	55	55
27 There should be a redistribution of wealth by means of a wealth tax.	23	41	32
37 These days scientists have more to contribute to our lives than priests.	5	46	63
Max. no. of respondents	84	267	1,189
Estimated population weights	84	7,991	40,168

Source: Hornsby-Smith, 1978c.
Note: Don't Knows and no responses have been omitted.
[a] Data available in three parishes only.

question, Catholics have disproportionately given their allegiance to the Labour Party. Gallup omnibus survey data confirmed that this tendency persisted at the time of the national survey in 1978. Roman Catholics who claimed to have voted for the Labour Party numbered 57% at the last election compared to 47% among the population generally. This relationship held for all age groups, Mass attendance categories and all social classes with the exception of the upper middle class where there were no differences between Catholics and the rest of the population (Hornsby-Smith and Lee, 1979: 37–9, 174–5).

Given some latent sympathy for the nationalist minority in Northern Ireland it is of note that the strongest levels of agreement on 13 social and moral issues considered were recorded against violence in the pursuit of political ends and in favour of an obligation to work for racial harmony. There was some readiness, in theory at least, to accept a lower standard of living for the sake of poorer nations but these redistributive sentiments were much weaker when applied at an individual level of giving to the poor even when finding it difficult to make ends meet (ibid.: 52–3, 192). The ambivalence of Catholics on the role of the Church on political issues was further indicated by the contrast between the strong support in general terms, especially among young Catholics, for a greater involvement of the Church in issues like housing, poverty and race relations, and the slight majority against the Church taking active steps to promote social justice if it means becoming involved in politics. 'On balance Catholics in England appear to prefer a "domesticated Gospel" to a "political Christianity"' (ibid.: 55, 194).

In the previous chapter some aspects of the progressivism of English Catholics were considered in the case of the delegates to the N.P.C. Among the clusters of attitudes reviewed, those of particular relevance to this chapter included the orientation towards nuclear-defence strategies, the relative emphasis on liberating people from oppressive structures and the extent to which religion should be concerned with political issues and this-worldly considerations. Unfortunately we do not have identical data on all these issues for the Catholic population as a whole although a limited number of comparisons can be made (table 8.2). These indicate first that there were no significant differences in the responses of the priest and lay delegates to the Congress. Secondly, they indicate that the delegates were more traditional than the average Catholic on matters of personal morality, such as divorce, abortion and euthanasia, but also more progressive on social issues such as relations with the Third World countries and the relationship between religion and politics. This gap between grass-roots Catholics and leadership groups within

Table 8.2 *Selected social, political and moral attitudes by religious group
(N.P.C. Delegates and R.C.O. National sample; % Agreement)*

Attitude	N.P.C. delegates		All Catholics (*Roman Catholic Opinion*)
	Priests	Laity	
7c The Church should speak out more clearly on the grave social injustice of unemployment and seek ways to help the unemployed.	82	87	na
7h The Church should condemn the possession and use of nuclear weapons.	64	69	na
14d If a person in his right mind is suffering from a painful disease which can't be cured and he wants to die, termination of life should be permitted.	4	4	44
14e Except where the life of the mother is at risk, abortion is wrong.	78	84	65
14f Catholics should be allowed to divorce.	19	26	63
14g The rich nations have a duty to accept a lower standard of living for the sake of poorer nations.	98	90	53
14h The Church should take active steps to provide (= promote) social justice even if it means getting involved in politics.	88	92	33
N = 100% (max.)	179	958	1,036

Source: Hornsby-Smith and Cordingley, 1983: 42–3.

the Church suggests that it would be difficult to mobilise the whole
Catholic community on any of these issues.

Interestingly, in a recent small study of the attitudes of the priests
in one diocese in the affluent south-east of England to the Campaign
for Nuclear Disarmament (C.N.D.), it was reported that half the
responding priests were either paid-up members of C.N.D. or
sympathetic to its aims. Even so, opinions varied widely and one in
seven were strongly opposed to the C.N.D. position, some even
commenting that they would not follow their bishops should they ever
recommend a unilateralist position (Hornsby-Smith, 1985). This is a
further example of the difficulty of mobilising English Catholics
around any political issue.

8.4 POLITICS IN THE CHURCH

The participating People of God ideology and the stress on religious freedom and personal conscience legitimated by the Second Vatican Council have resulted in the cooption of lay people into the bureaucratic machinery of the Church. We have previously noted that since the late 1960s lay people have been members of the bishops' commissions and advisory bodies (Hornsby-Smith and Mansfield, 1975). The clerical leadership in the Church, however, has always been at pains to insist that the Church is not a democratic institution. Inevitably, therefore, there are conflicts over decision-making (Mansfield and Hornsby-Smith, 1975) and policies of sponsorship, cooptation, pre-emption and so on (Harrison, 1959; Selznick, 1966) are likely to have been widely employed at every level in the Church: national, diocesan and parochial, to ensure that radical dissent is suppressed or managed to give the semblance of institutional consensus. A fuller analysis than can be given here would also, no doubt, provide examples of 'techniques of neutralisation' (Matza, 1964). None of this is surprising; there is no reason to claim that the Catholic Church is any different from any other social organisation in these respects.

None of these areas have been systematically studied in this present research. We will, therefore, confine ourselves to the consideration of the issue of the role of women in the Church, gender discrimination and the feminist movement. Although this issue is currently of latent concern only, it is suggested that it might well become more important over the next decade. Accordingly, a preliminary consideration of the embryonic Catholic feminist movement has been offered. Secondly, a brief consideration of some aspects of pastoral policy has been given, in order to indicate the potential for conflict and contestation. The wider issues of the nature of religious authority in the Church (Mansfield and Hornsby-Smith, 1982) will be considered in a separate publication.

8.4.1 Sexism and the feminist critique

It is appropriate to comment briefly on Catholic attitudes to the traditional gender division of labour in the home and in the Church because these are areas of traditional male power often treated as sacred and unproblematic both by men generally and by the clerical leadership in the Church in particular. While the feminist critique is still very much in its infancy in this country, it is clearly a major matter of contemporary concern in the more pluralist situation in the Church in the United States and can reasonably be anticipated to emerge in this country after a time lag. I originally placed this section at the end of chapter 5 on Catholic Marriage and Family Life but it was pointed out to me that this itself appears to offer a tacit agreement that this is women's only proper place. I accept the view that women's proper place in the Church can legitimately be said to be contested at the present time and that therefore it might more properly be treated in the context of justice and peace issues. As Angela West has written: 'Without ultimate justice, the ultimate liberation for all the powerless, there can never be any true liberation for women' (West, 1983a: 85–6). This section is, therefore, a very tentative contribution to an emergent agenda.

Dr Ursula King, reflecting as a Christian on the role of women in contemporary society, recently observed that 'sad to say, traditional attitudes to women are frequently sanctioned and further reinforced by Christian leaders' (King, 1977: 271). It is not surprising, therefore, given the male hegemony in the Church, that in the preparations for the N.P.C. in 1980, parish and diocesan reports on the whole showed a comparative lack of interest in the matter of the role of women in the Church although 'reports from special groups and organisations submit[ted] firm proposals and strong comment' (Anon., 1981: 64). The Congress itself considered the role of women in the Church and in the report made by the president of sector B, the request was made for 'a more detailed exploration of the possibility of admitting women to the ordained ministries' and that 'the eventual ordination of women ... be explored seriously at this time' (Anon., 1981: 156, 158).

However, in *The Easter People* the bishops rather lamely took refuge in *The Declaration on the Question of the Admission of Women to the Ministerial Priesthood* published in 1976 by the Sacred Congregation for the Doctrine of the Faith at the request of Pope Paul VI which had concluded 'that the Church in fidelity to the example of the Lord, does not consider herself authorised to admit women to priestly ordination' (Anon., 1981: 348). As if to soften the blow, the bishops later, addressing women directly, thanked 'God for the many distinctive gifts and talents that women offer to the Church', recognised 'their part in the history of salvation, pre-eminently of course in the

person of the Blessed Virgin Mary, Mother of God' and acknowledged 'with regret that you have often been permitted to play mainly
a limited, and often inferior, part in the Church' and that 'traditional
and unquestioning attitudes towards women and your role may have
to be changed'. They further appealed that 'we ourselves and our
clergy may well have to be persuaded gently of our insensitivity and
our assumptions of male dominance' (Anon., 1981: 383).

This no-doubt well-intentioned paternalism prompted a member
of the Catholic Peoples' Weeks to respond:

First we thank God for the many gifts and talents with which She has
undoubtedly endowed the male sex. The history of salvation reveals that
indeed men have made a significant contribution. Christian baptism
enhances the positive masculinity invaluable in your mission. As generators
of life you complement the pre-eminent role of women in this sphere. You are
characteristically strong and wise and capable of single-minded pursuit of
objectives. Your gift of a rational logical mind makes you alive to what needs
to be done. Relationships within the community are enriched by the
masculine dimension. Your sisters believe that the time is ripe for more
positive attitudes towards your participation in the life of the Church. The
limited and inferior role we have permitted you is a matter of genuine and
authentic heart searching and regret to most of us! (Hewson, 1980)

Rather late in the day in comparison with their sisters in the
United States, English Catholic women in the early 1980s were
beginning to raise important theological questions about their role in
the Church. One woman theologian, in anticipation of the Pope's
visit in 1982, wanted to know whether the Pope would be meeting any
women on his visit and who would speak for English women as
Theresa Kane had done in the United States (Murphy, 1982). The
answer was that the Pope met and talked to few women (indeed to
few lay people generally), including those who had been prominent at
the N.P.C.

It might be noted that whereas in 1978 over half of Catholics
generally would accept married priests, only one-quarter would
accept women priests. In the case of the more activist lay Catholics
who were delegates at the N.P.C., the proportions were over two-
thirds and over one-third, respectively. Whereas half of Catholics
generally would approve of 'letting women play a further part in the
life of the Church', over four-fifths of the lay delegates would do so
(Hornsby-Smith and Cordingley, 1983: 44).

It should be stressed, however, that the Catholic feminist

movement in England and Wales, which is still very much in its infancy, has not in any overt fashion been especially concerned with contraception, abortion or even ministerial priesthood. Angela West, for example, has articulated a feminist theology which denounces the idolatrous societies which produce the holocaust or threaten the world with nuclear destruction in these terms:

As a feminist I am therefore also a Catholic claiming membership of the universal church and of the communion of saints that it represents. What does that mean? It means being 'in one body' with all those past and present for whom Christ, dying and raised, prefigures the meaning of our ultimate human liberation: it carries with it the obligation of the traditional Christian practices, to pray together, to preach the gospel and to celebrate the eucharist ... Taking upon ourselves as a community the meaning of the eucharist as a participation in the dying and rising of Christ has served to powerfully reinterpret our experience as the powerless under patriarchy, the childbearers and those whose insights and skills are normally only valued domestically. To preach the gospel means to stand up front and be heard where formerly one sat at the back and made tea. It has meant to read, study and comment on the Bible where formerly theology was reserved for men; it has meant to bring woman's perspective into public moral debate; it has been to discover how praying together (as opposed to discussion, etc.) allows us to cast off the roles and statuses accorded us by patriarchy; it has meant turning again to the Bible and discovering it as an exciting and scandalous book ... (which) speaks to women ... because ... it is the story of an oppressed people who were always getting kicked around by those who were politically more powerful – a people who in the face of their hopeless history preserved a vision of God who would in the endtime redeem them from their earthly humiliation by sending a Messiah to set history right with the coming on earth of God's ultimate justice ... This then is what it means to be a Christian and a feminist: the Christ event is that alone which can give real meaning to the liberation of women (West, 1983a: 86–8)

A number of distinct strands can be identified in the Catholic feminist movement. The longest established, St Joan's Alliance, grew from the Catholic Woman's Suffrage Society which was founded in London in 1911. Over the years it has achieved consultative status with U.N.E.S.C.O. and seeks the elimination of discrimination against women in all countries. Currently, however, it only has a tiny membership and the new wave of radical Catholic feminists regard it as having become over-cautious in its approach to contemporary problems although deserving of recognition for its pioneering work in the areas of female circumcision, the bride price and child prostitution.

Roman Catholic Feminists was founded in 1977 and was represented at the N.P.C. It aims to unite and support women in their struggle to live with both their Roman Catholicism and their feminism. It publishes an occasional newsletter but its membership is only about 200. It holds meetings, 'occasionally Eucharistic', in order to share ideas and develop feminist theology, and it has engaged in a number of lively debates in the Catholic press. The Dorcas Group, an autonomous group of women in South London, also dates from 1977. It is loosely connected with other women's groups, both Catholic and ecumenical, and studies topics affecting the laity in general and women in particular, and engages in the consultative processes that the bishops occasionally inaugurate. There are other London-based groups, including an ecumenical group given considerable ideological and moral support by Rosemary Radford Ruether, the American Catholic feminist theologian whose writings (1975, 1979, 1981, 1984) and conference papers have become widely disseminated and influential among Christian feminists in this country. One product of this growing interest was the inauguration of the ecumenical Women in Theology group in 1984. In the same year a Catholic Women's Network was established to link Catholic feminists in Scotland and England and Wales. The initial newsletter had a distribution of 600.

Apart from the London-based groups, there is a very lively group of Catholic feminists in the Oxford area, where the Dominicans have provided significant encouragement and the regular consideration of feminist theology in their monthly review *New Blackfriars* (see, e.g. on a Christian feminist perspective on abortion, Campbell, 1980; the motherhood of God debate, Hebblethwaite (1984), Middleton (1984), Morley (1982) and Pepper and Hebblethwaite (1984); on the Church and Family throughout history, Ruether (1984); on Genesis and Patriarchy, West (1981); on sexual justice and eucharistic community and the emergence of the Oxford Catholic Women's Group, West, 1983b). Some members of the Oxford group have close links with the Greenham Common peace movement. Also based at Blackfriars in Oxford is the Christian Women's Information and Resources (C.W.I.R.E.S.) centre. There is a small but significant involvement of religious sisters in the feminist movement. Finally, reference might be made to the Catholic Lesbian Sisterhood (Redding, 1983).

Broadly speaking, it seems that from the origins of the movement in the previous decade two distinct groups of Catholic feminists may have emerged in the early 1980s:

(a) *The politicos*: stressing the themes of liberation theology in response to structures of sexual injustices and linking feminist critiques to other forms of oppression. This group places much emphasis on the Magnificat (Lk 1: 46–55) and the proclamation of the Good News to the poor (Lk 4: 16–21). They are strongly influenced by Ruether's theology and the need for a wider prophetic critique of contemporary society. In many ways they might also be regarded as 'theologicos'.

(b) *The scriptural reinterpreters*: who draw attention, in particular, to the key role of women in the life of Jesus: at the well, the woman with the haemorrhage, the discussion with Martha and Mary as equals, the first manifestation of the risen Christ to Mary Magdalene, and so on. This group is more concerned than the former with the institutional matters such as sexist language in the liturgy and the ordination of women (see, e.g. Warner, 1978: 338).

It is perhaps premature to attempt an evaluation of the social significance of the growing number of Catholic feminist groups in England and Wales. They remain small in number and, on the basis of taped interviews with several members in Oxford and London, they appear to be more concerned with the issues of inadequate theologies and the inequalities in access to power and authority in the Church than with the more restricted concerns of liturgy and priesthood *per se*. They can, it is tentatively suggested, be regarded as part of the much wider movement of change from a highly centralised, authoritarian Church towards a much looser structure of networks of small communities (Haughton, 1980: 70).

8.4.2 Mission stillborn

It would be no exaggeration to say that there is not as yet a political sociology of the Roman Catholic Church in England and Wales. For example, there has been no systematic and comprehensive analysis of the appointments of bishops, taking into account the representations of different interest groups such as the diocesan Senate of Priests and disparate lay groups. What evidence there is seems to be largely anecdotal and there are not the data available to evaluate competing claims to have exerted the dominant or determining influence. The political influence of the Catholic Union on parliamentary legislation has also not been fully explored and it seems likely to have been of no more than marginal importance (Scott, 1967: 71–5).

Within the Church itself other questions about pastoral strategy need to be considered. The time is perhaps opportune to evaluate the consequences of the obsessive drive to provide a Catholic schooling for all Catholic children at the primary and secondary levels. At one level Catholic schools have been marginally successful in the sense that survey evidence shows a positive (albeit very small) relationship between the amount of Catholic schooling and subsequent adult religious behaviour (Hornsby-Smith and Lee, 1979: 76–105, 212–31). But perhaps more importantly there has been no serious attempt to evaluate the latent functions of such a single-stranded pastoral strategy, for example considering the consequences of starving alternative pastoral efforts (such as parish-based catechesis, adult education or youth programmes etc.) of both human and intellectual and also financial resources. Implicit in the report of Bishop Konstant's working party in 1981 was the need to take such considerations into account.

Another related matter is the relative emphasis given to missionary activity by the Church, to the evangelisation of the unbeliever and the catechesis of the believer as against the maintenance of the institutional Church and, in particular, its physical plant: schools, churches, halls etc. It is now generally conceded that the balance between what Michael Winter called *Mission or Maintenance* (1973) needs to be redressed. For the best part of a century the Catholic parish priest was partly the manager of a sacrament-dispensing organisation and partly a building entrepreneur. Indeed, the pennies of the poor contributed to the enormous growth of Catholic churches and schools in the century after the restoration of the hierarchy. Religious orders, too, accumulated huge country mansions. In the more critical days of the late twentieth century the question is seriously being asked (Winter, 1979, 1985) if it is time to reconsider the baptismal call to mission and world transformation according to the Gospel emphases on social justice. It is to be hoped that a serious analysis of the Church's distribution of resources at the parish, diocesan and national levels will soon be undertaken in order to evaluate the extent to which the rhetoric of a concern for social justice is being met by significant shifts in the allocation of resources of time, people and money.

8.5 THE PROPHETIC CHALLENGE

It has been the major theme of this chapter that English Catholics have not played the part that might have been expected of them, given their size and socio-economic achievements and the decline of overt hostility, in the political processes of this country. It has been suggested that for historical reasons Catholics as an embattled minority learned to keep a low political profile. Other-worldly theological emphases reinforced the segregation of religion and politics so that there has been a deep suspicion among many Catholics of the Church 'meddling in politics.' Although the historical bias of support in favour of the Labour Party continues, Catholic attitudes on social, moral and political issues have converged with those of the general population. Over a wide range of issues there are no significant differences between Catholics and other citizens.

It would, however, be misleading to suggest that this situation is uncontested among English Catholics. The report of the justice sector at the N.P.C. confessed: 'We regret our failure as a Church to combat the prevailing national mood of insularity, to identify with the poor in our midst and to work vigorously for a more peaceful world'. It continued to condemn membership of the National Front as incompatible with membership of the Church, the scandal of overcrowded prisons and the possession and use of nuclear weapons. The report also urged the transformation of social and economic structures in the world, the search for credible non-violent alternatives to war and taking seriously the poor and powerless (Anon., 1981: 290–5; see also Forbes and Cosgrave, 1985).

An early attempt to offer a critical analysis of the social and cultural problems in modern Britain and then to define the attitudes of the Christian Church towards them and the actions demanded was a Downside Symposium on *The Committed Church* held 20 years ago. In proclaiming the rediscovery of theology the editors criticised the fact that:

English Catholics . . . are unwilling to mix religion and politics. Issues that concern the larger world outside the Christian *diaspora* are excluded from pulpit, retreat house, and the religious press (except where it is felt that someone has been unfair to 'us'). Such attitudes have survived even the recent intensive theological exploration of the nature of the Church: we recognize that the Church is a community of people, the people of God, but we are still disinclined to recommend that they should march in step with the people of the world. We are unwilling to recognize that political commitment is forced on us by our Christian belief itself; we think that a Christian is free to belong to almost any political party or none. We dream up forms of Christian social teaching which presuppose that Church and world exist apart and that the Church can discover 'solutions' to the world's problems which can then be applied...Sacred and secular have been kept apart, and related in purely external ways. (Bright and Clements, 1966: xii)

Bright and Clements urge that the Church must become committed to action through political structures and institutions for the betterment of the human condition. A similar stance was taken recently by Michael Dummett in his robust rejection of the position taken by Edward Norman in his treatment of the relationship between religion and politics in the 1978 Reith Lectures (Norman, 1979). Dummett rejected the view that there is a division between personal and social morality and insisted that we have a personal responsibility for the consequences of the economic and political structures of oppression in the world. He argued:

It should be obvious that the misery which is suffered by so many in our world as it is now is not to be effectively alleviated simply by the adoption by business men and politicians of a strict standard of personal morality though it would indeed be mitigated by that: it is due to the systems which have been created and in which we are all, in one way or another, enmeshed. These systems ... were created by men lusting after power and wealth and usually quite unscrupulous about how they obtained them. We owe these systems no loyalty: we owe it to those who suffer under them to think how to reform or replace them. (Dummett, 1979: 16–17)

A particular evil, still rampant in this country, according to Dummett, is racism, 'this greatest of all our failures'. The bishops of England and Wales have proclaimed a commitment to an 'irreversibly multiracial, multicultural society'. The Catholic Commission for Racial Justice has tentatively analysed racial discrimination in Catholic schools (C.C.R.J., 1975) and a working party has suggested ways in which Catholic education might best respond to the needs of a multicultural society (Department for Christian Doctrine and Formation, 1984). A report of the Bishops' Conference has reviewed the workings of the Nationality Act 1981 and made recommendations to the government (Department of Christian Citizenship, 1985). It cannot be claimed that these various reports reflect a consensus within the Catholic community. Rather they illustrate the point that there are radical groups within the Church in this country who are concerned to present a challenge to existing social and economic relationships.

This can be seen clearly in the two Catholic contributions in the book *Agenda for Prophets* which was seeking a political theology relevant for contemporary Britain. Fr Herbert McCabe, O.P. argued that participation in the class struggle, which is intrinsic in the human antagonism of capitalism,

is not only compatible with Christian love but is demanded by it ... Christianity is not an ideal theory, it is a praxis, a particular kind of practical challenge to the world ... we do have capitalism, we do have class war; and the Christian job is to deal with these facts about our world (McCabe, 1980: 156, 164)

A fellow Dominican, and until recently provincial in South Africa, has insisted that the Christian imperative to love means taking sides against oppressors. He rejected as erroneous the view that reconciliation means that Christians should always seek harmony and a 'middle way'. Where there is structural conflict between the oppressor and the oppressed:

Structurally, the cause of the poor and the oppressed is right and just, no matter what individual poor people may be like ... And the cause of the rich and oppressor is wrong no matter how honest and sincere and unaware they may be ... Within this situation of structural conflict the only way to love everyone is to side with the poor and the oppressed. Anything else is simply a way of siding with oppression and injustice ... Those who maintain an unjust distribution of wealth and power and those who prop up their thrones are in fact ... everybody's enemies. (Nolan, n.d.: 9–11)

The second Catholic contribution in *Agenda For Prophets* was by an Ampleforth Benedictine monk who has written and spoken widely on the issues of social justice and the Christian response. He argued that

the Church will be an agent for radical change in what Helder Camara has called her small Abrahamic groups. These are groups of people in any walk of life who by choice or necessity throw in their lot together, abandon what is stable and secure and set out like pilgrims to seek what God is really saying in their concrete situation within our modern society.

These prophetic and contemplative groups will generate alternative lifestyles and engage in a constant process of reflection and analysis, face up to hard questions about property, poverty and contemporary social structures, foster direct community action which will enable people to enliven their image of themselves, and not be afraid to get their hands dirty in concrete political options, even though this involves ambiguity, uncertainty and risk, for 'to keep one's hands clean is in fact to opt for the status quo' (Cullinan, 1980: 137, 141).

The development of a network of justice and peace groups along these lines is being promoted actively by C.A.F.O.D., the official agency for overseas development of the Bishops' Conference of England and Wales, its Scottish counterpart, S.C.I.A.F., Pax Christi which promotes campaigns on a wide range of peace issues, and the Catholic Institute for International Relations, C.I.I.R., which is an independent Catholic research organisation working to promote a better understanding of justice and peace issues (Anon., 1984).

The justice and peace movement within the Catholic community is still very much in its infancy. Support for it is very patchy and not all dioceses have commissions which promote this work actively and with the encouragement of the bishop. However, the influence of the movement is to be seen in the increasing concern of the bishops with such issues as unemployment, the Nationality Act, the nuclear deterrent, and so on. At the national level, the massive and spontaneous support given to Mgr Bruce Kent, then Secretary of C.N.D., when he was publicly attacked by the Apostolic Delegate, and at the local level, the increasing references to issues of justice and peace in liturgies, for example in the bidding prayers at Mass might be noted. Particularly active in promoting reflections on more Christian life styles has been the Justice and Peace Commission in the Leeds diocese. More generally there is in the movement an attempt to relate Third World concerns with domestic issues, such as unemployment and racism, and the arms race.

In general terms the justice and peace activists attempt to relate injustices in three distinct areas in their critique of contemporary society:

    (a) relations with the Third World countries, frequently inspired by the radical reports of the Latin American bishops at Medellin (C.E.L.A.M., 1979) and Puebla (C.E.L.A.M., 1980) and their articulation of the 'preferential option for the poor';

    (b) domestic issues such as racism, unemployment, structural inequalities and inner-city decay (Smith, 1983; Tanner, 1980); and

(c) the issues of peace, defence and disarmament, inspired by the American bishops' peace pastoral (U.S. Catholic Conference, 1983; see also Ruston, 1981; Wicker, 1985).

The embryonic movement has drawn much of its ideological legitimation from the documents of the Vatican Council, particularly the Pastoral Constitution on the Church in the Modern World, *Gaudium et Spes* (Walsh and Davies, 1984: 77-140), and subsequent papal encyclicals. A frequently quoted teaching is the statement of the bishops at the 1971 Synod in Rome:

Action on behalf of justice and participation in the transformation of the world fully appear to us as a constitutive dimension of the preaching of the gospel, or, in other words, of the Church's mission for the redemption of the human race and its liberation from every oppressive situation (Walsh and Davies, 1984: 190).

There is evidence that the small number of justice and peace activists were disproportionately represented among the delegates to the N.P.C. But, given the historical legacy of substantial withdrawal from the political process and a pre-Vatican theology and spirituality which underemphasised this-worldly concerns, a considerable leeway remains to be made up. With the dissolving of the defensive walls around the fortress Church, radical Catholics may perhaps be less likely than in the past to seek to transform unjust social structures from a base within Catholic organisations such as Pax Christi or C.I.I.R. but may equally well do so from within C.N.D. or the World Development Movement. In any case it can safely be suggested that a growing minority of Catholics has been challenging the image of a 'domesticated denomination' and urging that the 'preferential option for the poor' be adopted in the praxis of the Church and not just in its rhetoric.

8.6 COMPARATIVE PERSPECTIVES

Before completing this discussion about English Catholics and politics, it is profitable to consider the matter from a comparative perspective. In his recent analysis of the political behaviour of Catholics in 13 Western democracies, John Whyte distinguishes between open and closed Catholicism (Whyte, 1981: 7-8). As an ideal type *open Catholicism* exists where there is no Catholic party, social organisations exist on a non-confessional basis and the clergy play no part in politics. He suggests that the period from the French Revolution to the First Vatican Council can be characterised as the beginning of closed Catholicism, from the First Vatican Council to the end of the First World War as the development of closed Catholicism with the subsequent period up to the Second Vatican Council as the peak period of closed Catholicism. During this period there was 'a revived readiness on the part of hierarchies to give guidance for their flocks in political matters'. In Britain, as in the United States and Australia, 'bishops made repeated complaints about the financial difficulties of Catholic schools' (ibid.: 97). While the direction of movement from open to closed Catholicism was the same in both continental Europe and the Anglo-American countries, it was much more vigorous in the former so that the gap between the two groups of countries reached its widest point by the early 1960s.

According to Whyte the period since the Second Vatican Council manifests the decay of *closed Catholicism*. In all countries there was a decline in the distinctiveness of Catholic social teaching, much questioning of the traditional policy on Catholic schools, an erosion of the demographic base of Mass-attending Catholics and their increasing social mobility. In Britain, as in the United States, the Association of Catholic Trade Unionists appeared to be moribund and in England the Catholic Social Guild was wound up (ibid.: 113). The similarities in the trends in different countries points to similarities in the nexus of forces generating them. In broad terms one might suggest a post-war striving for both individual freedom and more egalitarian societies, the spread of democratic participation into the previously sacred areas of industry, family, school and Church, the ending of the colonial period, the transformation of technologies and the revolution of rising expectations, the emergence of rapid global communications and the intrusion of television with its potential to challenge directly authority figures, and the growth of urbanism, together with the religious changes within the Church and legitimated by the Second Vatican Council, such as the stress on the People of God model, lay participation and collegiality, have all contributed to a general decline of closed Catholicism. As we have seen, this has resulted in an erosion of the distinctiveness of English Catholicism and a general convergence of their political attitudes and behaviour with those of the rest of the population.

On the basis of the evidence reviewed in this chapter it is concluded that there do not appear to be adequate structural or cultural bases in English Catholicism in the 1980s upon which a resurgence of a closed Catholicism might be built, no matter how much this might be urged by a strong pope and a centralist Roman bureaucracy.

CHAPTER 9

THE COMMUNAL INVOLVEMENT OF ENGLISH CATHOLICS

9.1 INTRODUCTION

The distinction between the associational involvement and the communal involvement of a Catholic derives ultimately from Tönnies' contrast between *Gesellschaft* (or Society, characterised by public impersonal forms of association) and *Gemeinschaft* (or Community, characterised by private, intimate social relationships) (Tönnies, 1957). In his study of socio-religious groups in Detroit, Lenski used the frequency of attendance at corporate worship services, for Catholics the Mass, to measure associational involvement, and marital endogamy and commensality, that is the restriction of friendships in the main to members of the same socio-religious group, as measures of communal involvement (Lenski, 1963: 23). The importance of Mass attendance was considered above in the development of a typology of English Catholics in chapter 3 and variations between marriage types were reported in chapter 5.

In table 9.1 a number of measures of the declining communal involvement of Catholics have been given. In the past half-century the proportion of Catholics in England and Wales appears to have grown from around 7% before the Second World War to around 11% now, as indicated by the Gallup omnibus survey in 1978. From the data reported in *Roman Catholic Opinion* (Hornsby-Smith and Lee, 1979) it appears that the proportion of Catholics marrying other Roman Catholics has declined from over 70% before the war to around 30% now. Comparing the estimates of different age cohorts there have been significant reductions in the proportions of Catholics

Table 9.1 *Estimates of communal involvement over time*

Indicator of involvement	Late 1930s	Late 1950s	Late 1970s
1 Proportion of Roman Catholics in England and Wales (p%).	7	10	11
2 Proportion of Roman Catholics marrying Roman Catholics (m%).	72	60	31
3 Proportion of valid marriages (v%).	85	80	68
4 Proportion of Roman Catholics with half or more friends Roman Catholic (f₁%).	59	48	39
5 Proportion of Roman Catholics with half or more friends Roman Catholic at 17 (f₂%).	68	37	35
6 Index of marital endogamy (m/p).	10	6	3
7 Index of current in-group friendship (f₁/p).	8	5	4
8 Index of early in-group friendship (f₂/p).	10	4	3

Source: Hornsby-Smith, 1983b.

Notes

1. Estimates of the proportion of Roman Catholics in England and Wales have been based on Currie, R., Gilbert, A., and Horsley, L. (1977), *Churches and Churchgoers: Patterns of Church Growth in the British Isles since 1700*. Oxford: Clarendon Press, pp. 153–5.
2. Estimates of communal involvement have been made from the analysis of age differences reported in Hornsby-Smith, M.P. and Lee, R.M. (1979) *Roman Catholic Opinion: A Study of Roman Catholics in England and Wales in the 1970s*. Guildford: University of Surrey. For Catholics marrying in the late 1930s the 65 and over cohort has been considered; for those marrying in the late 1950s the 35–49 year old cohort has been taken; for those marrying in the late 1970s the 15–29 year old cohort has been taken.

reporting that half or more of their friends were Roman Catholics both now and in retrospect when they were aged 17. From these figures three indices of communal involvement and identity have been calculated in terms of the actual choices and the distributions one might expect simply in terms of the proportion of Catholics in the population generally, that is on the basis of chance. All three indices have declined to between one-half and one-third of the pre-war estimates. This measures the extent to which Catholics have in the post-war years diffused throughout British society as a result of their increasing participation in the processes of social mobility facilitated by educational expansion and the general economic prosperity of three decades. At the same time, it is worth noting that Catholics are still something like three times as likely to choose Catholic friends and a Catholic marriage partner from their own community as one would expect from their concentration in the population generally.

In this chapter we will review the evidence from both the parishes study and the national survey on the communal involvement of Catholics at the end of the 1970s. In the first place the parish data showed that, not unexpectedly, the various indicators of communal involvement were all greater in the case of the activist leadership core groups when compared to Catholics generally. Evidence from the national survey will focus on the two main strategies of the Catholic subculture described by Coman (1977): the emphasis on the separate Catholic school system and the support for religious endogamy. Four types of communal involvement and three types of religious commitment will then be distinguished and their relationship to demographic and religious variables explored.

Finally, the chapter will conclude with some observations about the parish as a key social institution. In particular it will be argued that it is likely to have only limited success in generating community-like characteristics in a highly urban, industrial society characterised by high levels of both social and geographical mobility. For most Catholics the parish is unlikely to be a salient institution in relation to workplace, family and kin, and neighbourhood. Its quest for community, in the sense of high levels of social interaction, shared values and mutual aid, is unlikely to be achieved. The most that can be expected are a few *Gemeinschaft*-like oases among the small groups which periodically emerge within the Catholic community either at levels below that of the parish itself or increasingly extraparochially in interest groups such as the justice and peace movement.

9.2 EVIDENCE FROM FOUR PARISHES

In the surveys undertaken in four parishes in the mid-1970s, a number of measures of communal involvement were used (table 9.2). On all the measures available the parish activists scored more highly than Catholics generally. They were much more likely than Catholics generally to have married a Catholic spouse, all of them were actively involved in parish life compared to one-quarter of Catholics generally, they were twice as likely to regard religious endogamy as important and much more likely to stress the importance of the religious socialisation of children. On average the parish activists had lived in their present residence for a longer period of time. This might be thought to have increased their chances of involvement in parish activities and social interaction.

Table 9.2 *Selected measures of communal involvement (Four parishes, weighted averages %)*

Characteristic	R.C. activists	R.C. electors	Other electors
Spouse R.C.	90	61	8
Active participation	100	26	16
Marriage within religion very or fairly important	81	42	39
Upbringing of children in same religion very or fairly important	98	75	60
Residence: 15 years and over	46	28	32
Maximum number of respondents	84	267	1,189
Estimated population weights	84	7,991	40,168

Source: Hornsby-Smith, 1978c.

The non-Catholic electors generally scored lower than the Catholic electors on the various measures though they had similar residential patterns and, in the case of religious intermarriage, their stress on its importance did not differ markedly from that of Catholics generally.

9.3 THE NATIONAL SURVEY

It has been pointed out that historically, in England and Wales until recently, Catholics have been a small minority subject to considerable amounts of hostility. The fight against the legal disadvantages and official discrimination was long, slow and not infrequently painful. Not surprisingly, Catholics reacted defensively to maintain their hard-won social position in British society and to preserve and transmit to the next generation their religious heritage. These goals were promoted by maintaining a siege mentality and defending the fortress Church from any dangerous contact with outsiders who might seduce Catholics away from their own precious heritage. Thus the tremendous stress on two strategies in particular:

(a) *Separate Catholic schools*: the provision of an all-embracing Catholic ethos for the religious socialisation of Catholic children and the insistence on their education only in Catholic schools staffed by Catholic teachers; and

(b) *Religious endogamy*: the insistence, buttressed by imposing religious and social sanctions, on marriage to another Catholic, encouraged and facilitated by a wide range of social and religious obligations which effectively ensured that Catholics normally only met other Catholics in their non-work hours, typically in parish-based activities.

In this section we will consider some evidence relating to the communal involvement of English Catholics which can be extracted from the 1978 national survey. Some relevant data on intermarriage patterns have been considered above in section 5.3. It must be remembered that the national survey was not specifically designed to explore in great detail the nature of interaction between Catholics at the parish level, at work, in leisure activities, and so on. All the same, there is much that can be gleaned from this source. We will consider the findings on such matters as the respondents' membership of parish organisations and their assessment of the number of activities in their parishes; their stress on a separate Catholic school system; the proportion of their friends who were Catholics both at the age of 17, that is in the key adolescent years when friendship choices were likely to determine whether or not they would marry a fellow Catholic, and now; the religious identification of their spouse; their attachment to their local parish and their evaluation of their priests on different aspects of their work; and their involvement with a variety of small-group activities.

In *Roman Catholic Opinion* a review of the evidence relating to members of Catholic parish organisations was given (Hornsby-Smith and Lee, 1979: 45–51, 188–91). Briefly about one in eight of all Catholic adults claimed to be a member of a parish organisation. Excluding those who have very tenuous links with any parish the proportion rose to just under one-fifth. Of these the majority were also involved in a range of other organisations such as political parties or trade unions. Members of parish organisations were disproportionately female, over the age of 35, married or widowed, converts, middle class, and Conservative voters. They were more likely than Catholics generally to rate their priests favourably and this was particularly true of office holders. They were also likely to be traditionalist in the sense that disproportionately they thought there had been too many changes since the Second Vatican Council.

Of those Catholics with some contact with their parish, about one-third reported that their parish had a lot of activities, just under one-half that it had a few, and one-fifth almost none. Activities reported most frequently were social or sporting activities; this was followed by fund raising and women's organisations. Prayer groups or parish council work were mentioned by only 1% of Catholics.

Clearly one factor which affects the involvement of people in parish life is the length of time they have lived in the parish. It is well known that there is a considerable amount of mobility in contemporary Britain. This is reflected in the length of time our respondents had lived in their present house. Nearly one-quarter had only been in their present house for two years or less and two-fifths for five years or less. Two-fifths had lived in their present house for 10 years or more, one-fifth for 15 years or more and only one in ten had lived there more than 20 years. The length of time in their present home has been taken to reflect reasonably accurately the length of time lived in the parish. In Fichter's study of southern parishes in the United States it was reported that only 23% of moves were either into or out of the parishes studied (Fichter, 1954: 97) but it is unlikely that this short-distance mobility is so significant in this country.

The evidence from the national survey indicated that while there was a positive relationship between attendance at Catholic schools and adult religious behaviour and attitudes, the effect was really rather small and was dwarfed by the significance of the religious characteristics of the parental home and of the spouse (Hornsby-Smith and Lee, 1979: 76–105, 212–31). The ambivalence of Catholics on the question of separate Catholic schools was reported in *Roman Catholic Opinion*. Briefly, Catholics largely wished to send their own children to Catholic schools and reported favourably both on their own experiences and those of their children in Catholic schools. At the same time only two-fifths favoured a separate Catholic school system compared with nearly one-half who disagreed with the 'dual' system. Without longitudinal data it is difficult to ascertain whether or not Catholics are less inclined than in the past to defend the principle of 'a Catholic school with Catholic teachers for every Catholic child'. What the survey showed clearly, however, was a strong age gradient in the support. Broadly speaking only one-quarter of those born in the post-war period favoured separate Catholic schools compared to three-fifths of those born before the 1930s. It is also interesting to note that the support was also weakest among those most likely to have benefited from the massive expansion of educational opportunities in the post-war period, a point which Joan Brothers first addressed in the early 1960s (Brothers,

1964). Thus only 29% of upper-middle-class respondents supported Catholic schools compared to 43% of the lower working class. It seemed, therefore, that the traditional securities of the Catholic school were most attractive to those whose social and economic lives were often least secure.

Given the very significant social changes which have taken place in British society over the past 30 years, the extent to which Catholics continue to maintain close friendships primarily within their own religious community remains high. Although Catholics in England and Wales comprise only about 11% of the total population, three-fifths of the Catholic adult respondents who were surveyed in 1978 reported that when they were 17 years old half or more of their friends were Catholics; the corresponding proportion now was 45%. As one might expect, younger Catholics were less likely to find most of their friends from within the Catholic community; for example whereas the proportion of the under 35s with half or more of their friends Catholic was between one-third and two-fifths, it was between one-half and three-fifths in the case of the over 50s. There was also a slight social-class gradient; two-fifths of the upper middle class compared with one-half of the lower working class found most of their friends from within the Catholic community – probably a reflection of their greater social and geographical mobility. There was a strong relationship between the proportion of Catholic friends and attachment to the parish though it is not clear whether the fact of having a large number of Catholic friends led to a strong attachment to the parish or whether an attractive parish led to an increase in the number of Catholic friendships.

On the question of Catholic marriage it was reported above in chapter 5 that whereas for Catholic marriages before 1960 about one in nine was invalid, in the sense of not having been solemnised before a priest, and about one-third of Catholics were married to a non-Catholic partner, in the 1970s nearly two-fifths of Catholics married invalidly and two-thirds married non-Catholics. These figures are indicative of the dissolution of the boundaries surrounding the Catholic community in England and Wales and the collapse or ending of the defensive strategies which had previously sustained the Catholic community in this country since the Reformation. All the same, as was indicated in table 9.1, Catholics are still three times more likely to marry other Catholics than they would be on the assumption of no association between the religious identifications of husbands and wives. It remains to be seen what evidence there is for the maintenance of any sort of Catholic 'community' in the sense of shared values, beliefs and behaviour, of strong face-to-face inter-action, of mutual support and encouragement, and so on.

Given the amount of social and geographical mobility in British society the level of attachment to their parish by our respondents was impressive. They were asked: 'Supposing you had to move to another part of the country. How sorry would you be to leave the parish?' Four alternative responses were given, ranging from 'very sorry' to 'not at all sorry'. Overall two-fifths of those of our respondents who attended church said they would be very sorry to leave their parish. There was a strong age gradient, one-fifth of the under 30s compared to three-fifths of the over 50s would be very sorry to leave. This largely reflects the length of time lived in their present house. Similarly, the married, particularly housewives, and working-class Catholics express stronger than average attachment to their parish.

Catholics were asked a battery of 11 questions about the way they rate their parish clergy. Two of these questions are relevant for our present purposes: 'the way in general that they do their job' and 'the amount of visiting they do to parishioners in their own homes'. Respondents were asked to rate their priests on four-point scales from 'excellent' to 'poor'. Overall priests were rated 'excellent' on the way they do their job by one-third of Catholics who answered. Just over one-half rated them 'excellent' or 'good' on their visiting. On both questions there was again a strong age gradient, older Catholics being twice as likely as younger Catholics to rate the priests highly. Again, married Catholics, especially housewives (who may be the group with the time and opportunity to participate more in parish activities and have greater direct contact with priests), were more favourable in their ratings than average, though in this case there were few social-class gradients. Again there was a strong relationship between the evaluation of the priest and the attachment to the parish, though the nature and direction of the relationship remains unclear.

Another measure of the strength of communal ties in the Catholic parish is the frequency of serious interaction between priests, as the religious leaders of the community, and their parishioners. Catholics were asked whether they had 'had a serious discussion with a priest about religious problems' within the last two years. Overall, just over one-quarter replied that they had. There were the expected age and social-class gradients and signs of a relative loss of contact, or weaker communal ties, with the younger Catholics and with the working class (Hornsby-Smith and Lee, 1979: 203).

Finally, Catholics were asked about their participation (within the previous two years) in a number of activities which reflected new styles of activism in the Church: going to a charismatic or pentecostal prayer meeting (6%), attending a house Mass (17%), attending a religious discussion group (17%), attending an ecumenical service (13%), and attending some other small group of a religious nature (19%). On all these measures there were the expected age and social-class gradients though, in general, the sex differences were not significant.

9.4 TYPES OF COMMUNAL INVOLVEMENT

In order to explore the nature of communal involvement further, four types have been distinguished in terms of the two dimensions: personal involvement or the density of Catholic friendships and institutional vitality or the level of parish activities (figure 9.1). Two scales to measure these dimensions, CATHFNDS and ACTIVPAR, were constructed in the following way:

CATHFNDS: one point was scored if half or more of the respondent's friends were Roman Catholics both at the age of 17, regarded as a key formative age prior to marriage, and at the time of the survey. A score of 0 or 1 was regarded as low and 2 as high.

ACTIVPAR: one point was scored for each of the following: if the respondent reported a lot of activities in the parish; very sorry to leave the parish; the priests in the parish in general do their job excellently; the amount of parish visiting is excellent or good. A score of 0 or 1 was regarded as low and 2 or more as high.

When the two scales were dichotomised as indicated, four types of communal involvement were distinguished.

| | | Institutional vitality (Level of Parish Activities) ACTIVPAR | |
		Low	High
Personal involvement (Proportion of Catholic friends)	High	Individual	Total
CATHFNDS	Low	Detached	Marginal

Fig. 9.1 A typology of communal involvement (CMSCAL)

Table 9.3 *Communal involvement by age, social class, sex, immigrant generation and type of Catholic (%)*

Characteristic	COMMUNAL INVOLVEMENT				N = 100%
	Detached	Individual	Marginal	Total	
Personal involvement	Low	High	Low	High	
Institutional vitality	Low	Low	High	High	
Age:					
15–24	56	28	9	8	188
25–34	60	17	17	6	249
35–49	49	18	20	13	295
50–64	36	18	25	22	190
65+	30	12	29	29	113
Social class:					
AB	48	19	22	11	112
CI	55	14	19	12	224
C2	48	18	20	14	345
DE	45	21	18	16	355
Sex:					
Male	49	20	17	14	451
Female, housewife	48	15	22	15	525
Female, other	48	35	12	6	60
Irish generation:					
First gen. Irish	35	23	19	24	151
Second gen. Irish	46	19	21	14	158
Not Irish	53	17	20	11	658
Type of Catholic[a]:					
Involved traditionalists (A)	11	10	41	38	26
Involved non-traditionalists (B)	16	19	36	29	67
Non-involved traditionalists (C)	19	21	35	25	61
Orthodox attenders (D)	34	20	23	22	163
Heterodox attenders (E)	48	25	11	17	54
Orthodox non-attenders (F+H)	64	15	15	6	88
Heterodox non-attenders (G+J)	73	20	5	2	220
Non-identifiers	94	6	0	0	25
All	49	19	19	14	1036

Source: National Survey, 1978.
[a] The types of Catholics were those derived in Hornsby-Smith, Lee and Turcan (1982). Non-attenders include irregular attenders, i.e. all who do not attend weekly or more frequently.

Table 9.3 indicates that about one-half of the sample of adult Roman Catholics surveyed in 1978 had a low personal involvement and were in an inactive parish. Approximately one-fifth of Catholics reported a high personal involvement but low parish activism and a further one-fifth reported that although their personal involvement was low, they lived in an active parish. About one Catholic in seven, using our measures, reported a total communal involvement in the sense that they had both a high personal involvement score and lived in an active parish. The table also reports the distributions of these four types of communal involvement by a number of demographic variables and by the type of Catholic. Thus younger Catholics were much more likely to have a detached, and to a lesser extent an individual involvement than older Catholics who more frequently reported a marginal or total involvement.

On the whole, social-class differences were relatively slight though there was a tendency for the lower working class to report a total involvement to a greater extent than other classes and for the lower middle class (c1) to report a detached rather than an individual type of involvement. The biggest sex differences in fact were those between housewives and other females and it may be that this is an important distinction, relevant for the consideration of parish activities and interaction which has not been given sufficient attention in the sociology of the parish. It is significant that well over one-third of housewives reported an active parish, that is a total or a marginal form of involvement, twice the proportion of other females (two-thirds of whom were under 21) who were twice as likely to report an individual type of communal involvement.

When the figures were considered in greater detail some interesting variations emerged. There were differences in the patterns reported for personal involvement (in terms of the density of Catholic friendships) and institutional vitality (in terms of parish activity levels). Whereas there seemed to be a sharp rise in the level of Catholic friendships among the over 50s, the pre-war generation, reported institutional vitality varied steadily with age cohort. The parish activity levels did not vary by social class but the personal friendships level was lower for the lower middle class than all other classes. Housewives reported the lowest level of Catholic friendships but also the highest level of parish activities. It could be that they perceived their parishes as being active but remote so that their own friendships were not especially found with other Catholics. Both personal involvement and institutional vitality were significantly related to the Irish immigrant generation and the convergence with the levels of the non-Irish by the second generation supported arguments about the processes of assimilation discussed in chapter 6 above. Variations of personal involvement appeared to depend chiefly upon the level of practice. Mass attenders, whether they held orthodox or heterodox beliefs and whether or not they were members of parish organisations, had high levels of Catholic friendships. On the other hand, there was a steady decline in the reported level of institutional vitality as one moved from type A Catholics (the involved traditionalists) to the non-identifiers.

In further analyses by country of birth a number of interesting differences emerged. Irish Catholics from both the Irish Republic and Northern Ireland reported the highest levels of total involvement of any immigrant group. On the other hand, the Catholics from western Europe (Italy, Spain, etc.) reported an active parish life less frequently than any other group; they also had the largest proportion with a detached communal involvement. By contrast, those from eastern Europe (for example, the Poles) had a relatively tiny proportion reporting a detached form of communal involvement but a proportion of those with an individual form of involvement which was well over twice the average for all Catholics. In all probability this indicated the importance of close kinship and friendship ties, especially for those who were first-generation immigrants in a society very different from their country of birth. It might be anticipated that the second-generation Catholics from eastern Europe would converge more to the norms for England and Wales. Such a process of assimilation could clearly be seen in the case of Irish Catholics. Over two generations the proportion of those with a detached involvement increased at the expense of those with a total involvement. As might have been expected, converts generally scored low on the scale of Catholic friendships and hence were underrepresented in the individual and total cells; the proportion of converts with a marginal involvement was twice that for Catholics generally.

Those with a *total* communal involvement were most likely to stress the importance of the Sunday Mass obligation, praying regularly and receiving the sacraments, marriage in a Catholic Church, sending their children to Catholic schools, an active concern for others, and obeying the teaching of the Church. In contrast, those with a *detached* form of involvement were least likely to stress these characteristics but were most critical of some aspects of Catholic schools such as their academic standards. They were also most likely to complain that Catholic schools made parents feel like intruders and to urge sex education in the curriculum. It might also be noted that it was those with a *marginal* involvement, and not those with a total involvement, who stressed most strongly the importance of being politically aware and active.

Finally, in table 9.4 a number of demographic and religious characteristics of those Catholics with the four types of communal involvement have been summarised. There is a consistent age gradient between the four types with half of those who reported a detached or individual involvement being under 35. On the other hand, those with a detached or marginal involvement and a low density of Catholic friendships included a higher than average proportion of middle-class Catholics. It can be seen that on the measures of associational involvement (Mass-attendance fre-

Table 9.4 *Selected demographic and religious variables by type of communal involvement (%)*

Variable	Detached	Individual	Marginal	Total	All
Demographic attributes					
Age (% under 35)	51	49	30	21	42
Social class (% ABC1)	35	28	34	27	32
Sex (% male)	44	47	39	43	44
Spouse (% R.C.)	42	66	64	78	55
Marriage Type (% valid)	69	84	88	93	79
Religious attributes					
Mass freq.					
(% weekly or more)	22	42	55	64	38
Doctrinal orthodoxy (%4)	38	48	69	76	52
Sexual orthodoxy					
(% 1 or more)	28	48	59	72	43
Member of parish org. (%)	5	10	26	27	13
Evaluation of priests					
(% 6 or more)	1	3	51	49	18
New style activism					
(% 2 or more)	12	20	33	26	20
Favours political involvement					
of Church (% agree)	41	37	36	30	38
N = 100% (max)	502	192	199	143	1,036

Source: National Survey, 1978.

quency), doctrinal and sexual orthodoxy, and measures of communal involvement (a Catholic spouse and canonically valid marriage), there was a clear progression from those with a detached, though an individual and marginal involvement, to a total involvement.

Those who reported a high level of parish activity, that is a marginal or total involvement, were twice as likely as the average Catholic to be members of parish organisations, very much more likely to evaluate their priests highly and more likely to report new styles of religious activism. On the other hand, it was those who reported a total communal involvement who were least likely to endorse the view that 'the Church should take active steps to promote social justice even if it means getting involved in politics'. The fact that it was those with a detached involvement who most strongly supported such a view suggests the possibility that in spite of the recent rhetoric about striving for social justice (Walsh and Davies, 1984), in practice parochial life is commonly organised in such a way that the goals for social justice may be largely ignored for the more immediate rewards of interpersonal relationships within the parish and that those most concerned to promote such goals were either driven to the periphery of the institutional Church or sought to achieve them primarily outside it.

This review of the differences between the four types of communal involvement indicated that both dimensions: Catholic friendship density and parish activism, were of importance to a wide range of religious attitudes, beliefs and practices in the Church in England and Wales today. In other words, increasing both the density of Catholic friendships and the perceived number of activities in the local parish were likely to increase the various measures of religious life of Catholics. Of the two dimensions, that of the activism of the local parish seems to be the more important. This suggests that there are good reasons for attempting the reform of parish life in this country. It is true that we have no *direct* measures of parish activity levels but only the perceptions of our respondents. All the same, it is a sociological truism that, as W.I. Thomas indicated: 'if men define situations as real they are real in their consequences'. Hence it seems important to change people's 'definitions of the situation' in their parishes. It is easier, in principle, to modify the parish activism variable since the density of Catholic friendships is likely to be dependent in part on the level of parish activities and interaction, but also to be limited by the broad patterns of social and geographical

mobility which Catholics increasingly experience as they assimilate
more and more successfully to British society.

What remains to be explored is the distinction between involvement within Catholic institutional life, parish, schools, friendships,
marital partners, and so on, and Catholic involvement in the political
and social life of the nation, in a critical way but supported by a
renewed local, small-group and parish communal life. It seems that
at the moment there are two tendencies which appear likely to
weaken such a radical and critical involvement in the life of British
society; one tendency is for Catholic institutional life to deteriorate so
that a detached communal involvement is the major outcome; the
other tendency is for active Catholics to develop an uncritical, total
communal involvement which provides high levels of affective
rewards and interpersonal bonds (Stark and Bainbridge, 1980b), but
in a way which consumes all their interests and energies so that their
critical contribution to the life of the nation is negligible by default. In
these circumstances the institutional church will have become what
Coser has called a 'greedy institution' (1974).

9.5 TYPES OF RELIGIOUS COMMITMENT

In his book *Homo Religiosus*, Towler has distinguished three distinct
types of religious commitment to a socio-religious community: local,
where the salient context is the parish or neighbourhood; party,
where the salient ethos is that of the particular denomination; and
pragmatic, characterised by detachment and non-involvement
(Towler, 1974: 166–71). In an attempt to complete an analysis of the
communal involvement of English Catholics, these three types of
commitment (TOWL) were operationalised in the following way:

A *party* or denominational commitment was defined as having an
exclusive unity (UTY) orientation (see above, pp. 104–6) but
without being strongly attached to their parish (i.e. not very sorry
if they had to leave it).

A *local* commitment was expressed by respondents who stressed
the salience of local 'roots' in response to a question asking why
they would not want to leave their parish.

A *pragmatic* commitment was expressed by those respondents for
whom Christian Unity was 'unimportant' or 'didn't matter'.

Although under two-fifths of the respondents could be classified in
this way it is suggested that the findings are of interest and that
further empirical work designed at the outset to explore the nature of

Table 9.5 *Selected demographic and religious variables by type of religious commitment (%)*

| Variable | Type of religious commitment | | | |
	Party	Local	Pragmatic	All
Age: 15–29	20	11	40	29
30–34	10	11	19	13
35–49	32	28	25	29
50+	37	50	16	29
S.E.S.: ABC1	35	27	32	32
Sex: Male	48	39	58	44
Irish:				
first generation	25	12	6	16
second generation	20	20	18	16
Marriage type:				
BC	14	18	6	9
CB	5	13	9	9
BB	42	35	39	36
VM	25	25	18	24
IM	7	3	25	17
Mass Freq. (% Weekly or More)	54	64	19	38
Doctrinal Orthodoxy (% 4)	81	70	29	52
Sexual Orthodoxy (% 2 or 3)	34	42	15	19
Member of Parish Org. (%)	14	23	4	13
Evaluation of Priests:				
(% 6 or more)	22	33	11	18
New Style Activism:				
(% 2 or more)	27	27	9	20
Proportion of Cath. Friends:				
(% half or more)	55	63	40	45
New-style Ministries:				
(% 2 or more)	16	27	33	38
Attended Ecum. Service in				
past 2 years.	19	23	5	14
N = 100% (max.)	115	134	132	1,036

Source: National Survey, 1978.

the religious commitment of Catholics would be well worthwhile. As it is we are limited by the data from the national survey which was not designed specifically for this purpose.

In table 9.5 a number of demographic and religious attributes of Catholics with the three types of commitment have been summarised. Catholics with a *party* commitment were chiefly distinguished by having a higher proportion of both first- and second-generation Irish than English Catholics generally. Associated with this was a relatively low proportion in invalid marriages. They reported higher than average levels of religious practice and both doctrinal and sexual orthodoxy. On the other hand, they had higher than average scores on the scale of new styles of activism in the Church though they were the most traditional group in their resistance to new types of ministry such as married or women priests.

Half of those Catholics with a *local* commitment were aged 50 or over, much above the average. They were disproportionately women and working class with a high proportion of second-generation Irish and a much higher than average proportion of convert marriages (both BC and CB), and a very small proportion in invalid marriages. They had the highest proportions of regular Mass attenders, the sexually orthodox, members of parish organisations and those with a high density of Catholic friendships. They rated their priests more highly than the other categories and were high scorers on both the new-style activism and new ministries scales. They had attended ecumenical services more than the other categories.

Those with a *pragmatic* commitment were disproportionately young and male. Few of them were first-generation Irish and as many as one-quarter were in invalid marriages. They scored lowest of the three categories on all the religious variables except that of new-style ministries where they were much more prepared to innovate than the other two categories. Interestingly they also had low scores on new styles of activism and attendance at ecumenical services. This suggests that their attachment to institutional religion generally was weak.

In table 9.6 the relationship between communal involvement, religious commitment and unity orientation has been given. Whereas three-fifths of those with a party or local commitment were orthodox attenders, three-fifths of those with a pragmatic commitment were non-practising. Nearly half of those with a party commitment were non-involved orthodox attenders which seemed to be related to the

Table 9.6 *Type of Catholic, communal involvement and unity orientation by type of religious commitment (%)*

	Type of religious commitment			
Variable	Party	Local	Pragmatic	All
Type of Catholic				
Involved Orthodox Attenders (% A and B)	13	20	3	10
Non-Involved Orthodox Attenders (% C and D)	47	41	13	23
Irregular Attenders (% F and G)	24	24	21	26
Non-Practising (% H and J plus Non-Ident.)	15	8	60	35
Communal involvement				
Detached	45	22	63	49
Individual	27	13	19	19
Marginal	16	36	11	19
Total	12	29	6	14
Unity orientation				
Ambivalent	0	27	45	33
Inclusive	0	19	33	32
Exclusive	100[a]	38	14	23
Invitational	0	16	8	11
N = 100%	115	134	132	1036

[a] By definition.
Source: National Survey, 1978.

fact that a much higher proportion of them reported an individual form of communal involvement than in the other two groups. Two-thirds of those with a local commitment reported high levels of parish activities and hence proportions of those with marginal or total communal involvement twice that for Catholics generally. Their unity orientations were disproportionately exclusive and invitational, that is they placed a high emphasis on the papacy. Nearly two-thirds of the pragmatic Catholics had a detached communal involvement and nearly half of them expressed an ambivalent orientation towards Christian Unity. This appeared to confirm the earlier impression that their attachment to institutional religion in all its forms was generally weak and unconcerned.

9.6 THE PARISH AND ITS QUEST FOR COMMUNITY

So far in this chapter we have reviewed some empirical data relevant for the consideration of the nature of the communal involvement and religious commitment of English Catholics. In the years since the Second Vatican Council there has been a significant reduction in the levels of suspicion and antagonism between the different religious traditions and a decided dismantling of the boundaries previously erected to insulate Catholics from non-Catholics. Apart from the changing religious climate we have also noted that socio-economic changes have contributed to greater mobility, both social and geographical, among Catholics. Inevitably, therefore, the Catholic parish as a major institution has had to adjust to a totally new social context over the past three or four decades. Whereas in the pre-war years the parish frequently provided an all-embracing or total environment for the religious socialisation of its members, with religious, educational, social welfare and entertainment functions for all circumstances and needs, in the post-war years with the provision of secondary education for all, the development of the Welfare State, the improvements in home circumstances, the ubiquity of television viewing and the growth of mass, urban leisure industries focussed particularly on the teenage consumer, many of these functions have been irretrievably lost. In these circumstances the quest of the parish for 'community' has become much more problematic.

In this final section of this chapter a few general observations will be offered on this quest. There are few words more highly prized among Catholics than 'community'. References to the 'parish community' abound. In Butterworth and Weir's well-known phrase: it is a 'God-word' before which we abase ourselves. It is one task of the sociologist to demythologise. If essential characteristics of 'community' include shared core values, close face-to-face social interaction, and mutual aid and support, then any empirical study of the typical Catholic parish will indicate unambiguously the absence of community in this sense. The most that can be claimed is that there is in many parishes a serious attempt to develop community-like characteristics. It is important, however, to distinguish the rhetoric of community from the reality in most parishes. Given the reality of the social pressures in a highly urbanised, modern, industrial, mobile, cosmopolitan society such as ours, it might realistically be suggested that attempts to create community-like characteristics in parishes are inevitably doomed to failure. At the very least it is necessary to recognise the reality of the constraints on them including the declining salience of the parish for Catholics in the post-war years.

Something of the flavour of the unrealistic expectations of the parish have been well summarised by Denys Turner commenting on the preparatory work for the N.P.C. which showed

a very widespread desire that the parish should become something more like a 'real community'. Indeed ... quite unrealistic demands were made upon the parish to be, simultaneously, a liturgical community capable of satisfying the varied liturgical tastes of all its members, a community capable of sustaining all its marriages, a community capable of transcending the class and racial cleavages of society, a community which takes up the burdens of unemployment, handicap, loneliness and sickness of its members. (Turner, 1983)

Turner goes on to warn against a 'warm, comforting, supportive and yet utterly *self-centred* community' and 'a tendency to merely ecclesial communitarianism in our Church today', with 'abstract gestures' towards the injustices in the world in the bidding prayers and in mere posturing.

Similarly, Fr Austin Smith in his *Passion For the Inner-City* has insisted that the inner-city parish must be open and responsive to the needs of the poor, deprived and oppressed in our own society. He has observed that

The Christian Church has named itself a community; this was a key notion in the attempts of Vatican II to rewrite theology. If this is true one cannot simply accept certain inherited structures and shape them more to the pattern of authentic community. The parish is a perfect example of this. Can the sociological unit of the parish, as we know it today, ever project the ideal of community? It cannot if one simply takes the parish and renames it a community. One must ask many questions about 'the people' and of 'the people'. If it is really to respond to the definition of community then there must be a sense of shared power over destiny. If this is so then the word of the few must carry as much weight as the word of the pulpit. Both words must be brought together to search for the Word of God in life. (Smith, 1983: 114)

These remarks are not intended to decry the sometimes valiant attempts to create *Gemeinschaft*-like characteristics in an overwhelmingly *Gesellschaft*-like context (see, e.g. Lovell and Widdicombe, 1978: 76–90; O'Sullivan, 1979). It is, however, to suggest that the cosy model of the largely Irish parish in Liverpool in the late 1950s (Ward,

1961) cannot be regarded as the norm in England and Wales today. In the past three or four decades there have been major transformations in contemporary Roman Catholicism, as a case study of a parish outside Liverpool in the 1970s indicated (Koopmanschap, 1978). The parish remains the major social institution in the Church but it cannot carry the load expected of it in the modern world. There are limits to its community-building potential. Urging *The Liberation of the Church* from the parochialism which imprisons it within territorial boundaries, David Clark has argued that 'if the Church is to be genuinely engaged with a secular world it must come to terms with the fact that the importance of community of place is now more than equalled by that of community of concern' (Clark, 1984: 35).

Some see the quest for community as being met largely through 'basic Christian communities' (Clark, 1984; Winter, 1973, 1979, 1985). Whatever the outcome, it is clear from the evidence presented in this chapter that the achievement of high levels of communal involvement by its members is becoming increasingly problematic at a time of rapid social change and this raises further questions about the salience of institutional religion generally in a secular, urban, industrial society.

CHAPTER 10

THE DISSOLUTION OF THE ENGLISH CATHOLIC SUBCULTURE

———— ⚜ ————

10.1 INTRODUCTION

In this final chapter we will attempt to summarise the findings from the various empirical studies reviewed in this present work and interpret them in the light of post-war social change and the global developments which have been taking place in the Roman Catholic Church since the Second Vatican Council. In this book three levels of reporting have been considered:

(a) *Description*: The first purpose has been simply descriptive, to provide a factual basis to replace hunches and unsubstantiated assertions about English Catholics and so contribute to the understanding of the current state of the Roman Catholic Church in England and Wales. At the end of the 1970s Roman Catholics comprised over one-half of the adult members of the Christian Churches and one-third of adult church attenders in England. There were more Catholics at Mass on Sunday than attenders at the established Church of England (Anon., 1980a: 23). It is claimed that the data presented in this study provide the best empirical basis so far available for the understanding of the English Catholics in the last quarter of the twentieth century.

(b) *Hypothesis testing*: The second purpose of this present study was to test a number of hypotheses about English Catholics formulated at the outset. In particular it was hypothesised that English Catholics were disproportionately immigrant (particularly Irish) and working class in their social origins and that in the post-war years, with the expansion of educational opportunities and the economic boom of the 1950s and 1960s, they experienced a social 'mobility momentum' and a convergence in occupational distribution with that of the population generally. It was also hypothesised that with the upward social mobility of Catholics, traditional relationships between lay people and the parochial clergy would be transformed. This study has provided the necessary data base for the testing of hypotheses such as these.

(c) *Theory construction*: A third and much more ambitious purpose might have been to contribute to the body of sociological theory for the understanding of social change. For example, English Catholics might have been regarded as a suitable test case for theories of secularisation. Could one identify a distinctive 'Catholic ethic' to contrast with Weber's classic analysis of the 'Protestant ethic' and, if so, what are its social correlates and implications for economic relations? Could one develop a comprehensive theory of the relationships between religion and politics? While it must be admitted that in the absence of Weberian insights these purposes were not primary at the outset of the research reported here, nevertheless it seems possible that there exists in the empirical findings outlined, the basis for further theoretical development.

Three main themes in particular will be suggested in this concluding chapter. First, it will be suggested that all the evidence reviewed in this book points to the conclusion that in the post-war years there has been a dissolution of the boundaries which previously protected the fortress Church with its distinctive English Catholic subculture. Secondly, it will be argued that while English Catholics have experienced in some measure a process of socio-economic embourgeoisement during this period, it can be interpreted best in terms of normative convergence in a secular society rather than as a process of protestantisation. Thirdly it will be concluded that in general terms, English Catholicism can be regarded as a 'domesticated denomination' even though, as with the other Christian Churches in Britain today, it contains a number of significant prophetic groups.

10.2 SUMMARY OF FINDINGS

The hunches and hypotheses with which the present research programme was undertaken were outlined in chapter 1. Chief among these was the examination of the social mobility experiences of Catholics (largely working class, many with recent Irish ancestry, living primarily in inner-city parishes often with co-cultural priests) as a consequence of the large expansion of educational opportunities. A second consideration was the implications of such social changes, and also the religious changes legitimated by the Second Vatican Council, on the community life of Catholics, particularly at the parish level, and especially the transformations anticipated as a consequence of these changes in the authority relationships between priests and lay people. Thirdly, an examination of the model of the monolithic, hierarchically organised Church, homogeneous in its beliefs and practices and rigidly disciplined to a tight conformity by a dominant priesthood, with powerful religious and social sanctions at its disposal, in a distinctive Catholic subculture, was to be undertaken. Among other related points it was proposed to investigate was the relative weakness, given its size and resources, of the Catholic contribution to political decision-making in British society.

A review of the historical roots of contemporary English Catholicism suggested that there never has been a golden age when Catholics were united, conflict-free, and substantially coerced or socialised into a uniformity of conforming practice and belief by a dominant clergy. Consequently great care had to be taken in drawing inferences about institutional decline on the basis of the cross-sectional data of recent research in the 1970s and 1980s. Trend data, for example of Mass attendance rates in the century since the restoration of the hierarchy, were not reliable or comprehensive. Furthermore, it could be argued that there had been shifts in the selection of the criteria of religious adherence and commitment regarded as relevant in recent years. Theories of secularisation were therefore difficult to substantiate because of the problematic nature of the relevant criteria for the measurement of the 'religious' and as a result of the changes in the meaning and significance of traditional practices which appeared to have taken place over the past two decades.

A comparison of the social and demographic characteristics of English Catholics with those of the population as a whole shows that they continue to bear many of the marks of an immigrant community. Indeed, one-quarter of them were first-generation immigrants, six times the proportion in the rest of the population. They are younger and have lower socio-economic status characteristics than the population generally. This is reflected in their lower levels of home ownership and their much greater propensity to vote Labour. On the other hand, it has been suggested that, given the low social origins of the millions of mainly Catholic Irish immigrants to this country over the past century and a half, the current socio-economic position of English Catholics represents a success story of upward social mobility with a substantial convergence towards the occupational distribution of British society. One measure of this was the relatively high proportion of Catholics who had had some form of further or higher education. Another indicator of their socio-economic achievements is the extent to which they have moved out of the inner-city parishes and into the new suburban estates, and also a general redistribution of the Catholic population so that whereas at the time of the restoration of the hierarchy Catholics were significantly concentrated in the North-West, now two fifths are to be found in the London and South-East Region.

However, in spite of the apparent socio-economic convergence of Catholics and the population generally, in the only research where we had directly comparable data on the social mobility experiences of Catholics and other people living in the same area, that is in our four parishes study, there was no support for a mobility momentum thesis. In none of the four parishes did the differences in social mobility experiences between Catholic electors and other electors reach the level of statistical significance. Indeed the data suggested that fewer Catholics were upwardly mobile and more were downwardly mobile than in the rest of the population in the two London and two Preston parishes considered. Similarly, the mean mobility movement for Catholic men from the national survey was about one-half that for men generally, as judged from the Oxford Mobility Study data. However, the picture looked rather different when account was taken of the immigrant origins of many Catholics. Thus Catholic men who had been born in Great Britain had mobility experiences comparable to those of men generally. It seemed, though, that immigrant Catholics were much less likely to have experienced upward social mobility. Somewhat contrary to our original expectations, however, social and geographical mobility experiences had a relatively limited effect on the wide range of religious variables considered.

Since the immigration of Irish Catholics has played such an important part in the growth and development of English Catholicism, the process of their assimilation in England and Wales was given particular attention. Data from the G.H.S. were used to explore patterns of occupational achievement over two generations, considering migrants from the Irish Republic and Northern Ireland and men and women separately. The evidence suggested that there were few barriers to occupational achievement for Irish immigrants to England and that there was a substantial measure of structural assimilation of the Irish by the second generation. Contrary to earlier suggestions in *Roman Catholic Opinion*, (Hornsby-Smith and Lee, 1979), however, the type of Irish parentage did not appear to be a key variable in the process of assimilation. Rather, what appeared to be a much more significant factor was the degree of ethnic endogamy maintained and the extent to which both first- and second-generation Irish migrants married out. In all cases the mean upward social mobility movement was greater where there was a non-Irish spouse. It might be inferred from this evidence that Irish Catholics are likely substantially to assimilate both structurally and culturally over a period of two generations. This process is mediated in particular by the patterns of social and religious intermarriage. Marriage to a British spouse appears to enhance social mobility and accelerate structural assimilation while religious intermarriage (to a non-Catholic) accelerates cultural assimilation and convergence to the norms of religious belief and practice of English Catholics by the second generation.

The second broad question addressed in this present work was the validity of the model of the monolithic Church. Apart from the historical evidence which had indicated that since the restoration of the hierarchy in 1850 and the large influx of Irish Catholics in the nineteenth and twentieth centuries there always had been a considerable amount of heterodoxy of belief and practice among English Catholics, the empirical data reported in this present study have also indicated clearly that the model of the homogeneous, disciplined and conforming English Catholic community has little basis in reality at the present time. The heterodoxy of English Catholics is a social fact which has been fully documented in the various chapters of this book.

In chapter 3 a typology of English Catholics was developed which classified them in terms of their religious identity, practice, doctrinal and moral orthodoxy, and their institutional involvement. This typology has been used throughout the rest of this book to indicate patterns of differentiation by mobility experiences, marriage type and communal involvement, and the important variations between the activist Catholics and grass-roots Catholics. The study of the delegates to the N.P.C. enabled the heterogeneity of this particular sample to be investigated further in terms of differences of ecclesiology, morality and this-worldly emphasis. In general the evidence suggests that while there is no deep-seated antagonism between lay people and their priests, there does appear to be a more serious conflict between those who broadly favour and those who broadly oppose the changes which have taken place in the Church over the past two decades.

Apart from the latent conflict between the traditionalists and the progressives, this study has also reported on other lines along which Catholics may be strongly differentiated. Generally differences between the sexes did not appear to be very important though women other than housewives were likely to be rather more heterodox than men or housewives. On the other hand, age differences appeared to be highly significant with large variations in religious outcome measures between the more orthodox and conforming older Catholics and the more heterodox and non-conforming younger Catholics. Social-class differences were not as great as age differences. Nevertheless there were strong indications, notably in the demographic characteristics of the bishops' advisers or the delegates to the N.P.C., that contemporary institutional Catholicism is disproportionately attractive to the educated middle class. There seems to be a real danger of a cleavage between the activist and the traditional mass of relatively passive, grass-roots, working-class Catholics without clear representation in the decision-making processes in the more open and participative Church in the post-Vatican era. This is a different cleavage from the one addressed by Hadden (1970) in the American Protestant Churches over the civil rights issue which focussed on clergy–lay conflict. But the cleavages between the generations and between the progressive activists and the mass of ordinary Catholics are likely to have serious implications for the Church in the future.

10.3 THE DISSOLUTION OF A DISTINCTIVE SUBCULTURE

It is time to reflect on the significance and implications of the findings reported in this study for the understanding of the nature and importance of English Catholicism in the last two decades of the twentieth century. A useful starting point is the notion of a distinctive Catholic subculture which was said to have characterised English Catholicism up to the 1950s. John Bossy interpreted the restoration of the hierarchy in 1850 as being designed 'to reinforce the monarchical authority of the bishops over their clergy' and refers to the 'more general hardening of lines and narrowing of sympathies' entailed (Bossy, 1975: 361, 363). Writing of the period nearly 90 years later, immediately before the Second World War, the biographer of Cardinal Hinsley has given a flavour of this English Catholicism with its near fusion of old English and Irish cultures:

there was yet time before 1939 for the larger parish communities to indulge in a triumphalist efflorescence of faith which compacted their own solidarity while still proclaiming separation from the world outside. Week by week they continued throughout the liturgical year, the indoor and outdoor processions, rhythmically swaying their way by aisle and nave, through terraced street and suburban avenue, safely girt about by the episcopal *cordon sanitaire* of Catholic Action and the confident certainty of doctrinal belief. The serried ranks of the faithful in the sashes and regalia of their individual parish organisations thundered forth the four-square Victorian hymnody.

> Faith of our Fathers, Holy Faith
> In spite of dungeon, fire and sword . . .

. . . All life was there: colour, sound, ritual, liturgy, devotion, worship, community, not excluding ostentation, management and authoritarianism for those so minded. Never had the English and Welsh Catholic body seemed so secure, *so united, so insulated* . . . (Moloney, 1985: 242; italics added)

It is this all-embracing Catholic institutional life with its own norms, values and beliefs which can be characterised as a subculture within the wider society. In mid-twentieth century English Catholics

constituted a subculture by virtue of their specific norms and values in sexual, marital and familial morality, their allegiance to Rome, the importance attached to the Mass, their belief in life after death and their numerous distinguishing symbols such as Friday abstinence. Catholic social teaching . . . was consistent with the endeavour of English Catholics to develop 'subsocietal institutions' to preserve their subculture by segregating the young in educational terms through the maintenance of a separate denominational education system. Similarly, group endogamy sought to provide an all-Catholic milieu within the family. Such educational segregation and marital endogamy in combination with an array of other Catholic associations . . . were designed to protect the Catholic subculture. (Coman, 1977: 4–5)

Immigration experiences and the struggle for survival in the host society while avoiding a disloyalty to Ireland, encouraged isolation and produced 'a mentality in which Catholics ... accepted the fact of separation from the rest of society as being an integral part of their faith as Catholics' (Hickey, 1967: 169).

It is a major conclusion of this present book that the sort of distinctive Catholic subculture described in these accounts had largely *dissolved* by the mid-1980s. The process was not cataclysmic – the dramatic collapsing of the fortress walls as a result of a single explosive attack from without. Rather it was a gradual change which had taken place over several decades as a result of the steady dissolving of the walls in the solvent of rapid external social change after the global trauma of the Second World War and the internal religious *aggiornamento* encouraged in the 1960s by Pope John XXIII. With hindsight it is clear that the process was well under way by the 1960s in cities such as Liverpool (Ward, 1961) and Cardiff (Hickey, 1967). The belated tolerance of the Welfare State by English Catholics is attributed by Coman to 'the internal divisions and dissent, characteristic of a declining culture and increasing anomie...the weakening of the traditional Roman Catholic sense of boundary and demarcation in relation to the wider community...(and) the weakening of a general Roman Catholic identity' (Coman, 1977: 106).

The elements of the religious changes which have characterised this dissolution of a distinctive subculture are

The gradual assimilation through education and mixed marriage, the dissent over traditional teaching in birth regulation, the questioning of the limits of papal authority, the gradual substitution of English for Latin in the liturgy, the tentative movements towards ecumenism, the softening of traditional disapproval of mixed marriages and the abolition of Friday abstinence ... (ibid.: 105)

The anthropologist, Mary Douglas, has pointed to a lack of awareness of a sense of history and 'the need for symbolic solidarity with the past and present body of the Church' which some of these modifications manifested. Thus she bemoans the fact that

Friday no longer rings the great cosmic symbols of expiation and atonement: it is not symbolic at all, but a practical day for the organisation of charity. *Now the English Catholics are like everyone else.* (Douglas, 1973: 67; italics added)

Many of the data reported in this book bear on precisely this point, that in many respects English Catholics are now like everyone else.

The process of reaching this state from the position of distinctive difference immediately after the Second World War can be regarded as one of dissolution, a process which is likely to be irreversible. In the four decades since the Second World War English Catholics have very largely converged both structurally and culturally to the norms of the wider society. It cannot be said that no differences remain. We have noted, for example, that they are still a distinctly immigrant group with six times the national proportion of first-generation immigrants. As a major religious denomination they have a relatively inclusive membership definition and high weekly attendance ratio which continues to differentiate them clearly from the other Christian Churches, quite apart from their distinctive religious beliefs and authority structures.

The demonstration of the heterogeneity of English Catholics in terms of beliefs and practices has been a major aim of this present study. The implication of this heterogeneity is that there is a considerable overlap in the beliefs and patterns of church attendance between Catholics and non-Catholics in England and Wales in the 1980s. This is confirmed directly in the comparisons between the Catholic electors and other electors in our surveys in four parishes, and can be inferred more indirectly from the national survey data reported in *Roman Catholic Opinion* and other survey data. The evidence of a considerable disaffection with the institutional Church on the part of the young is a problem which is common to all the larger denominations which rely for membership recruitment primarily on the socialisation of the children of existing members. The alienation of the working class has also become more apparent with the ending of large-scale immigration from Ireland; this had always given the Catholic Church the misleading appearance of being able to retain the allegiance of the working class. The growing gap between the educated middle-class activists in the Church and the ordinary Catholic in the pew is also a phenomenon familiar to the other Christian Churches. Although it is still in its infancy, the emergent feminist movement in the Catholic Church has many similarities with the same movement among Anglicans.

The detailed analyses of social mobility experiences which we have reviewed, at first glance suggested that the mean upward mobility movement of Catholics was no greater than and may even have been less than that experienced in the population generally. However, elaboration of the data by taking into account the country of birth of the respondent indicated that Catholic men born in Great Britain had indeed a slight 'mobility momentum' relative to men in England and Wales generally but that first-generation immigrants, especially the non-Irish Catholics, experienced either lower mobility movement or even net downward mobility. In sum the evidence suggested that structural assimilation on the part of immigrant Catholics might take several generations but that for Catholics born in Great Britain the process had very largely been achieved. When considering patterns of religious practice and belief, there appeared to be some differences between Irish Catholics, who came to Britain from a tradition of high levels of religious practice, and other Catholic immigrants who appeared to bring with them a norm of non-practice. Whereas there was strong evidence of cultural assimilation on the part of the Irish Catholics by the second generation, in the case of other immigrants it seemed that there might be a growing alienation from the institutional Church over two generations.

It is when considering the changing marital norms of English Catholics that the full extent of the dissolution of the distinctive subculture is most apparent. Whereas under one-third of Catholics married before 1960 were in religiously mixed marriages and around one in eight in canonically invalid marriages, by the 1970s these proportions had increased dramatically to two-thirds in exogamous unions and well over one-third in invalid marriages. These figures are eloquent testimony to the fact that, even if the Catholics were still three times as likely to marry other Catholics as their proportion in the general population would warrant, by the 1980s there had been a major dissolution of the boundaries which for decades had safeguarded the religious identity of Catholics and ensured the distinctiveness of their separate subculture by the enforcement of religious and social sanctions against out-marriage. The evidence also showed that mixed marriages and, to a very much greater extent, invalid marriages were associated with deviation from the official norms of belief and practice. Apart from the evidence from marriage patterns, changes in the degrees to which Catholics selected their friends primarily from among other Catholics also indicated clearly the extent to which the boundaries separating the Catholic community from the rest of the population have steadily been dissolved over the past four or five decades.

By drawing on the analyses of G.H.S data and inferring that nearly all the immigrants from the Irish Republic were Roman Catholics, it was possible to explore further the processes of structural assimilation to British society. It was shown that well over half the first-generation and nearly all the second-generation Irish married non-Irish, mainly British, spouses and that such intermarriage greatly facilitated processes of structural assimilation. There was also a substantial convergence towards the English norms of religious intermarriage and canonically invalid marriage by the second generation. The Irish who contracted religiously endogamous marriages seemed able to retain distinctive patterns of religious beliefs and practices through to the second generation while for those with non-Catholic spouses, assimilation to the norms of British Catholics in exogamous unions was complete by the second generation. One might infer, therefore, that the dissolution of the distinctiveness of the Catholic subculture might be retarded by the migration experience but only where religious endogamy was maintained.

The evidence from the study of Catholic elites, both the activists at the parish level and also the advisers at the national level, including the delegates to the N.P.C., showed that close involvement with the institutional Church was also associated with a strong attachment to the traditional norms of the Roman Catholic Church, not only in the areas of religious practice and doctrinal orthodoxy, but also, to a considerable extent, to the official norms of sexual and marital morality in such matters as contraception, divorce and abortion. In general, the evidence we have reviewed supports the general proposition that *the maintenance of a distinctive socio-religious subculture is facilitated by marital endogamy, exclusivity of friendship ties, and high levels and inclusive patterns of institutional involvement and activity.* The corollary is that the dissolution of the boundaries surrounding the English Catholic socio-religious group is facilitated by increasing levels of marital exogamy, the cultivation by Catholics of inclusive friendship ties, and the maintenance of a detached communal involvement and only nominal links with the institutional Church.

It seems likely that the shift from the sect-like characteristics of exclusivity and strong internal discipline of the days of 'closed Catholicism' to the more inclusive, more tolerant and less judgemental characteristics of the 'open Catholicism' of the post-Vatican period, has had serious consequences for the political power which the Roman Catholic Church can wield in British society. With the dissolution of the boundaries surrounding a disciplined Church which could be relatively easily mobilised to defend its own interests, as they were defined by a clerical leadership, it has become increasingly difficult to persuade the membership of the Church that there are specific goals for which it ought to strive and interests it ought to defend which are distinct from those over which there is generally institutionalised conflict in a pluralist society. Paradoxically, therefore, the dissolution of the boundaries surrounding the English Catholic subculture associated with the decline of hostility and the cultivation of ecumenical relationships, has substantially reduced the potential for independent political action. This political impotence is shared with the other Christian bodies in a basically secular society. One likely result might be greater ecumenical cooperation between the Churches in areas of social concern. This seems already to be evident, for example in the closeness of the collaboration between Archbishop Worlock and Bishop Sheppard in Liverpool. A second possibility is the greater involvement of Catholics in the major political institutions in British society, rather than primarily within their own confessional organisations. The service of Mgr Bruce Kent as General Secretary of C.N.D. is an obvious example of this strategy.

In sum, the evidence reviewed in this book points clearly to the conclusion that the transformations which have taken place in English Catholicism over the past three or four decades can best be interpreted as a process of dissolution of the boundaries which once defended a distinctive Catholic subculture from contamination in a basically secular society. It is too simplistic to regard such a process as one of decline. Rather it indicates that far-reaching changes have taken place in the relationships between the Church and British society since the Second World War. These have necessarily entailed radical changes in the nature of the Catholic identity in England and Wales today.

10.4 FINAL REFLECTIONS

This book has been concerned with the five-and-a-half million Roman Catholics living in England and Wales in the 1970s and 1980s. It has reported and attempted to interpret, generally on the basis of survey findings, 'structural' features of English Catholicism, that is the broad patterns of religious beliefs, attitudes and practices and the social and demographic characteristics of English Catholics. It has not addressed a number of important questions about the subjective meanings which Catholics attribute to their religion or the nature of the Catholic identity or sense of 'belonging' or how these are patterned among different groups of Catholics. There are indeed wide variations according to the levels of institutional involvement of Catholics (Hornsby-Smith, 1983a). There are also wide variations in the interpretations given to the nature of religious authority in the Church. All these issues concerned with meaning, belonging, and authority will be considered in a subsequent publication.

Care must be exercised in making inferences about social change substantially on the basis of the mainly cross-sectional type of survey data with which this study has chiefly been concerned. However, such problems should not mesmerise us and prevent our drawing reasonable inferences about the major transformations which have clearly taken place in English Catholicism since the Second World War. Historical evidence relating to the everyday lives of Catholics up to the 1950s is limited. However, we have been able to build up some sort of picture of the 'closed Catholicism' of the earlier period and this picture is consistent with the analysis of cohort differences which we have been able to undertake. That major transformations have taken place seems irrefutable. Their interpretation, however, is more difficult because of the complexities of the processes concerned. We have noted the existence of conflict and accommodation: between patterns of change and continuity, progressive activity and traditional passivity. If a sign of maturity is the emergence of independent judgement and responsible action, then one might judge that English Catholics, while they might quite happily be more ready than in previous years to 'make up their own minds' on religious and moral matters, are nevertheless too passive or lethargic to make a proportionate contribution to the political decision-making of British society.

The initial concern of this study was the embourgeoisement of the English Catholic community in the post-war years. While duly cognizant of the strictures of Goldthorpe and Lockwood (1963), there is a sense in which the data we have reviewed can be said to indicate a process of group mobility, a success story for this socio-religious group. In terms of socio-economic measures, English Catholics can be said very largely to have 'made it' in post-war Britain. We have indicated the extent to which there has been a substantial breakdown of their distinctive subculture so that a process of normative convergence with the wider society can be said to have take place. In relational terms, the barriers which formerly segregated Catholics from their fellow citizens have largely disappeared and the evidence is to be found in increasing intermarriage and ecumenical collaboration.

Can one any longer conceive of a distinct 'Catholic ethic', perhaps to contrast with the Weberian ideal-type of 'Protestant ethic' (Mueller, 1978, 1980; Weber, 1930)? On the basis of the evidence we have reviewed it seems extremely doubtful. Rather the data indicate a high level of convergence between Catholics and non-Catholics on a wide range of social, moral, political and religious issues. For this reason it seems more appropriate to regard this process as one of 'normative convergence' in a predominantly secular society rather than a process of the 'protestantisation' of English Catholicism. The latter model would misleadingly imply that Catholics have simply assimilated to a clearly identifiable static model of 'protestantism'. The reality is clearly more complex because Catholics retain aspects of a 'customary' religion (Hornsby-Smith, Lee and Reilly, 1985) with identifiable elements of an earlier Catholic upbringing learned in the socialising institutions of family, school and parish. On the other hand, the strong emphasis on 'making up their own minds' about aspects of Catholic teaching, so evident at the time of the papal visit (Hornsby-Smith, Brown and O'Byrne, 1983), suggests a strong element of private decision-making which is one mark of protestantism.

One final question which must be addressed related to the evaluation of the English Catholics as a sizeable political constituency. To the extent that there has been a process of embourgeoisement and socio-economic assimilation, English Catholics share in large measure the values and prejudices of British society generally. In this sense they can be regarded as a 'domesticated denomination', unlikely to rock the boat of British complacency to any marked extent, content rather with the status quo and marginal social engineering to file down the most pointed injustices. There is no evidence in this work that English Catholics *per se* are likely to mount a sustained attack on the weaknesses and injustices of our form of mixed economy and representative democracy. The powerful in Britain can sleep safely, confident that there will be no prophetic uprising of five-and-a-half million English Catholics determined to bring the 'Good News to the Poor'!

In focussing on the patterned beliefs and practices of English Catholics there has been a neglect in this book of many of the major institutions of importance in the Church. Thus there has been no consideration of the role of the bishops or of the religious orders or of the numerous Catholic organisations. No political sociology of English Catholicism has been attempted which might have addressed questions of financial and other forms of resource allocation. There has been no systematic examination of ecumenical collaboration in all its official and unofficial forms at every level in the Church. There has been no ethnographic study of the day-to-day workings of Catholic schools or Catholic parishes. In their report on the N.P.C., the ecumenical observers noted questions of social control in the Church: 'it was also observed that the laity appeared to wish to be controlled' (Anon., 1980b: 12). The nature of clergy–lay relations and the exercise of such social control, especially at the parish level, also remain to be systematically examined. None of these issues was considered in this present study, yet they are clearly all important for the full understanding of the Roman Catholic Church in England and Wales two decades after the Second Vatican Council. The research agenda for a comprehensive sociology of English Catholicism is formidable indeed. This present study of English Catholics is a first contribution to this.

SCALES OF RELIGIOUS
BELIEFS AND PRACTICES

Apart from the typology derived in section 3.2 it was found to be useful to construct a limited number of scales for some of the analyses of religious beliefs, attitudes and practices in order to report the variety of data available in a parsimonious manner. In the 1978 survey in *Roman Catholic Opinion* (Hornsby-Smith and Lee, 1979) it was reported that 333 discrete variables were measured for each of the 1,023 respondents. In order to simplify the analysis of such a large amount of information, 14 main scales were constructed. Fuller details of these scales will be reported separately (Hornsby-Smith, 1987). For our present purposes it is sufficient to note that in the main they were derived following factor analysis of attitude batteries. In the construction of the scales consideration was paid not only to the achievement of good levels of face validity and reliability but also to the existence of comparable data, both in the studies of American Catholics by Greeley (1966; 1976) and in our own study of the delegates to the N.P.C. (Hornsby-Smith and Cordingley, 1983). A brief indication of the 14 scales follows.

1 DOCORTH: Doctrinal Orthodoxy (score 0–4)

This scale measures belief in orthodox doctrines concerning God, heaven, the Resurrection of Jesus and the consecration of the bread and wine at Mass. Each response of 'certainly true' was scored one point.

2 ADREL: Adult Religious Behaviour (score 0–2)

This scale measures the frequency of attendance at Mass and reception of Holy Communion. Respondents scored one point if they

went to Mass weekly or more often and one point if they received
Holy Communion monthly or more frequently.

3 PRAYER: Frequency of private prayer (score 0–2)

Respondents scored one point if they prayed weekly or more often
and one point if they stopped in church to pray weekly or more often.

4 CHCHINV: Church commitment (score 0–5)

Respondents scored one point for each affirmative response on the
questions of a serious discussion with a priest about religious
problems within the last two years, receiving Holy Communion at
least monthly, praying at least weekly, membership of a parish
organisation and having read a spiritual book within the last two
years.

5 NEWACT: New-style activism (score 0–5)

One point was scored for each of the following types of religious
behaviour within the previous two years: attendance at a charismatic
or Pentecostal prayer meeting, a house Mass, a religious discussion
group, an ecumenical service and at some other small group of a
religious nature.

6 VALTRAD: Liturgical traditionalism (score 0–3)

Respondents were asked their level of approval of the Mass in
English, folk Masses, lay people distributing communion at Mass, the
reduction of devotions, novenas and benedictions, and receiving communion under the form of both bread and wine at Mass. For each item
approval scored one point, mixed feelings two points and disapproval
three points. The total score constituted the scale TRADVAL. A second
question asked respondents what they thought about recent changes
in the Church. Those who considered there had been too many
changes in the Church and scored less than or equal to six on the
TRADVAL scale scored one point on the VALTRAD scale; greater than six
but less than or equal to twelve on the TRADVAL scale scored two
points on the VALTRAD scale; and greater than twelve on the TRADVAL
scale scored three points on the VALTRAD scale. This scale thus
measured opposition to recent liturgical changes in the Church.

7   SXLORTH: Sexual orthodoxy (score 0–3)

Those disagreeing with the remarriage of divorced people or artificial birth control each scored one point. Those who agreed that pre-marital sexual intercourse is wrong also scored one point.

8   THWLJUST: World justice orientation (score 0–2)

Respondents scored one point if they considered rich nations should accept a lower standard of living for the sake of poorer nations and one point if they thought the Church should take active steps to promote social justice even if it meant getting involved in politics.

9   PRSTSCAL: Evaluation of priests (score 0–2)

Respondents rated priests on four-point scales on eleven aspects of their work. Each rating of excellent scored one point. A score between one and five was counted as one point on PRSTSCAL and six or more, two points.

10   NEWPRST: New-style ministries (score 0–3)

Respondents scored one point each for acceptance of married priests and women priests and one point for approval of women playing a further part in the life of the Church.

11   CATHCHAR: Conformity to institutional identity (score 0–2)

Respondents rated 15 characteristics of being a Catholic on five-point scales. Each rating of 'very important' for going to Sunday Mass, regular and frequent prayer, regular and frequent Holy Communion, financial support for the Church, making Easter duties, sending children to a Catholic school, getting married in a Catholic Church, supporting Church activities and obeying the teaching of the Church scored one point. An aggregate score from one to three scored one point on CATHCHAR and a score of four to nine scored two points on this scale.

12   BEWARE: Salience of religious sanctions (score 0–5)

This scale attempted to measure some aspects of the fear of religious retribution for sinful behaviour. One point was scored for each of the following beliefs as 'certainly true': hell, the devil, voluntary missing of Sunday Mass as a serious sin, papal infallibility and eternal punishment for evil people.

13 PAPACY: Papal authority (score 0–2)

One point was scored if the respondent considered Jesus directly handed over the leadership of His Church to Peter and the popes as 'certainly true' and an additional point if the respondent also considered that it is certainly true that the pope is infallible under certain conditions.

14 LAYSAY: Lay participation (score 0–3)

One point was scored if the respondent agreed strongly with each of the propositions that the hierarchy should share more control over the affairs of the Church with ordinary Catholics, that ordinary Catholics should have a greater say in the choice of their parish priest and in the way his financial contributions to the Church are spent.

APPENDIX II

SUPPLEMENTARY TABLES

Apart from the tables given in the text, a number of additional tables have been appended here. While the details reported are not necessary in order to follow the argument in the text, they may be of value for those who wish to undertake secondary analysis. It should be noted that all the survey data analysed in this present study will be deposited with the Economic and Social Research Council Data Archive at Essex University.

Table A1 Social and demographic characteristics by sex, age, social class, terminal education age and associational involvement (%)

Social and Demographic characteristic	Sex M	Sex F HW	Sex F Other	Sex F All	Age 15–24	Age 25–34	Age 35–49	Age 50–64	Age 65+	Social class AB	Social class C1	Social class C2	Social class DE	T.E.A. <15	T.E.A. 15–16	T.E.A. 17–18	T.E.A. 19+	Assoc. invol. Org. Mems.	Assoc. invol. Parish attac.	Assoc. invol. Not	All Caths. R.C.O.	N.P.C. Lay dels.
Sex, % Male	—	—	—	—	58	33	41	48	41	42	24	75	38	51	41	29	51	32	44	48	44	55
Marital status, % single	25	6	88	14	72	8	4	7	14	12	17	12	14	22	17	19	17	5	20	22	19	30
Soc. class, % AB (Prof. & Manag.)	18	18	21	19	11	23	20	15	17	—	—	—	—	8	12	36	73	23	17	17	19	68
Age, % under 35	43	37	84	42	—	—	—	—	—	42	49	36	31	20	53	53	56	18	41	55	42	27
T.E.A., % 19 or over	8	6	3	6	5	11	6	4	4	29	4	3	0	—	—	—	—	8	7	6	7	47
Communal Assoc.: % half or more friends. R.C.	44	46	47	46	42	33	48	53	59	36	36	41	40	56	41	37	41	69	48	29	44	75
% all Catholic schools	55	56	63	56	49	52	58	61	60	47	50	60	65	65	53	53	32	55	59	51	60	65
% Converts	8	13	1	11	1	9	13	15	12	13	10	11	10	10	10	12	9	22	9	6	10	15
Irish immigrants: % first generation	17	16	6	15	5	15	19	20	18	15	13	17	21	20	12	19	12	14	19	10	15	6
% second generation	17	15	24	16	23	16	13	14	20	15	18	17	15	15	17	17	18	18	17	14	15	7
N = 100% (max)	451	525	60	585	188	249	295	190	113	173	281	210	285	339	501	128	68	125	560	317	1036	959

Table A2 Religious types and scale scores by sex, age, social class, terminal education age and associational involvement (%)

Religious type or scale score	Sex — M	Sex — F HW	Sex — F Other	Sex — F All	Age 15–24	Age 25–34	Age 35–49	Age 50–64	Age 65+	Social class AB	Social class C1	Social class C2	Social class DE	T.E.A. <15	T.E.A. 15–16	T.E.A. 17–18	T.E.A. 19+	Assoc. invol. Org. Mems.	Assoc. invol. Parish attac.	Assoc. invol. Not	All Caths. R.C.O.	N.P.C. Lay dels.
R.C. types:																						
Involved orth. attenders (% A+B)	8	13	3	12	1	4	16	13	19	13	9	10	9	11	8	11	13	99	0	0	9	74
Non-Inv. orth. attenders (% C+D)	25	22	25	22	13	17	23	32	48	28	23	23	22	30	16	33	27	0	39	3	22	24
Irregular attenders (% F+G)	24	28	25	28	29	33	26	17	14	21	29	26	28	20	28	29	27	0	37	13	24	1
Non-practising (% H+J+non-ident.)	37	34	34	34	42	42	29	34	16	32	37	35	40	31	43	21	23	0	14	83	32	1
Scale scores (% high):																						
DOCORTH (% 4)	50	55	41	54	42	55	68	74	74	57	53	51	52	59	48	55	45	77	55	31	52	na
ADREL (% 1–2)	46	50	48	50	30	37	53	56	75	60	53	43	46	59	37	56	61	92	61	7	48	99
PRAYER (% 2)	12	13	9	13	2	6	15	18	28	12	14	9	14	18	8	13	16	37	12	2	12	65
CHCHINV (% 3–5)	31	37	37	37	19	27	39	39	48	47	41	31	30	41	26	42	52	93	36	7	34	96
NEWACT (% 1–5)	33	38	41	38	30	26	43	37	23	50	45	29	33	38	29	48	51	75	39	15	36	96
VALTRAD (% 1–3)	15	16	17	16	8	13	17	21	23	44	19	15	15	16	18	18	18	18	19	8	16	10
SXLORTH (% 1–3)	41	46	33	45	20	18	47	64	82	44	43	36	50	33	38	43	43	65	48	27	43	73
THWLJUST (% 2)	27	19	16	18	22	18	24	24	25	29	24	20	21	22	21	21	26	42	20	18	22	72
PRSTSCAL (% 2)	15	21	6	19	9	10	18	30	31	14	18	17	19	24	15	17	8	38	19	6	18	48
NEWPRST (% 2–3)	40	36	46	37	55	47	37	28	12	52	40	39	32	30	41	44	48	23	35	50	38	63
CATHCHAR (% 2)	34	37	24	35	18	18	54	51	66	31	33	29	43	47	29	28	30	62	37	20	35	na
BEWARE (% 3–5)	34	38	22	35	13	22	40	51	55	33	35	30	39	44	33	33	34	62	39	16	35	na
PAPACY (% 2)	33	38	23	36	11	24	40	51	55	34	34	32	38	41	30	36	31	62	40	14	35	na
LAYSAY (% 1–3)	24	24	20	23	19	26	24	25	22	23	20	26	24	22	24	29	17	18	24	25	24	na
N = 100 % (max)	451	525	60	585	188	249	295	190	113	173	281	210	285	339	501	128	68	125	560	317	1036	959

Table A3 *Religious types and scale scores by social mobility experiences*

Religious type or scale score	Stable middle	Social mobility experience Upwardly mobile	Downwardly mobile	Stable working	Signi- ficance
R.C. types					
Involved orthodox attenders (% A+B)	13	10	7	10	
Non-inv. orthodox attenders (% C+D)	31	24	22	22	
Irregular attenders (% F+G)	19	25	30	27	
Non-practising (% H+J+non-ident.)	32	38	34	36	
Scale scores (% High)					
DOCORTH (%4)	58	48	43	54	*
ADREL (% 1–2)	55	46	46	47	*
PRAYER (%2)	16	11	11	12	
CHCHINV (% 3–5)	46	32	26	34	
NEWACT (% 1–5)	48	36	35	33	**
VALTRAD (% 1–3)	21	17	15	14	*
SXLORTH (% 1–3)	47	33	47	45	
THWLJUST (%2)	26	23	23	21	
PRSTSCAL (%2)	15	14	14	18	
NEWPRST (% 2–3)	42	44	33	37	
CATHCHAR (%2)	32	28	32	38	
BEWARE (% 3–5)	39	32	31	35	
PAPACY (%2)	37	37	30	34	
LAYSAY (% 1–3)	22	23	21	25	
N = 100% (max.)	159	172	156	549	

Significance levels: *** p<.001 **p<.01 *p<.05
Source: National Survey, 1978.

Table A4 *Religious types and scale scores by geographical mobility experiences*

Religious type or scale score	English	2nd gen. British	1st gen. British	2nd gen. Irish	2nd gen. Other[a]	1st gen. Irish	1st gen. other	Significance
R.C. types								
Involved orthodox attenders (% A+B)	10	4	6	13	3	9	10	
Non-inv. orthodox attenders (% C+D)	22	9	22	23	17	35	21	
Irregular attenders (% F+G)	24	27	26	23	37	30	30	
Non-practising (% H+J+non-ident.)	38	51	42	33	43	17	38	
Scale scores (% high)								
DOCORTH (%4)	51	31	47	52	46	62	56	*
ADREL (% 1–2)	46	29	42	53	38	62	39	**
PRAYER (%2)	13	5	13	12	9	16	4	**
CHCHINV (% 3–5)	34	38	26	35	32	36	33	
NEWACT (% 1–5)	35	22	41	39	29	39	40	
VALTRAD (% 1–3)	16	15	16	14	15	22	8	
SXLORTH (% 1–3)	41	23	42	43	30	57	48	*
THWLJUST (%2)	22	27	32	27	21	15	22	
PRSTSCAL (%2)	16	9	13	17	24	22	12	
NEWPRST (% 2–3)	39	52	45	40	32	30	35	
CATHCHAR (%2)	35	25	37	36	29	40	26	
BEWARE (% 3–5)	33	22	30	36	26	44	36	
PAPACY (%2)	32	25	31	38	21	46	33	*
LAYSAY (% 1–3)	25	25	27	19	32	23	20	
N = 100% (max.)	555	27	44	156	34	151	69	

[a] including two respondents with Irish mothers 'other' fathers.
Significance levels: ***p<.001 ** p<.01 * p<.05
Source: National Survey, 1978.

Table A5 *Religious types and scale scores by marriage type (%)*

Religious type or scale score	Born R.C. with born R.C. spouse BB	Convert with born R.C. spouse CB	Born R.C. with convert spouse BC	Valid mixed VM	Invalid mixed IM	All types
R.C. types						
Involved Orthodox Attenders (% A+B)	13	26	17	9	1	11
Non-Involved Orthodox Attenders (% C+D)	32	25	43	20	4	24
Irregular Attenders (% F+G)	28	21	20	31	17	26
Non-Practising (% H+J+non-Ident.)	22	23	11	36	77	35
Scale scores (% high)						
DOCORTH (% 4)	59	68	79	50	27	55
ADREL (% 1–2)	58	64	75	45	9	48
PRAYER (% 2)	13	21	28	10	4	13
CHCHINV (% 3–5)	41	54	53	28	10	34
NEWACT (% 1–5)	39	56	46	29	19	35
VALTRAD (% 1–3)	22	13	25	11	5	16
SXLORTH (% 1–3)	56	52	71	34	21	45
THWLJUST (% 2)	20	38	29	21	15	22
PRSTSCAL (% 2)	19	29	22	16	9	18
NEWPRST (% 2–3)	30	35	21	44	55	38
CATHCHAR (% 2)	46	42	58	29	15	37
BEWARE (% 3–5)	45	40	56	31	17	37
PAPACY (% 2)	47	39	68	34	9	38
LAYSAY (% 1–3)	26	23	16	23	24	24
N = 100% (max.)	305	73	73	204	144	799

Source: National Survey, 1978.

Table A6 *Progressive orientations by delegate group (%)*

Variable	Orientation	Priests	Female religious	Laity	All
1. SUBMAST	We are utterly dependent on God and should completely submit ourselves to His will for us.	26	32	43	40
	God created us to master the world and to work for its transformation into His Kingdom.	69	67	54	58
2 RELCONC	Religion is mainly concerned with the way I live my life in this present world.	70	78	57	61
	Religion is mainly concerned with the salvation of my soul for everlasting life in the next world.	26	22	39	36
3 EVIL	Evil in the world is essentially the result of individual personal sin.	66	61	72	70
	Evil in the world is essentially the result of sinful social structures.	29	36	27	28
4 RELIGPOL	Religion has nothing to do with politics or with social and economic issues.	2	2	5	4
	Religion cannot be divorced from politics and from social and economic issues.	97	98	95	95
5 MISSION	Our primary missionary concern is to liberate people from oppressive structures.	9	13	16	15
	Our primary missionary concern is to change the hearts of individual people.	86	87	83	83
6 NATGOD	God is the all-knowing and all powerful Lord of all creation.	29	6	36	33
	God is the Divine Presence in this world whom I discover through people, things and events.	65	93	60	63
7 WORLD	The World is good, and God's creative activity continues throughout the development of man and his culture to make it even better.	77	71	48	54
	The World is the arena where man proves himself for God by trusting in His Providence and following his Will.	20	28	51	44
8 HSPIRIT	The Holy Spirit speaks to all men of good will in different ways and under different circumstances throughout history.	81	90	73	75
	The Holy Spirit proceeds from God the Father and God the Son and distributes grace to men.	11	5	24	21

Table A6 (*Cont.*)

Variable	Orientation	Priests	Female religious	Laity	All
9 MINISTER	A Christian Minister is someone ordained to the priesthood and thereby authorized to celebrate the Eucharist and administer the sacrament of Penance and Anointing the sick.	36	24	37	36
	A Christian Minister is someone who has been authorized by the People of God to build Christian community, lead it in its celebration of God's grace and inspire it to share actively in the world's concerns.	60	75	61	62
10 MACTIVY	The purpose of Missionary Activity is to convert people to the Catholic Church through preaching, teaching catechetics, administering the sacraments etc.	22	9	24	22
	A purpose of Missionary Activity is to help man develop his own resources to fulfil total human needs i.e. religious, economic, educational, political	74	89	74	75
11 MASSEMP	In the Mass the priest offers up Christ's sacrifice on behalf of the faithful.	21	13	31	28
	In the Mass the whole community comes together to worship God and celebrate His goodness.	72	86	65	68
12 NATCHCH	The Church is essentially a visible organisation of believers with clearly specified religious leaders.	11	7	17	15
	The Church is essentially a community of believers all of whom have different ministries.	83	94	82	83
N = 100 % (max.)		176	94	958	1276

Note: respondents indicating both alternatives or neither have been omitted.
Source: Hornsby-Smith and Cordingley, 1983: 45).

BIBLIOGRAPHY

——— ❊ ———

Abbott, W. M. (ed.) (1966) *The Documents of Vatican II*, London: Geoffrey Chapman.

Abrams, M., Gerard, D. and Timms, N. (eds.) (1985) *Values and Social Change in Britain*, London: Macmillan.

Albion, G. (1950) 'The Restoration of the Hierarchy', in Beck, G. A. (ed.) *The English Catholics: 1850–1950*, London: Burns Oates, 86–115.

Ambler, R. and Haslam, D. (eds.) (1980) *Agenda for Prophets: Towards a Political Theology for Britain*, London: The Bowerdean Press.

Anon. (1980a) *Prospect for the Eighties* (from a Census of the Churches in 1979 undertaken by the Nationwide Initiative in Evangelism), London: Bible Society.

Anon. (1980b) *National Pastoral Congress: Observers' Report*, London: British Council of Churches.

Anon. (1981) *Liverpool 1980: Official Report of the National Pastoral Congress*, Slough: St Paul Publications.

Anon. (1984) *Action for Justice and Peace: A Handbook for Groups*, London: C.A.F.O.D., C.I.I.R., Pax Christi and S.C.I.A.F.

Argyle, M. and Beit-Hallahmi, B. (1975) *The Social Psychology of Religion*, London: Routledge.

Barker, E. (ed.) (1982) *New Religious Movements: A Perspective for Understanding Society*, New York: Edwin Mellen.

Barker, E. (1984) *The Making of a Moonie: Choice or Brainwashing?* Oxford: Blackwell.

Baum, G. (1980) 'The Sociology of Roman Catholic Theology', in Martin, D., Mills, J. O. and Pickering, W. S. F. (eds.) *Sociology and Theology: Alliance and Conflict*, Brighton: Harvester Press, 120–35.

Beck, G. A. (ed.) (1950a) *The English Catholics: 1850–1950*, London: Burns Oates.

Beck, G. A. (1950b) 'Today and Tomorrow' in Beck, G. A. (1950a), 585–614

Beck, G. A. (1955) *The Case for Catholic Schools*, London: C.E.C.

Beckford, J. A. (1975) *The Trumpet of Prophecy: A Sociological Study of Jehovah's Witnesses*, Oxford: Blackwell; New York, Halstead Press.

Beckford, J. A. (1985) *Cult Controversies: The Societal Response to New Religious Movements*, London: Tavistock.

Bell, C. (1968) *Middle Class Families: Social and Geographical Mobility*, London: R.K.P.

Berger, P. L. (1971) *A Rumour of Angels: Modern Society and the Rediscovery of the Supernatural*, Harmondsworth: Penguin.

Berger, P. L. (1973) *The Social Reality of Religion*, Harmondsworth: Penguin.

Berger, P. L. and Luckmann, T. (1971) *The Social Construction of Reality*, Harmondsworth: Penguin.

Besanceney, P. H. (1965) 'Interfaith Marriages of Catholics in the Detroit Area', *Sociological Analysis*, 26 (1) Spring, 38–44.

Bishops' Conference of England and Wales (1971) *Commissions: Aid to a Pastoral Strategy – Report of a Review Committee*, Abbots Langley: C.I.S.

Bishops' Conference of England and Wales (1983) *The Review of the Structures and Procedures*, Abbots Langley: C.I.S.

Bishops' Conference of England and Wales (1985) *Submission to the Synod Secretariat, Briefing* (Supplement 2), London: Catholic Media Office.

Blau, P. M. (1956) 'Social Mobility and Interpersonal Relations', *American Sociological Review*, 21 (3) 290–5.

Bode, J. G. (1970) 'Status and Mobility of Catholics Vis-a-Vis Several Protestant Denominations: More Evidence', *Sociological Quarterly*, 11 (1), 103–11.

Bossy, J. (1975) *The English Catholic Community: 1570–1850*, London: Darton, Longman and Todd.

Bright, L. and Clements, S. (eds.) (1966) *The Committed Church*, London: Darton, Longman and Todd.

Brothers, J. B. (1964) *Church and School: A Study of the Impact of Education on Religion*, Liverpool: Liverpool University Press.

Brothers, J. (1984) 'English Catholics Surveyed', *The Tablet*, 238 (7492), 11 February, 134.

Bumpass, L. and Sweet, J. (1972) 'Differentials in Marital Stability', *American Sociological Review*, 37, 754–66.

Burns, T. and Stalker, G. M. (1966) *The Management of Inovation*, London: Tavistock.

Butler, C. (1981) *The Theology of Vatican II*, London: Darton, Longman and Todd.

Butler, R. A. (1971) *The Art of the Possible: Memoirs of Lord Butler*, London: Hamish Hamilton.

Campbell, Liz (1980) 'Abortion: A Christian Feminist Perspective', *New Blackfriars*, 61, September, 370–7.

Canon Law Society of Great Britain and Ireland (1983) *The Code of Canon Law*, London: Collins.

Carr, E. H. (1964) *What is History?*, Harmondsworth: Penguin.

Cartwright, A. (1976) *How Many Children?*, London: Routledge and Kegan Paul.

Catholic Commission for Racial Justice of the Bishops' Conference of England and Wales (1975) *Where Creed and Colour Matter: A Survey on Black Children and Catholic Schools*, Abbots Langley: Catholic Information Office.

Catholic Education Council (1984) *Summary of Pastoral Statistics: England and Wales*, London.

Catholic Information Services (1980) 'Synod '80: "The Family Today" No. 1' *Briefing*, 10 (32), 5–7.

Caulfield, B. and Bhat, A. (1981) 'The Irish in Britain: Intermarriage and Fertility Levels 1971–1976', *New Community*, 9 (1) Spring–Summer, 73–83.

C.E.L.A.M. (Second General Conference of Latin American Bishops) (1979) *The Church in the Present-Day Transformation of Latin America in the Light of the Council: The Medellin Conclusions*, Washington, D.C.: Secretariat for Latin America, National Conference of Catholic Bishops.

C.E.L.A.M. (Third General Conference of Latin American Bishops) (1980) *Puebla*, Slough: St Paul Publications.

Chadwick, O. (1975) *The Secularization of the European Mind in the Nineteenth Century*, Cambridge: Cambridge University Press.

Cheetham, J. (1976) 'Surveys which include information about Roman Catholics' attitudes towards legal abortion', University of Oxford (mimeo).

Clark, D. (1984) *The Liberation of the Church: The Role of Basic Christian Groups in a New Re-Formation*, Birmingham: National Centre for Christian Communities and Networks.

Coleman, J. A. (1978) *The Evolution of Dutch Catholicism, 1958–1974*, Berkeley, Los Angeles, Ca: University of California Press.

Coman, P. (1977) *Catholics and the Welfare State*, London: Longman.

Comerford, M. and Dodd, C. (1982) *Many Ministries: Lay People in Neighbourhood Care: A Practical Guide* (S361), London: C.T.S.

Connolly, S. J. (1982) *Priests and People in Pre-Famine Ireland: 1780–1845*, Dublin: Gill and Macmillan.

Coser, L. A. (1974) *Greedy Institutions: Patterns of Undivided Commitment*, New York: Free Press; London: Collier Macmillan.

Coventry, J. (n.d.) *Mixed Marriages Between Christians* (S327), London: C.T.S.

Cullinan, T. (1980) 'The Church as an Agent of Social Change – From the Edge' in Ambler, R. and Haslam, D. (eds.) (1980), 135–43.

Cumming, J. and Burns, P. (eds.) (1980) *The Church Now: An Inquiry into the Present State of the Catholic Church in Britain and Ireland*, Dublin: Gill and Macmillan.

Currie, R., Gilbert, A. and Horsley, L. (1977) *Churches and Churchgoers: Patterns of Church Growth in the British Isles since 1700*, Oxford: Clarendon Press.

Dale, A., Gilbert, G. N. and Arber, S. (1985) 'Integrating Women into Class Theory', *Sociology*, 19 (3) August, 384–408.

Daly, G. (1980) *Transcendence and Immanence: A Study in Catholic Modernism and Integralism*, Oxford: Clarendon Press.

Daly, G. (1981) 'Faith and Theology (2) The Ultramontane Influence', *The Tablet 235*, 18–25 April, 391–2.

Denzin, N. K. (1970) *The Research Act in Sociology: A Theoretical Introduction to Sociological Methods*, London: Butterworths.

Department for Christian Citizenship of the Roman Catholic Bishops' Conference of England and Wales (1985) *Immigration and Nationality: A Review of Policy and Practice with Recommendations*, Godalming: Catholic Media Office.

Department for Christian Doctrine and Formation of the Bishops' Conference of England and Wales (1984) *Learning From Diversity: A Challenge for Catholic Education*, Godalming: Catholic Media Office.

Douglas, M. (1973) *Natural Symbols: Explorations in Cosmology*, Harmondsworth: Penguin.

Dulles, A. (1976) *Models of the Church: A Critical Assessment of the Church in all its Aspects*, Dublin: Gill and Macmillan.

Dummett, M. (1979) *Catholicism and the World Order: Some Reflections on the 1978 Reith Lectures*, London: C.I.I.R.

Evennett, H. O. (1944) *The Catholic Schools of England and Wales*, Cambridge: Cambridge University Press.

Fichter, J. H. (1954) *Social Relations in the Urban Parish*, Chicago: University of Chicago Press.

Fitzsimons, M. A. (1969) 'England', in Fitzsimons, M. A. (ed.), *The Catholic Church Today: Western Europe*, Notre Dame, London: Notre Dame Press, 309–44.

Fogarty, M., Ryan, L. and Lee, J. (eds.) (1984) *Irish Values and Attitudes: the Irish Report of the European Value Systems Study*, Dublin: Dominican Publications.

Forbes, A. and Cosgrave, A. (1985) *Justice 85: The National Pastoral Congress Revisited*, Leeds.

Garcia, J. and Maitland, S. (eds.) (1983) *Walking on the Water: Women Talk About Spirituality*, London: Virago.

Gay, J. D. (1971) *The Geography of Religion in England*, London: Duckworth.

Giddens, A. (1973) *The Class Structure of the Advanced Societies*, London: Hutchinson.

Gilbert, A. D. (1976) *Religion and Society in Industrial England*, London: Longman.

Goldthorpe, J. H. (1978) 'On the role of the Social Scientist', in Hirsch, F. and Goldthorpe, J. H. (eds.) (1978) *The Political Economy of Inflation*, London: Martin Robertson, 214–16.

Goldthorpe, J. H. (1980) *Social Mobility and Class Structure in Modern Britain*, Oxford: Clarendon.

Goldthorpe, J. H. (1983) 'Women and Class Analysis: In Defence of the Conventional View', *Sociology*, 17 (4) November, 465–88.

Goldthorpe, J. H. and Lockwood, D. (1963) 'Affluence and the British Class Structure', *Sociological Review*, 11 (2) 133–63.

Goldthorpe, J. H. and Hope, K. (1974), *The Social Grading of Occupations: A New Approach and Scale*, Oxford: Oxford University Press.

Gordon, M. M. (1964) *Assimilation in American Life*, Oxford: Oxford University Press.

Greeley, A. M. (1963) *Religion and Career*, New York: Sheed and Ward.

Greeley, A. M. (1972) 'The State of the Priesthood in the United States', *Doctrine and Life*, 22 (7) July, 351–80.

Greeley, A. M. (1975) *The New Agenda*, Garden City, N.Y.: Image Books.

Greeley, A. M. (1977) *The American Catholic: A Social Portrait*, New York: Basic Books.

Greeley, A. M., McCready, W. C., McCourt, K. (1976), *Catholic Schools in a Declining Church*, New York: Sheed and Ward.

Green, R. W. (ed.) (1959) *Protestantism and Capitalism: the Weber Thesis and its Critics*, Boston, Mass.: D. C. Heath.

Greene, G. (1962) *The End of the Affair*, (f.p. 1951), Harmondsworth: Penguin.

Gutierrez, G. (1974) *A Theology of Liberation*, London: S.C.M.

Gwynn, D. (1950) 'The Irish Immigration' in Beck, G. A. (ed.) *The English Catholics 1850–1950*, London: Burns Oates, 265–90.

Hadden, J. K. (1970) *The Gathering Storm in the Churches*, Garden City, N.Y.: Doubleday.

Haerle, R. K. (1969) 'Church Attendance Patterns Among Intermarried Catholics: A Panel Study', *Sociological Analysis*, 30, 204–16.

Harrison, J. (1983) *Attitudes to Bible, God, Church*, London: Bible Society.

Harrison, P. M. (1959) *Authority and Power in the Free Church Tradition: A Social Case Study of the American Baptist Convention*, London: Feffer and Simons.

Hastings, A. (1977) 'Some Reflections on the English Catholicism of the Late 1930s' in Hastings, A. (ed.) *Bishops and Writers: Aspects of the Evolution of Modern English Catholicism*, Wheathampstead: Anthony Clarke, 107–25.

Haughton, R. (1980) 'Is God Masculine'? in Elizondo, V. and Greinacher, N. (eds.), *Women in a Men's Church*, Edinburgh: Clark, 63–70.

Hay, D. (1982) *Exploring Inner Space: Scientists and Religious Experience* Harmondsworth: Penguin.

Heath, A. (1981) *Social Mobility*, Glasgow: Fontana.

Hebblethwaite, M. (1984) *Motherhood and God*, London: Geoffrey Chapman.

Hechter, M. (1975) *Internal Colonialism: The Celtic Fringe in British Development 1536–1966*, London: Routledge.

Herberg, W. (1960) *Protestant–Catholic–Jew: An Essay in American Religious Sociology*, Garden City, N.Y.: Doubleday.

Hewson, J. (1980) 'Comment on "The Bishops Speak"', *Roman Catholic Feminists Newsletter*, 18, October.

Hickey, J. (1967) *Urban Catholics: Urban Catholicism in England and Wales from 1829 to the Present Day*, London: Geoffrey Chapman.

Hoge, D. R. (1981) *Converts, Dropouts, Returnees: A Study of Religious Change among Catholics*, Washington, D.C.: United States Catholic Conference; New York: Pilgrim Press.

Hoge, D. R. (1986) 'Interpreting Change in American Catholicism: The River and the Floodgate', H. Paul Douglass Lecture, *Review of Religious Research*, 27 No. 4, June, 289–99.

Holmes, J. D. (1978) *More Roman than Rome: English Catholicism in the Nineteenth Century*, London: Burns and Oates.

Hopper, E. (1971) 'Educational Systems and Selected Consequences of Patterns of Mobility and Non-Mobility in Industrial Societies: A Theoretical Discussion' in Hopper, E. (ed.), *Readings in the Theory of Educational Systems*, London: Hutchinson, 292–336.

Hornsby-Smith, M. P. (1975) *A Feasibility Study of the Roman Catholic Community in England, Final Report to S.S.R.C. on Grant HR2667*, Guildford: University of Surrey.

Hornsby-Smith, M. P. (1978a) *Catholic Education: The Unobtrusive Partner*, London: Sheed and Ward.

Hornsby-Smith, M. P. (1978b) 'Irish Catholics in England: Some Sociological Perspectives', in *Irish Catholics in England: A Congress Report*, Dublin: Irish Episcopal Commission for Emigrants, March, 26–60.

Hornsby-Smith, M. P. (1978c) *Tradition and Change in the Roman Catholic Community in England: Final Report to the Social Science Research Council on Grant HR3444*, Guildford: University of Surrey.

Hornsby-Smith, M. P. (1982) 'Two Years After: Reflections on "Liverpool 1980"', *New Blackfriars*, 63, June, 252–60.

Hornsby-Smith, M. P. (1983a) 'Catholic Accounts: Problems of Institutional Involvement', in Gilbert, N. and Abell, P. (eds.) (1983) *Accounts and Action*, Aldershot: Gower.

Hornsby-Smith, M. P. (1983b) 'English Catholics and Christian Unity', *Insight*, 1 (3), March, 30–6.

Hornsby-Smith, M. P. (1985) 'Priests and C.N.D.: a Survey', *The Month*, 18 (9) September, 300–2.

Hornsby-Smith, M. P. (1986) 'The Immigrant Background of Roman Catholics in England and Wales: A Research Note', *New Community*, 13 No. 1, Spring–Summer, 79–85.

Hornsby-Smith, M. P. (1987) 'Research Instruments Used and Scales Constructed in Studies of English Catholicism', *Sociology Department Occasional Paper*, Guildford: University of Surrey (forthcoming).

Hornsby-Smith, M. P. and Mansfield, M. C. (1974), 'English Catholicism in Change', *The Newman*, 7 (3), September, 62–70.

Hornsby-Smith, M. P. and Mansfield, Penny (1975) 'Overview of the Church Commissions', *The Month*, 8 (3) March, 84–9.

Hornsby-Smith, M. P. and Lee, R. M. (1979) *Roman Catholic Opinion: A Study of Roman Catholics in England and Wales in the 1970s*, Guildford: University of Surrey.

Hornsby-Smith, M. P. and Turcan, K. A. (1981) 'Are Northern Catholics Different?', *Clergy Review*, 66 (7) July, 231–41.

Hornsby-Smith, M. P., Lee, R. M. and Turcan, K. A. (1982) 'A Typology of English Catholics', *Sociological Review*, 30 (3) August, 433–59.

Hornsby-Smith, M. P., Brown, J. and O'Byrne, J. (1983) 'Second Thoughts on the Pope's Visit', *The Month*, 16 (4) April, 131–3.

Hornsby-Smith, M. P. and Cordingley, E. S. (1983) *Catholic Elites: A Study of the Delegates to the National Pastoral Congress*, Occasional Paper No. 3, Guildford: University of Surrey.

Hornsby-Smith, M. P., Lee, R. M. and Reilly, P. A. (1984) 'Social and Religious Change in Four English Roman Catholic Parishes', *Sociology*, 18 (3) August, 353–65.

Hornsby-Smith, M. P., Lee, R. M., and Reilly, P. A. (1985) 'Common Religion and Customary Religion: A Critique and a Proposal', *Review of Religious Research*, 26 (3) March, 244–52.

Hornsby-Smith, M. P., Procter, M., Rajan, L., and Brown, J. (1985) 'A Typology of Progressive Catholics: A Study of the Delegates to the National Pastoral Congress'. Paper read at the Annual Meeting of the Society for the Scientific Study of Religion at Savannah, Georgia, 25 October 1985.

Hornsby-Smith, M. P., Turcan, K. A. and Rajan, L. T. (1985) 'Patterns of Religious Commitment, Intermarriage and Marital Breakdown Among English Catholics'. Paper read at the International Conference for the Sociology of Religion (C.I.S.R.) at Leuven, 20 August 1985.

Hornsby-Smith, M. P. and Dale, A. (1986) 'The Assimilation of Irish Immigrants to England: Some Data on Occupational Mobility and Intermarriage Patterns' (mimeo).

Hughes, P. (1950) 'The English Catholics in 1850', in Beck, G. A. (ed.) *The English Catholics: 1850–1950*, London: Burns and Oates, 42–85.

Inglis, K. S. (1963) *Churches and the Working Classes in Victorian England*, London: Routledge and Kegan Paul.

Jackson, J. A. (1963) *The Irish in Britain*, London: Routledge.

Jansen, C. (1969) 'Some Sociological Aspects of Migration', in Jackson, J. A. (ed.) *Migration*, Cambridge: Cambridge University Press, 60–73.

John Paul II (1982) *The Pope in Britain*, London: Catholic Truth Society/Catholic Information Services.

Jowell, R. and Airey, C. (eds.) (1984) *British Social Attitudes: the 1984 Report*, Aldershot: Gower.

Kennedy, R. E. (1973) *The Irish: Emigration, Marriage and Fertility*, Berkeley, Ca.: University of California Press.

Kerr, M. (1958) *The People of Ship Street*, London: Routledge.

King, U. (1977) 'The Role of Women in Today's Society: Reflections from a Christian Point of View', *The Month*, 10 (8) August, 268–72.

Kirby, P. (1984) *Is Irish Catholicism Dying? Liberating an Imprisoned Church*, Dublin: Mercier Press.

Kluegel, J. R. (1980) 'Denominational Mobility: Current Patterns and Recent Trends', *Journal for the Scientific Study of Religion*, 19 (1) March, 26–39.

Konstant, D. (Chairman) (1981) *Signposts and Homecomings: The Educative Task of the Catholic Community*, Slough: St Paul Publications.

Koopmanschap, T. (1978) *Transformations in Contemporary Roman Catholicism: A Case Study*, unpublished Ph.D. thesis, University of Liverpool.

Lasswell, H. D. (1958) *Politics: Who Gets What, When, How*, Cleveland, Ohio: Meridian Books.

Lawlor, M. (1965) *Out of This World: A Study of Catholic Values*, London: Sheed and Ward.

Lazerwitz, B. (1971) 'Intermarriage and Conversion: A Guide for Future Research', *Jewish Journal of Sociology*, 13 (1), 41–63.

Lees, L. H. (1979) *Exiles of Erin: Irish Migrants in Victorian London*, Manchester: Manchester University Press.

Lenski, G. (1963) *The Religious Factor: A Sociological Study of Religion's Impact on Politics, Economics and Family Life*, Garden City, N.Y.: Anchor.

Leslie, J. H. (1980) 'Some Theoretical Issues in a Sociological Analysis of Religious Ideology in a Roman Catholic Parish', in *Research Bulletin*, I.S.W.R.A., University of Birmingham.

Ling, T. (1973) 'Religion in England: Majorities and Minorities', *New Community*, 2 (2) Spring, 117–24.

Lodge, D. (1962) *The Picturegoers* (f.p. 1960) London: Pan.

Lodge, D. (1980) *How Far Can You Go?*, London: Secker and Warburg.

Lodge, D. (1983) *The British Museum is Falling Down* (f.p. 1965) Harmondsworth: Penguin.

Lovell, G. and Widdicombe, C. (1978) *Churches and Communities: An Approach to Development in the Local Church*, London: Search Press.

Luckmann, T. (1970) *The Invisible Religion: The Problem of Religion in Modern Society*, London: Collier-Macmillan.

Luckmann, T. and Berger, P. (1964) 'Social Mobility and Personal Identity', *European Journal of Sociology*, 5 (2) 331–44.

McCabe, H. (1980) 'The Class Struggle and Christian Love' in Ambler, R. and Haslam, D. (eds.) (1980), 153–69.

McLeod, H. (1974) *Class and Religion in the Late Victorian City*, London: Croom Helm.

McLeod, H. (1981) *Religion and the People of Western Europe: 1789–1970*, Oxford: Oxford University Press.

McRedmond, L. (1980) 'The Church in Ireland' in Cumming, J. and Burns, P. (eds.) *The Church Now: An Inquiry into the Present State of the Catholic Church in Britain and Ireland*, Dublin: Gill and Macmillan, 35–45.

McSweeney, Bill (1980) *Roman Catholicism: The Search for Relevance*, Oxford: Blackwell.

Mansfield, Penny and Hornsby-Smith, M. P. (1975) 'Consultation, Consensus and Conflict: Some Observations on the Structures and Working of the International Justice and Peace Commission', *The Month*, 8 (5) May, 138–45.

Mansfield, M. C. and Hornsby-Smith, M. P. (1982) 'Authority in the Church: The Individual Catholic's Interpretation', *New Blackfriars*, 63, November, 450–60.

Marcson, S. (1950) 'A Theory of Intermarriage and Assimilation', *Social Forces*, 29 (1), 75–8.

Marsh, D. and Chambers, J. (1981) *Abortion Politics*, London: Junction Books.

Martin, D. (1980) 'Age and Sex Variations of Church Attenders', in Anon. (1980a), London: Bible Society, 12–14.

Martin, D., Mills, J. O. and Pickering, W. S. F. (eds.) (1980) *Sociology and Theology: Alliance and Conflict*, Brighton: Harvester Press.

Mathew, D. (1955) *Catholicism in England: The Portrait of a Minority: Its Culture and Tradition*, 3rd ed, London: Eyre and Spottiswoode.

Matza, D. (1964) *Delinquency and Drift*, New York: Wiley.

Mays, J. B. (1965) *The Young Pretenders: A Study of Teenage Culture in Contemporary Society*, London: Michael Joseph.

Merton, R. K. (1957) *Social Theory and Social Structure*, New York: Free Press.

Merton, R. K. (1972) 'Intermarriage and the Social Structure: Fact and Theory' in Barron, M. L. (ed.) (1972) *The Blending American: Patterns of Intermarriage*, Chicago: Quadrangle, 12–35.

Michels, R. (1949) *Political Parties*, Glencoe, Ill.: Free Press.

Middleton, D. F. (1984) 'God as Mother: a Necessary Debate', *New Blackfriars*, 65, July–August, 319–22.

Mills, C. W. (1970) *The Sociological Imagination*, Harmondsworth: Penguin.

Moloney, T. (1985) *Westminster, Whitehall and the Vatican: The Role of Cardinal Hinsley 1935–43*, Tunbridge Wells: Burns and Oates.

Moore, J. (1975) 'The Catholic Priesthood', in Hill, M. (ed.), *A Sociological Yearbook of Religion in Britain*, 8, 30–60.

Morley, J. (1982) 'In God's Image?', *New Blackfriars*, 63, September, 373–81.

Mueller, G. H. (1978) 'The Protestant and the Catholic Ethic', *Annual Rev. of the Social Sciences and Religion*, 2, 143–66.

Mueller, G. H. (1980) 'The Dimensions of Religiosity', *Sociological Analysis*, 41 (1), Spring, 1–24.

Murgatroyd, L. (1982) 'Gender and Occupational Stratification', *Sociological Review*, 30 (4), November, 574–602.

Murphy, A. (1982) 'Woman's Status in the Church', *The Tablet*, 236 (7400) 8 May, 452–3.

Murphy, J. (1971) *Church, State and Schools in Britain: 1800–1970*, London: Routledge and Kegan Paul.

Musgrove, F. (1963) *The Migratory Elite*, London: Heinemann.

Neal, Sister Marie Augusta (1970) 'The H. Paul Douglass Lectures for 1970. Part I. The Relation between Religious Belief and Structural Change in Religious Orders: Developing an Effective Measuring Instrument.' *Review of Religious Research*, 12 Fall, 2–16.

Neal, M. A. (1971) 'The Relation between Religious Belief and Structural Change in Religious Orders: Some Evidence', *Review of Religious Research*, 12 (3) Spring, 153–64.

Nelson, G. K. and Clews, R. A. (1973) 'Geographic Mobility and Religious Behaviour', *Sociological Review*, 21, 127–35.

Newport, F. (1979) 'The Religious Switcher in the United States', *American Sociological Review* 44 (4) August, 528–52.

Noble, T. (1982) 'Recent Sociology, Capitalism and the Coming Crisis', *British Journal of Sociology* 33 (2) June, 238–53.

Nolan, A. (n.d., approx. 1983) *Taking Sides* (S372), London: C.T.S./C.I.I.R.

Norman, E. (1979) *Christianity and the World Order*, Oxford: Oxford University Press.

Norman, E. (1984) *The English Catholic Church in the Nineteenth Century*, Oxford: Clarendon Press.

O'Dea, T. F. (1958) *American Catholic Dilemma: An Inquiry into the Intellectual Life*, New York: Sheed and Ward.

O'Dea, T. F. (1968) *The Catholic Crisis*, Boston, Mass.: Beacon Press.

Office of Population Censuses and Surveys (1970) *Classification of Occupations*, London: H.M.S.O.

O'Sullivan, B. (1979) *Parish Alive*, London: Sheed and Ward.

Paul VI (1968) *The Regulation of Birth (Humanae Vitae)* (Do411) London: C.T.S.

Pepper, M. and Hebblethwaite, M. (1984) 'Finding Motherhood in God: Release or Trap?', *New Blackfriars*, 65, September, 372–84.

Price, C. (1969) 'The Study of Assimilation', in Jackson, J. A. (ed.) *Migration*, Cambridge: Cambridge University Press, 181–237.

Pro Mundi Vita (1973) 'Pluralism and Pluriformity in Religious Life: A Case Study', Bulletin 47, Brussels.

Pro Mundi Vita (1980) *The Roman Catholic Church in England and Wales*, Europe–North America Dossier II, Brussels, December.

Reardon, M. and Reardon, R. (n.d.) *What is A.I.F. For?*, Haywards Heath: Association of Interchurch Families.

Reardon, R. and Finch, M. (eds.) (1983) *Sharing Communion: An Appeal to the Churches by Interchurch Families*, London: Collins.

Redding, M. (1983) 'Everything the Pope Ever Wanted to Know About Sex and Didn't Dare to Ask' in Garcia, J. and Maitland, S. (eds.) (1983), 117–26.

Reidy, M. T. V. and White, L. C. (1977) 'The Measurement of Traditionalism among Roman Catholic Priests: An Exploratory Study', *British Journal of Sociology*, 28 (2) July, 226–41.

Rex, J. and Moore, R. (1967) *Race, Community and Conflict: A Study of Sparkbrook*, Oxford: Oxford University Press.

Richardson, C. J. (1977) *Contemporary Social Mobility*, London: Frances Pinter.

Robertson, R. (1970) *The Sociological Interpretation of Religion*, Oxford: Blackwell.

Roof, W. C. and Hadaway, C. K. (1979) 'Denominational Switching in the Seventies: Going Beyond Stark and Glock', *Journal for the Scientific Study of Religion*, 18 (4) December, 363–79.

Ruether, R. R. (1975) *New Woman, New Earth: Sexist Ideologies and Human Liberation*, New York: Seabury Press.

Ruether, R. R. (1979) *Mary: The Feminine Face of the Church*, London: S.C.M.

Ruether, R. R. (1981) *To Change the World: Christology and Cultural Criticism*, London: S.C.M.

Ruether, R. R. (1984) 'Church and Family', *New Blackfriars*, 65

    i, 'Church and Family in Scriptures and Early Christianity', January, 4–14.

    ii, 'Church and Family in the Medieval and Reformation Periods', February, 77–86.

    iii, 'Religion and the Making of the Victorian Family', March, 110–18.

    iv, 'The Family in Late Industrial Society', April 170–9.

    v, 'Feminism, Church and Family in the 1980s', May, 202–12.

Ruston, R. (1981) *Nuclear Deterrence – Right or Wrong?*, Commission for International Justice and Peace for England and Wales, Abbots Langley: C.I.S.

Ryan, W. (1973) *Assimilation of Irish Immigrants in Britain*, unpublished Ph.D. thesis: St Louis University.

Saunders, L. E. (1976) 'The Gradient of Ecumenism and Opposition to Religious Intermarriage', *Review of Religious Research*, 17, (2) Winter, 107–19.

Scarisbrick, J. J. (1971) *What's Wrong With Abortion?*, Kenilworth: LIFE.

Scott, G. (1967) *The R.C.s: Report on Roman Catholics in Britain Today*, London: Hutchinson.

Secretaria Status Rationarium Generale Ecclesiae, *Statistical Yearbook of the Church*, Rome (published annually).

Selznick, P. (1966) *T.V.A. and the Grass Roots: A Study in the Sociology of Formal Organization*, New York: Harper.

Sharratt, B. (1977) 'English Catholicism in the 1960s', in Hastings, A. (ed.) *Bishops and Writers: Aspects of the Evolution of Modern English Catholicism*, Wheathampstead: Anthony Clarke, 127–58.

Smith, A. (1983) *Passion for the Inner City: A Personal View*, London: Sheed and Ward.

Sobrino, J. (1978) *Christology at the Crossroads*, London: S.C.M.

Sorokin, P. A. (1959) *Social and Cultural Mobility*, New York: Free Press.

Spencer, A. E. C. W. (1966a) 'The Demography and Sociography of the Roman Catholic Community of England and Wales', in Bright, L. and Clements, S. (eds.), *The Committed Church*, London: Darton, Longman and Todd, 60–85.

Spencer, A. E. C. W. (1966b) 'On the Effects of Changing Social and Moral Beliefs on the Long Term Prospects of Fertility Among Catholics in Great Britain'. Paper read at Council of Europe European Population Conference, Strasbourg.

Spencer, A. E. C. W. (1971) *The Future of Catholic Education in England and Wales*, London: Catholic Renewal Movement.

Spencer, A. E. C. W. (1973) 'The Catholic Community as a British Melting Pot', *New Community*, 2 (2) Spring, 125–31.

Stark, R. and Bainbridge, W. S. (1980a) 'Towards a Theory of Religion: Religious Commitment', *Journal for the Scientific Study of Religion*, 19 (2) June, 114–28.

Stark, R. and Bainbridge, W. S. (1980b) 'Networks of Faith: Interpersonal Bonds and Recruitment to Cults and Sects', *American Journal of Sociology* 85 (6) May, 1376–95.

Stark, R. and Glock, C. Y. (1968) *American Piety: The Nature of Religious Commitment*, Berkeley, Ca: University of California Press.

Tanner, T. (1980) 'The Church and Social Responsibility' in Cumming, J. and Burns, P. (eds.) (1980), 161–9.

Thomas, K. (1973) *Religion and the Decline of Magic: Studies in Popular Beliefs in Sixteenth and Seventeenth Century England*, Harmondsworth: Penguin.

Thornes, B. and Collard, J. (1979) *Who Divorces?*, London: Routledge.

Tönnies, F. (1957, f.p. 1887) *Community and Society*, New York, Evanston and London: Harper.

Towler, R. (1974) *Homo Religiosus: Sociological Problems in the Study of Religion*, London: Constable.

Tumin, M. M. (1957) 'Some Unapplauded Consequences of Social Mobility in Mass Society', *Social Forces*, 36 (October), 32–7.

Turcan, K. A. and Hornsby-Smith, M. P. (1981) 'Further Analysis of Marriage Types from the Roman Catholic Opinion Data: the Elaboration of Non-Mixed Marriage Types', University of Surrey (mimeo).

Turner, D. (1983) 'The Relevance of Christian Values Today', *New Life*, 39 (4), 3–7.

U.S. Catholic Conference (1983) *The Challenge of Peace: God's Promise and Our*

Response, The U.S. Bishops' Pastoral Letter on War and Peace in the Nuclear Age, London: C.T.S./S.P.C.K.

Vaillancourt, J. G. (1980) *Papal Power: A Study of Vatican Control over Lay Catholic Elites*, Berkeley, Ca: University of California Press.

Varacalli, J. A. (1983) *Toward the Establishment of Liberal Catholicism in America*, Washington, D.C.: University Press of America.

Wadsworth, M. E. J. and Freeman, S. R. (1983) 'Generation Differences in Beliefs: A Cohort Study of Stability and Change in Religious Beliefs', *British Journal of Sociology*, 34 (3) September, 416–37.

Wallis, R. (1976) *The Road to Total Freedom: A Sociological Analysis of Scientology*, London: Heinemann.

Wallis, R. (1982) *Millennialism and Charisma*, Belfast: Queen's University.

Walsh, M. and Davies, B. (eds.) (1984) *Proclaiming Justice and Peace: Documents from John XXIII to John Paul II*, London: Collins/C.A.F.O.D.

Ward, C. (1965) *Priests and People: A Study in the Sociology of Religion*, Liverpool: Liverpool University Press.

Warner, M. (1978) *Alone of All Her Sex: the Myth and the Cult of the Virgin Mary*, London,: Quartet Books.

Weber, M. (1930) *The Protestant Ethic and the Spirit of Capitalism*, London: Allen and Unwin.

Weber, M. (1949) *The Methodology of the Social Sciences*, New York: Free Press.

Weber, M. (1966) *The Sociology of Religion*, London: Methuen.

Welch, M. R. and Baltzell, J. (1984) 'Geographical Mobility, Social Integration and Church Attendance', *Journal for the Scientific Study of Religion*, 23 (1), 75–91.

West, A. (1981) 'Genesis and Patriarchy', *New Blackfriars*, 62,
i, January, 17–32.
ii, 'Women and the End of Time', October, 420–32.

West, A. (1983a) 'A Faith for Feminists?' in Garcia, J. and Maitland, S. (eds.) (1983), 66–90.

West, A. (1983b) 'Bodiliness and the Good News', *New Blackfriars*, 64,
i, May, 204–14.
ii, June, 261–9.

Whyte, J. H. (1981) *Catholics in Western Democracies: A Study in Political Behaviour*, Dublin: Gill and Macmillan.

Wicker, B. (1985) *Nuclear Deterrence: What Does the Church Teach?* (S374), London: Catholic Truth Society.

Wilson, B. (1970) *Religious Sects: A Sociological Study*, London: Weidenfeld and Nicolson.

Wilson, B. (1982) *Religion in Sociological Perspective*, Oxford: Oxford University Press.

Winter, M. M. (1973) *Mission or Maintenance: A Study in New Pastoral Structures*, London: Darton, Longman and Todd.

Winter, M. M. (1979) *Mission Resumed?*, London: Darton, Longman and Todd.

Winter, M. M. (1985) *What Ever Happened to Vatican II?*, London: Sheed and Ward.

Woolf, M. (1971) *Family Intentions: An Enquiry Undertaken for the General Register Office*, O.P.C.S. Social Survey Division, London: H.M.S.O.

Woolf, M. and Pegden, S. (1976) *Families Five Years On: A Survey carried out on behalf of Population Statistics 1 of the Office of Population Censuses and Surveys*, London: H.M.S.O.

Wuthnow, R. and Christiano, K. (1979) 'The Effects of Residential Migration on Church Attendance in the United States', in Wuthnow, R. (ed.) *The Religious Dimension: New Directions in Quantitative Research*, New York: Academic Press, 257–76.

Wyatt, J. F. (1976) 'Residential Stability in an Inner Urban Housing Block: A Re-Study after 18 years', *Sociological Review* 24, (3) August, 559–76.

Zimmer, B. G. (1970) 'Participation of Migrants in Urban Structures', in Jansen, C. J. (ed.) *Readings in the Sociology of Migration*, Oxford: Pergamon, 71–83.

INDEX